CARTAGE
& COLOM___
CARIBBEAN
COAST

OCEAN MALANDRA

Contents

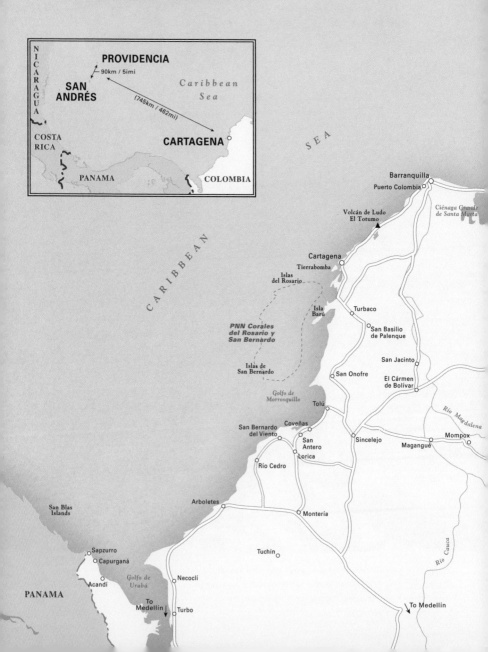

CARTAGENA AND COLOMBIA'S CARIBBEAN COAST

NICARAGUA

PROVIDENCIA

90km / 5imi

SAN ANDRÉS

Caribbean Sea

(745km / 462mi)

COSTA RICA

CARTAGENA

PANAMA

COLOMBIA

SEA

Barranquilla
Puerto Colombia

Ciénaga Grande de Santa Marta

Volcán de Ludo
El Totumo

C A R I B B E A N

Cartagena
Tierrabomba

Islas del Rosario

Isla Barú

Turbaco

San Basilio de Palenque

PNN Corales del Rosario y San Bernardo

San Jacinto

San Onofre

El Cármen de Bolívar

Islas de San Bernardo

Golfo de Morrosquillo

Tolú

Río Magdalena

Coveñas

San Bernardo del Viento

San Antero

Sincelejo

Magangué

Mompox

Lorica

Río Cedro

San Blas Islands

Arboletes

Montería

Sapzurro

Capurganá

Tuchín

Acandí

Golfo de Urabá

Necoclí

Río Cauca

PANAMA

To Medellín

Turbo

To Medellín

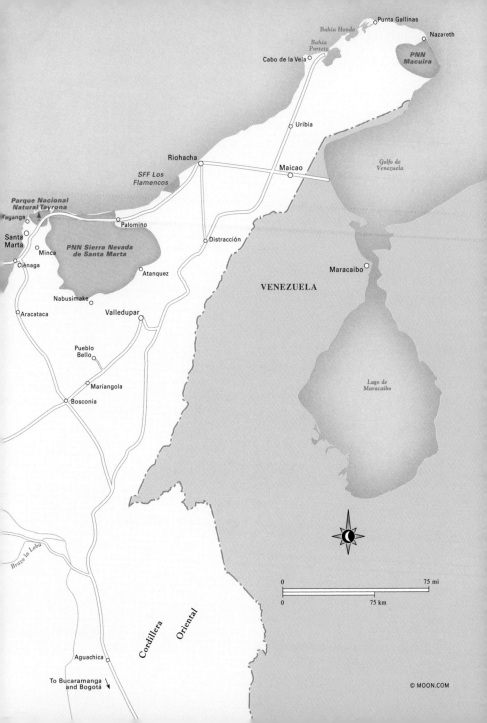

Punta Gallinas
Bahía Hondo
Nazareth
Bahía
Portete
PNN
Cabo de la Vela
Macuira

Uribia

Golfo de
Venezuela

Riohacha

SFF Los
Flamencos

Maicao

Parque Nacional
Natural Tayrona

Taganga

Palomino

Distracción

Santa
Marta

Minca

PNN Sierra Nevada
de Santa Marta

VENEZUELA

Ciénaga

Maracaibo

Atanquez

Nabusimake

Aracataca

Valledupar

Lago de
Maracaibo

Pueblo
Bello

Mariangola

Bosconia

Brazo la Loba

Cordillera   Oriental

0   75 mi
0   75 km

Aguachica

To Bucaramanga
and Bogotá

© MOON.COM

DISCOVER

Cartagena &
Colombia's
Caribbean Coast

Colombia is a whirlwind of colors and sensations; magical realism pervades the entire country's varied terrain. Its Caribbean coast in particular is a tropical dreamscape. Reigning over it in sultry majesty is Cartagena, an architecturally stunning seaport ringed by colonial walls, lined with cobblestone streets, and filled to bursting with nightlife.

Stretching west and east of the city are a kaleidoscope of landscapes and cultures, from the beachfront Afro-Colombian villages of Capurganá and Sapzurro to the red desert bluffs of La Guajira, home to the matriarchal Wayúu people. In between, you'll find laid-back bohemian villages and flamboyant Carnaval celebrations that last for weeks. Snorkeling, diving, and otherwise playing in the turquoise sea are options, but so are hiking and bird-watching in the Sierra Nevada, the world's highest coastal mountain range.

Sun worshippers will never run out of devotional opportunities. Unspoiled islands with sugar-sand beaches beckon, from the luxurious Islas del Rosario just offshore from Cartagena to the harder-to-reach, calypso-driven San Andrés Archipelago.

Clockwise from top left: caiman; bougainvillea-covered house in Cartagena; doorknocker; Alquímico bar; Kogi girl from the Sierra Nevada; Johnny Cay.

In this multifaceted jewel of the South American continent, you'll discover flavorful cuisine and dawn-breaking fiestas that can happen any night of the week. It's the Colombian people themselves who steal the show. Always ready to jump up and dance to the near-constant backdrop of music, their profound passion for life is always on full display. Join them.

Clockwise from top left: Santuario de San Pedro Claver; *palenquero* dancers; hammocks and hats for sale; beach in San Andrés.

10 TOP
EXPERIENCES

1 **Wander Along Cartagena's Walls:** Stroll *las murallas,* part of the largest series of fortifications in South America (page 38), and cap off your ramble with an alfresco drink at sunset (page 46).

2 **Live on Island Time:** Just off the coast you'll find the **Islas del Rosario** (page 73) and **Islas de San Bernardo** (page 132), strings of islands with white-sand beaches that let you live out your Caribbean dreams.

>>>

3 **Dance Until Dawn at Carnaval:** Join the throngs on the streets during **Carnaval de Barranquilla** (page 84), a centuries-old festival that's recognized by UNESCO, or celebrate at a more off-the-beaten path Carnaval along the coast (page 87).

>>>

∧
∧ ∧
∧ ∧

4 **Chill Out in Hippie Heaven:** Lounge on the beach, go for a hike, or just hang in a hammock in bohemian getaways like **Taganga** (page 96), **Minca** (page 99), **Palomino** (page 107), and **Capurganá and Sapzurro** (page 136).

5 **Explore Parque Nacional Natural Tayrona:** Pitch a tent or rent a *cabaña* and play on the wilderness coastline of Colombia's most popular natural area (page 102).

^^
^
^

6 **Have an Epic Night Out:** Whether you're lounging at bars or dancing at discos and salsa clubs, you'll learn why Cartagena's nightlife is legendary (page 46).

7 **Indulge in Caribbean Cuisine:** From the freshest ceviche to aphrodisiacal seafood stews, dining on the coast is a true feast for the senses (page 26).

>>>

∧
∧ ∧
∧

8 **Snorkel and Dive:** Head out on underwater explorations of the **Seaflower Biosphere Reserve** in the San Andrés Archipelago (pages 150 and 162).

9 **Trek to the Lost City:** Climb through the jungle to **Ciudad Perdida,** the ruins of the ancient Tayrona civilization in the Sierra Nevada (page 112).

10 **Discover the Remote Sands of the Alta Guajira Desert:** Head out on a 4x4 to explore an otherworldly landscape where the desert meets the sea (page 122).

Planning Your Trip

Where to Go

Cartagena

Cartagena is a tropical, pastel-hued fortress city straight out of a fairytale and full of sensory experiences. In this sparkling city by the sea, you can feast on **Caribbean cuisine** and admire **colonial architecture** in the form of impressive churches, plazas, and fortifications. Catch the sunset along the water from *las murallas,* the stone walls that surround the **Old City,** for a good introduction, and soak up the atmosphere in **Getsemaní,** the city's bohemian district full of **mural-lined streets.** Nightlife in the city is epic, so plan on exploring the **lounges, discos, and salsa clubs.** Cartagena also makes a great base for day trips or overnights to the **Islas del Rosario,** a string of postcard-worthy Caribbean islands just off the coast, or the peaceful riverside city of **Mompox,** a slice of yesteryear that exudes pure magical realism.

Santa Marta and La Guajira

East of Cartagena along the coast lies an outdoor lover's paradise. **Santa Marta** is often a base for adventures in the region, but you'll also find compelling bohemian villages you may want to visit or stay longer in: **Minca,** set in the mountains, where you can visit coffee farms and go bird-watching along hiking trails; and **Taganga** and **Palomino,** offering laid-back beachfront vibes. Colombia's famous **Carnaval de Barranquilla** also takes place in the vicinity. Farther east you'll find the country's most famous national park, **Parque Nacional Natural Tayrona,** full of rugged cove beaches along the edge of the Sierra

Cartagena's Old City

Nevada, the world's highest coastal mountain range, and can embark on a multiday trek to **Ciudad Perdida (Lost City)**, the ruins of the ancient Tayrona civilization. Farther along is the isolated coastline of **La Guajira,** the only real **desert landscape** in the entire Caribbean region, set strikingly against the sea. This area is home to the matriarchal Wayúu indigenous people and celebrated for its rugged beauty.

Western Caribbean Coast

The less-visited Caribbean coast west of Cartagena is where you can go to get away from it all. Hop on a boat out to the **Islas de San Bernardo,** offshore islands with inviting white sands and crystalline waters. Also only accessible by boat are the car-free Afro-Colombian communities of **Capurganá and Sapzurro,** set on idyllic crescent-shaped bays. Beaches are isolated and wild here, backed only by the pristine rainforest and the clear blue sky, and trails along the coast and through the jungle offer lovely opportunities to hike.

San Andrés and Providencia

Reggae rhythms and gently swaying palm trees typify life in the San Andrés Archipelago. Located far from the mainland, these three idyllic Caribbean islands are heaven on earth for sunseekers. Part of the UNESCO-designated **Seaflower Biosphere Reserve,** the islands offer excellent scuba diving and snorkeling. The most bustling

diver off the coast of San Andrés

reggae bar on San Andrés island

of the islands is San Andrés, with a lively beachfront boardwalk and enticing **reggae bars.** From San Andrés, you can day-trip to **Johnny Cay and Rose Cay,** the latter of which is also known as **The Aquarium (El Acuario)** for its pristine waters.

Providencia and **Santa Catalina**—connected by a pedestrian bridge—are more expensive and require additional travel but are where to go to get away from it all. Kayak through mangroves or hike through tropical forest.

When to Go

Because Colombia straddles the equator and the Caribbean region lies mostly along sea level, the temperatures and length of days are nearly constant year-round. There are, however, distinct dry and rainy seasons. Throughout most of the coast, the months of **December through February** and **July through August** are considered *verano* **(dry season).** *Invierno* **(rainy season)** is usually between **April and May** and again between **September and November.**

In San Andrés and Providencia, June-November is the rainy season and January-April is the dry season. In the arid La Guajira area, there is a short rainy season during June and

July, and another longer, more intense rainy season September-November, when it can be difficult to travel through the desert due to muddy conditions on the roads.

High tourist seasons run from **mid-December through mid-January,** during **Easter week (Semana Santa),** and, to a lesser extent, school vacations from **June to August.** During high season, hotel rates and airline ticket prices soar. Colombians from the interior flock to the Caribbean coast during the New Year's holidays, creating a party atmosphere. Hotels and flights may be hard to come by during this time and the 10 or so *puentes* (long weekends) of the year.

Many of the major **festivals and celebrations** take place between November and February, including the Hay Festival in Cartagena and the **Carnavals** in Barranquilla and other Caribbean towns. **Easter week** celebrations are popular in colonial cities such as Mompox, Santa Marta, and Cartagena.

Before You Go

Passports and Visas

U.S. and Canadian travelers to Colombia who intend to visit as tourists for a period of under 90 days will need only to present a **valid passport** upon entry in the country. You may be asked to show **proof of a return ticket.** Tell the immigration officer if you intend to stay up to 90 days, otherwise they will probably give you a stamp permitting a stay of 60 days. Language schools and universities will be able to assist those who may require a yearlong **student visa.**

Vaccinations

There are **no obligatory vaccination requirements** for visiting Colombia. However, proof of the **yellow fever vaccine** may be requested upon arrival at the Parque Nacional Natural Tayrona and, if you intend to travel onward to the Amazon, at the Leticia airport. This vaccination can be obtained at Red Cross clinics throughout the country. If you are traveling onward to countries such as Brazil, Ecuador, or Peru, you may have to provide proof of the vaccine upon entry to those countries.

The Centers for Disease Control and Prevention (CDC) recommends that travelers have all the **basic vaccinations** updated. In addition, for most travelers to Colombia, the CDC recommends the **hepatitis A** and **typhoid** vaccinations. **Hepatitis B, rabies,** and **yellow**

Carnaval de Barranquilla

fever vaccinations are recommended for some travelers. If you plan to visit the Amazon region, **antimalarial drugs** may be recommended. With infections of **mosquito-borne illnesses** such as malaria, dengue, chikungunya, and Zika possible in tropical areas of the country, visitors are encouraged to keep mosquito repellent close at hand.

Transportation

Most travelers arrive by plane to the Caribbean coast of Colombia, with the vast majority arriving at the modern but smallish **Rafael Núñez International Airport** (CTG) in Cartagena. There are numerous daily nonstop flights into Cartagena from New York, Miami, Fort Lauderdale, Orlando, and Atlanta. Amsterdam also has direct flights, though they're not daily. Within Latin America, Mexico City and Panama City have multiple daily flights to Cartagena.

There are **overland border crossings** into Colombia from Ecuador (to Ipiales); by boat from Peru or Brazil to the Amazonian port of Leticia; and by sea from Panama to Capurganá or Cartagena. There is an entry point to Venezuela at the town of Maicao, but the border is frequently closed, and this is considered one of the most dangerous border crossings.

Intra-country flights are easy, safe, increasingly more economical, frequent, and, above all, quick. Besides Cartagena, Barranquilla, Santa Marta, Riohacha, and Tolú all host local airports.

Taking the **bus** to just about anywhere on the Caribbean coast is an inexpensive and popular, but slower option.

In the major cities of Cartagena and Barranquilla, there are extensive **rapid bus networks. Private buses** and **taxis** are ubiquitous in cities—the taxi-hailing app **Easy Taxi** (http://cabify.com) is useful—although the best way to see the sights of most cities is usually **on foot.**

Renting a car, or even a **motorcycle,** is also a viable option, but it's not necessary or recommended for the region; parking will be problematic, and public transit is fast and easy.

What to Pack

Pack your beach gear, folks: this is the Caribbean at its finest. For jungle explorations, including the Ciudad Perdida (Lost City trek), **waterproof hiking boots** and **collapsible trekking poles** are musts. For exploring the watery environs, a **waterproof camera bag** and **silica gel** may prevent the heartache of a ruined camera. If you plan on spending much time underwater, bring your own **snorkeling gear;** rentals are often overused and not in the best shape. For spotting birds and other wildlife, especially in the Minca and Palomino areas, you'll be happy to have **binoculars.** A lightweight **sleeping sack** makes rustic sleeping conditions more comfortable.

To protect against the sun, pack a **wide-brimmed hat;** against the rain, a **lightweight rain jacket** and **compact umbrella;** against mosquitoes, lightweight and light-colored long-sleeved shirts and some strong **insect repellent.** For long bus rides, earplugs, eye masks, and **luggage locks** will make the trip more relaxing. A **Latin American Spanish dictionary** will help you get your point across.

Casual attire is fine at most restaurants and bars. In religious venues, theaters, and upscale restaurants, covered shoes and shirts with sleeves are expected. In larger cities, like Cartagena and Barranquilla, you'll want to **dress to impress** before going to a nightclub, or you might get turned away at the door.

The Best of Cartagena and the Caribbean Coast

DAY 1

Arrive in **Cartagena.** Once you change into the light and airy attire standard for the sultry city, get to know the area with a stroll along *las murallas,* the massive ramparts that once protected Cartagena against pirates, taking in views of the city and Caribbean. Enjoy a sunset cocktail at **Café del Mar,** a bar atop the seafront section of the wall. For dinner, head to the **San Diego** area and enjoy a Cartagenan-style seafood meal at **Santísimo** or the best steak of your life at **Marzola Parrilla Argentina.** Spend the night at **3 Banderas,** a friendly midrange option in a colonial building, or splurge on the breathtaking landmark **Sofitel Legend Santa Clara** hotel, a former monastery.

DAY 2

Walk the Old City streets, getting lost and found again as you amble from the divine **Parque de Bolívar** to the **Plaza de Santo Domingo.** Check out the **Palacio de la Inquisición** and the **Santuario de San Pedro Claver.**

If you have spare time be sure to take a cab or bus over to the impressive **Castillo de San Felipe** later in the afternoon.

For dinner it's Peruvian-Caribbean fusion at **Mar y Zielo.** For an after-dinner cocktail (or two), go to **Alquímico,** a lounge that exudes tropical cool. Once warmed up, check out **Donde Fidel** to get your salsa groove on and meet new friends.

DAY 3

For a change of pace, take a cab or bus to one of the beaches just south of the city on the **Bocagrande peninsula,** popular with vacationing Colombian families. Grab a beach umbrella and a fresh coconut and enjoy the people-watching.

balcony-lined street in Cartagena

palenqueras selling fruit in the Old City

Local Cuisine

Indulge in regional cuisine while you're on the Caribbean coast:

- *cazuela de mariscos*: This delicious, thick stew is piled with shellfish, including clams and mussels, and served throughout the coastal regions of Colombia, including both the Caribbean and Pacific sides. It's said to be aphrodisiacal and is often eaten before setting out on a weekend of partying or romance. The beachfront eatery **Kiosco el Bony** (page 62) in Cartagena's Bocagrande serves one of the most potent versions in the country, while upscale eateries in the Old City, like **Santísimo** (page 58), serve a more refined version.

- **ceviche costeño:** Coastal ceviche is the dish most associated with the Caribbean coast across Colombia, although in reality it's more like a "cocktail," different from most people's conception of ceviche (al la Peruvian or Mexican style); seafood items are boiled instead of cured, and then chilled. The dish starts with shrimp, and can be mixed with octopus, *caracol* (conch), fish, clam, and whatever else is fresh that day. It's tossed in chopped onions with a cocktail and mayonnaise sauce and served with *aji picante* (hot sauce) and soda crackers. Mostly a street food, it's also served on beaches and in shack-style eateries from Cartagena all the way up the coast to Riohacha. Cartagena's **La Cevichería** (page 58) is famous for its offerings, but **La Nacional** (page 57), part of a row of street *cevicherías*, offers stellar options as well.

- *posta negra:* A beef dish based on a thick black marinade made of molasses, *posta negra* is popular throughout the Caribbean region. In Cartagena it's often referred to as *posta cartagenera*. Seasoned with laurel, thyme, and cloves, this savory dish is a nice break from the seafood-centric fare of the region. Try an excellent *posta negra* at **Restaurante Coroncoro** (page 61) in Cartagena,

cazuela de mariscos at Kiosco el Bony

or get your maws on the *posta puyada momposina,* the regional version of Mompox, at the riverfront **Comedor Costeño** (page 77).

- *rondón:* Loosely translated from the local creole as the "rundown," this is the most famous dish of the San Andrés Archipelago. Made from just about everything grandma can get her hands on, including fish chunks, *caracol*, and pigs' tails, it's a rich coconut-based stew with local herbs and spices. A real *rondón* is so filling that you'll need a breather before standing up and walking away from the table. **Restaurante Lydia** (page 155) is famous for her version, but she is open only on Sundays and holiday Mondays; stop by the **Fisherman's Place** (page 155) for a solid alternative.

Spend the afternoon in the hip and happening neighborhood of **Getsemaní,** which has mural-lined streets filled with tapas bars and watering holes. Don't miss the *palenquero* dancers in the evening (starting around 7pm) at **Plaza de la Trinidad,** the neighborhood's beating heart, where you can also enjoy a beer from one of the many roaming vendors or at one of the bars with plaza seating. For dinner, head to **Caffé Lunático** for

Spanish tapas and inventive Mediterranean-Caribbean fusion cuisine.

DAYS 4-6

From the Muelle Turístico de la Bodeguita in town, take a boat to the **Islas del Rosario,** which has the area's finest beaches, and spend a couple of nights at an island hotel. A great choice is **Gente de Mar** on Isla Grande, but it's also worth splurging on the private island experience at **Isla Bendita.**

Return to Cartagena in the late afternoon and take one last walk on the walls, then enjoy a final cocktail at the funky and friendly **La Caponera** in Getsemaní.

EXCURSION TO SANTA MARTA AND LA GUAJIRA

For some nature therapy and quality beach time, head east along the coast. Give yourself at least five days if you can. From Cartagena it's a five-hour bus ride to **Santa Marta,** a convenient base to explore the enchanting area, including the nearby bohemian beach town of **Taganga** and hip mountain village of **Minca;** both also make for lovely overnight options. At Santa Marta you're also just a one-hour bus ride away from the country's celebrated **Parque Nacional Natural Tayrona,** to which you can take a day trip or camp overnight.

If you have an extra three days or want a different sort of adventure, head farther east to **La Guajira,** a desert peninsula that is home to the matriarchal Wayúu people and striking wilderness beaches. Start in **Riohacha,** the departmental capital of La Guajira, and join an organized tour group that'll take you out in a 4x4 to **Cabo de la Vela,** where you can take a dip in the Caribbean Sea or try your luck windsurfing or kitesurfing, and **Punta Gallinas,** the northernmost point of South America, where you'll find an unusual landscape of desert dunes that drop dramatically into the sea.

EXCURSION TO SAN ANDRÉS AND PROVIDENCIA

If you're looking to add a true Caribbean getaway, head to the San Andrés Archipelago. With five

kitesurfing at sunset in Cabo de la Vela

days, you can explore all three main islands, or choose one to focus on if you have less time. The islands offer beautiful beaches, excellent snorkeling and diving, and fresh seafood.

Fly into **San Andrés,** the most bustling of the islands, where you can take a boat tour to offshore cays and enjoy beachfront reggae bars.

To truly get away from it all, take a short flight or catamaran ride to **Providencia,** where you can relax on white sands, hike through the mountains, and kayak through mangroves, and from which you can walk to tiny **Santa Catalina** via pedestrian bridge.

The Wild Coast

This ambitious weeklong itinerary takes you to lesser-known points along the Caribbean coast. Be prepared to take several modes of transportation in order to get around. If you don't have a full week to spend here, prioritize a visit to either the Islas de San Bernardo or Capurganá and Sapzurro. Note that waters can be rough December-March.

DAY 1

From Cartagena, you can board a bus for the three-hour ride to sleepy **Tolú.** Upon arrival, head to the boardwalk to hang out along the beach, as well as set up a day trip to the **Islas de San Bernardo** for the next day; boat tours typically leave at 8:30am. Or, make accommodation reservations in advance to stay on one of the islands, and head directly via a 2.5-hour ride from Cartagena; some lodgings, such as **Casa en el Agua,** offer direct fast-boat service.

DAY 2

Today, day-trippers will take a tour of the Islas de San Bernardo, with stops at **Isla Múcura** for snorkeling and **Santa Cruz del Islote,** the most densely populated island in the world. Those who spent the night on one of the islands might spend the day lounging on the beach, playing in the water, or exploring nearby islands.

At the end of the day, take a boat back to Tolú and spend the night at **Hotel Casa Ines,** where you can relax at its terrace bar.

DAY 3

In the morning, take a minibus to **Bahía de**

Cispatá, a turtle and crocodile refuge run by local fishers near the town of San Antero. Once you've worked up an appetite, have a fresh seafood lunch at **Pesecar,** which is perched on Bahía de Cispatá.

From here, it's a three-hour trip to **Río Cedro.** Take a minibus from San Antero to Lorica, then transfer to a shared taxi and head for Moñitos. From there, you can arrange for a motorbike to the **Reserva Natural y EcoHotel Viento Solar.** You'll arrive at this private reserve on undeveloped coastline in time to take a walk on the secluded beaches and go for a dip in the calm waters. Settle into one of the thatched-roof cabins, lulled to sleep by the sounds of the jungle and sea.

DAYS 4-5

Wake up early and take a walk through the tropical dry forest of the reserve. If you're lucky, you may spot an *oso perezoso* (sloth) clinging to a tree. Enjoy a quiet breakfast before hitting the road to the **Darién Gap,** a region that straddles the Colombia-Panama border.

It's a multi-hour trip to the beach town of **Necoclí.** Take a motorbike to Montería, then hop on a bus headed for Necoclí. Check into the **Casa Neco** for the night.

The next morning, take a fast boat across the gulf to **Capurganá,** which takes about 1.5 hours. Once you arrive in Capurganá, stay at the lovely **Cabaña Darius** guesthouse or at the secluded, honeymoon-worthy **Bahía Lodge.**

DAY 6

Get up nice and early for a day of hiking

Social-Impact Tourism

The annual number of international visitors to Colombia increased from 600,000 in 2000 to 4.5 million in 2019. This boom has fostered a growth of community and ecotourism options. Here are several ways to support the local people, plants, or animals, all while having the vacation of your dreams.

- **Stay in a *posada nativa*.** The interior of **San Andrés** (page 156) is home to *posadas nativas* (native guesthouses) that are owned and operated by locals, many of whom have deep roots on the island. Stay at a *posada nativa* and you'll get to know the local culture.

- **Visit a national park.** Colombia's system of natural parks and protected areas covers around 13.4 percent of the country. The Parks Service actively engages local communities, with much of the ecotourism infrastructure being operated by community-based organizations. Some of the region's best parks are **Parque Nacional Natural Tayrona** (page 102) near Santa Marta, **Parque Nacional Natural Old Providence McBean Lagoon** (page 160) on Providencia, and **Parque Nacional Natural Corales del Rosario y San Bernardo,** which includes the Islas del Rosario (page 73) near Cartagena and the Islas de San Bernardo off the western Caribbean coast (page 132).

- **Save the animals.** At the **Bahía de Cispatá refuge** (page 134) in San Antero,

flamingos at Santuario de Fauna y Flora Los Flamencos

local fishers are helping to protect crocodiles and turtles, formerly hunted for their meat and eggs. Visit the **Santuario de Fauna y Flora Los Flamencos** (page 121), famous for its population of migratory flamingos. Here, conservationists also work to keep threatened sea turtles safe.

and exploration. Hike through the jungle surrounding Capurganá to **El Cielo waterfall** and splash around in the water before heading back into town. Next, take the two-hour hike to the neighboring town of **Sapzurro,** letting the howler monkeys guide you. Have lunch at the **Doña Triny.** Or continue walking north from Sapzurro for 15 minutes over the border into **Panama** (make sure you have your passport) into the village of **La Miel,** where you can enjoy a seafood lunch on the beach.

Head back to Capurganá and have a gourmet dinner on the beach at **Donde Josefina.**

For those more interested in playing in the water, spend the day on a **snorkel or dive trip.** This region has over 30 diving sites to choose from, so expect a full day on the water.

DAY 7

Today you return to Cartagena. Take a boat to Necoclí, and then a long bus ride back to Cartagena.

Cartagena

Magical Cartagena wastes no time in seducing its visitors. Sitting pretty on the edge of the glimmering Caribbean Sea, the majestic walled city is full of magnificent churches and palaces, picturesque balcony-lined streets, and lush plazas. This romantic historic-city-meets-tropical-beach-paradise combo makes Cartagena unrivaled in South America, and it frequently tops lists of the continent's most beautiful and coveted holiday destinations.

Cartagena is also a cultural heritage mecca, with its roots as a major port during the transatlantic slave trade nurturing a strong musical tradition that allowed for resistance and joy under even the most horrific circumstances. From the drum-driven *palenquero* dancers to the urban grinding of *champeta,* Cartagena ranks among other African

Highlights

Look for ★ to find recommended sights, activities, dining, and lodging.

★ **Wander Along *las Murallas*:** The best introduction to Cartagena is rambling the walls of the historic city and enjoying a *cerveza* accompanied by the Caribbean sunset (page 38).

★ **Visit a Monastery Turned Museum:** Explore the historic home of Latin America's "patron saint of the slaves" and see excellent Afro-Colombian artwork at **Santuario de San Pedro Claver** (page 38).

★ **Appreciate the Architectural Grandeur of the Palacio de la Inquisición:** The former headquarters of the Spanish Inquisition is now a museum (page 40).

★ **Admire Street Art in Getsemaní:** Walk the vibrant, mural-lined streets of this historic neighborhood (page 41).

★ **Explore the Continent's Largest Spanish Fortification:** You'll find mysterious underground tunnels and breathtaking views over the city at **Castillo de San Felipe** (page 43).

★ **Live *la Vida Loca*:** Whether you're partying in the city's bars or rooftop dance clubs, nightlife in Cartagena is not to be missed (page 44).

★ **Bask in Caribbean Wonderland:** A short boat ride from Cartagena brings you to the white-sand beaches of the spectacular **Islas del Rosario** (page 73).

© MOON.COM

★ **Step Back in Time:** At magical **Mompox,** a riverside city, you'll catch a glimpse of what Cartagena used to be like (page 75).

diaspora hot spots (think New Orleans and Rio de Janeiro) in terms of soul and flow.

Nightlife here is legendary. But it's also expensive compared to the rest of the country, as almost everything is geared toward tourists. Dining is also pricier, but this is where not only top Colombian chefs but leading kitchen stars from Latin American capitals like Mexico City, Lima, and Buenos Aires like to show off by opening up their second outposts. You can get an excellent five-star meal here for much cheaper than most places around the globe.

Just a stone's throw offshore, the Islas del Rosarios are a string of picture-perfect Caribbean islands easily visited by boat on day trips or epic overnight beach paradise getaways.

Far away from the constant tourist buzz, the *tranquilo* streets and plazas of the charming inland town of Mompox, southeast of Cartagena and perched on the banks of the Río Magdalena, await discovery by those looking to escape the coast and the crowds.

PLANNING YOUR TIME

There are a lot of sights to see in Cartagena, and the entire city feels like one big sensory indulgence. While a weekend will suffice to wander the streets of the Old City and soak up the history, beauty, and atmosphere, 3-4 days is ideal, especially if you want to hit the beaches at Playa Blanca or the Islas del Rosario—both require at least a full day and also offer several enticing options for staying the night right on the sands. Add two more days if you want to go to the riverside town of Mompox, which involves 6-8 hours of travel one-way.

Although the sheer grandeur of the walled Old City can't be equaled, the historic Getsemaní area, once home to the city's working classes, is also alluring, with bohemian flair and mural-lined streets; it's become the official backpackers' quarters.

Accommodation options in the city run the gamut, from budget hideaways to some of the most luxurious on the continent, so take your pick. You'll find the most options for the former in Getsemaní and the latter in Centro. Both are good, walkable neighborhoods in terms of restaurant and nightlife options, as well as safety considerations.

Cartagena

History

Cartagena de Indias was founded in 1533 by Spanish conquistador Pedro de Heredia on a small Carib indigenous settlement. During the 16th century the city was sacked by pirates numerous times, most notably by Sir Francis Drake in 1568. The city was walled and forts were constructed at various passage points in the harbor to stop intruders. The construction of the fortifications, the most extensive in South America, took almost two centuries and was completed by the mid-1700s. The effect is an almost castle-like city hovering over the turquoise Caribbean.

The city prospered as one of the main slave ports in Spanish America during the colonial era. It is estimated that more than one million enslaved people passed through the city; those who escaped created free communities known as *palenques.*

Cartagena formally declared independence from Spain in 1812. In 1815, it was

Previous: Torre del Reloj over Plaza de los Coches; mixed seafood cocktail; cannon at Castillo de San Felipe.

Cartagena

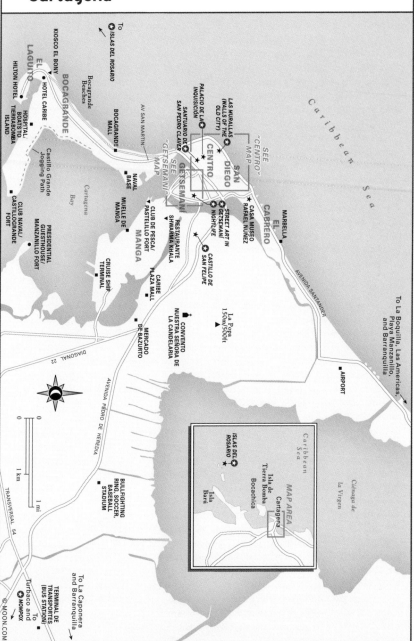

To ISLAS DEL ROSARIO

KIOSCO EL BONY
EL LAGUITO
HILTON HOTEL
HOTEL CARIBE
HOSPITAL
BOATS TO TIERRABOMBA ISLAND
Bocagrande Beaches
BOCAGRANDE
AV SAN MARTIN
BOCAGRANDE MALL
Castillo Grande Jogging Path
CLUB NAVAL/ CASTILLOGRANDE FORT
Cartagena Bay
NAVAL BASE
MUELLE DE MANGA
MANGA
PRESIDENTIAL GUESTHOUSE/ MANZANILLO FORT
CLUB DE PESCA/ PASTELILLO FORT
CRUISE SHIP TERMINAL
CARIBE PLAZA MALL
MERCADO DE BAZURTO
PALACIO DE LA INQUISICIÓN
LAS MURALLAS (WALLS OF THE OLD CITY)
SANTUARIO DE SAN PEDRO CLAVER
"GETSEMANÍ" MAP
SEE
CENTRO
SAN DIEGO
SEE "CENTRO" MAP
SEE "GETSEMANÍ" MAP
STREET ART IN GETSEMANÍ
NIGHTLIFE
RESTAURANTE SHWARMA KHALA
CASA MUSEO RAFAEL NÚÑEZ
EL CABRERO
MARBELLA
AVENIDA SANTANDER
CASTILLO DE SAN FELIPE
CONVENTO NUESTRA SEÑORA DE LA CANDELARIA
La Papa 150m/500ft
DIAGONAL 22
AVENIDA PEDRO DE HEREDIA
BULLFIGHTING RING, SOCCER, BASEBALL STADIUM
TRANSVERSAL 54
AIRPORT
To La Boquilla, Las Américas, Playa Manzanillo, and Barranquilla

Caribbean Sea

0   1 km
0   1 mi

To La Caponera and Barranquilla
TERMINAL DE TRANSPORTES (BUS STATION)
To Turbaco and Mompox
MOMPOX

ISLAS DEL ROSARIO
Caribbean Sea
Isla de Tierra Bomba
Bocachica
Cartagena
MAP AREA
Isla Barú
Ciénaga de la Virgen

© MOON.COM

recaptured by the Spanish, only to be retaken by revolutionaries in 1821. During the 19th century, Cartagena lost its status as one of Colombia's main Caribbean ports and nearby Barranquilla, closer to the mouth of the Magdalena River, rose to prominence. The economic decline had one good side effect: preserving the colonial past. The Old City remained largely intact through the 20th century, prompting UNESCO to declare it a World Heritage Site.

Cartagena remained relatively peaceful even during the worst periods of violence in the 1980s and 1990s. In the past couple of decades, Cartagena has become a major international tourist destination. It's a popular cruise ship port on the Caribbean circuit and boasts a proliferation of chic, five-star hotels in the Old City as well as glitzy condominiums and hotels in Bocagrande, a modern beachfront area to the south.

Safety

The historic Old City and Getsemaní areas of Cartagena are quite safe to visit and walk around even relatively late into the night. This is because they're an island separated from the rest of the sprawling city by a couple of bridges and are well policed. Because the old streets of the center are often packed, however, keep valuables close to your body. Also stay mindful while walking on the walls after dark, and be careful when leaving this secured area—the rest of Cartagena is one of the most insecure urban landscapes in the country due to high levels of inequality.

While reports are rare, police have been known to stop and frisk young non-Colombian men in the evening, purportedly out of suspicion of drug possession (Colombian law decriminalizes personal possession of all drugs), when in actuality they are looking for money. This has occurred most commonly late at night in Getsemaní. Some people have found that calling attention to the officer and getting others to record the episode on their phone defuses the situation.

Some of the poorer fishing communities near Cartagena, such as La Boquilla and the town center in the island of Tierrabomba, are best visited in a group. Keep an eye on drinks at late-night venues, especially outside of the historic center.

By far the greatest annoyances in Cartagena are persistent street vendors, who have even been known to latch on to walking tours. Some try to annoy you into buying something to make them go away, probably because that has worked in the past. Saying *"No, gracias,"* and making eye contact instead of ignoring them usually helps ward off these nuisances. Don't allow them to get under your skin.

Most taxi drivers, bartenders, and vendors are honest, but there are always a few who will try to take advantage of visitors by overcharging or not returning the proper amount of change to a non-Colombian visitor who may not hold a strong grasp of the language or be confused by the currency. Always try to pay street vendors with small notes or coins when possible—keep those COP$50,000 notes only for emergencies, or change them. Request to see the drinks menu (*carta de tragos*) at bars before ordering. Before getting into a cab, have an idea of what you'll be paying, and confirm the amount with the driver upfront.

Orientation

The city's tourist focus is a relatively small area: the Old City, the original Spanish settlement that was once completely enclosed by massive stone walls. The Old City comprises two main districts: the **Centro,** with its magnificent walls, narrow streets, colorful bougainvillea dangling from balconies, activity-packed plazas, and myriad churches and palaces; and **Getsemaní,** an old colonial neighborhood that was also enclosed by its own wall and fortifications. Newly mural-lined and spruced up, today it's a more relaxed counterpart to the Centro, with more bohemian-style lodgings, restaurants, and nightlife options.

CENTRO

The Centro (from *centro histórico;* also called the **Old City** or the **Walled City**) is the historic core of Cartagena; it's surrounded by the most impressive sections of the city walls. This is where most of Cartagena's sights are located, including its most famous churches and museums. Today, the Centro is where many upscale hotels, restaurants, shops, and nightclubs are found.

The northeastern half of the Centro is known as **San Diego**. The former home of the middle-class inhabitants of Cartagena, the architecture here is a bit more modest but still bursting with style and color. There are a few attractions in San Diego, notably the Iglesia de Santo Toribio de Mogrovejo and Las Bóvedas, a shopping arcade located in a section of the walls. The charm of San Diego lies in its quieter streets and leafy plazas, including Plaza de San Diego, and its high-end restaurants and bars, many tucked into former colonial houses.

The Centro is organized in a general grid with numerous plazas. Even many residents don't know or use official street names, as they change from block to block. Orient yourself by identifying the main squares—Torre de los Coches, Plaza de la Aduana, Plaza de Santo Domingo, Parque de Bolívar, and Plaza Fernández de Madrid—and making your way from one to the other. Walking these charming streets (and even getting lost on occasion) is a pleasure.

GETSEMANÍ

The neighborhood of Getsemaní lies southeast of the Centro, just outside the main walls. Also walled and just as old as the Centro, it's a bohemian alternative to the Old City, with hip cafés and independent hostels tucked down narrow, winding, mural-lined streets; the street art here is amazing. The epicenter of the neighborhood is the Plaza de la Trinidad, in front of Iglesia de la Santísima Trinidad, where Cartagena's independence was first declared. Backpackers, street artists, *palenquero*

dancers, and locals mingle in the open air over cold beers on a nightly basis.

In between Getsemaní and the Old City are the docks of the Muelle de los Pegasos and the Muelle Turístico de la Bodeguita, the latter of which is the departure point for tourist boats headed to the Islas del Rosario.

LA MATUNA

In the late 19th and early 20th centuries, the mangroves and marshes separating the Centro and Getsemaní were filled, resulting in the thin slice of modernity called La Matuna. Home to several high-rises, there is also a colorful open-air market feel to the pedestrian-only streets of La Matuna, a refreshingly local vibe that contrasts nicely with the rest of the Old City. It's full of cheap eats and shops.

MANGA

To the southeast of Getsemaní, across the Puente Roman (Roman Bridge), is the island of Manga, a historic residential district dotted with gorgeous 19th-century mansions. A handful of hostels have popped up here recently, and it's also home to the landmark Club de Pesca restaurant, housed in the well-preserved Fuerte de San Sebastián del Pastelillo, one of many forts that once protected the bay. The boardwalk along Calle 24, with its magnificent views across the bay, is a pleasant place to walk at sunset.

BOCAGRANDE

South of the Old City is flashy Bocagrande, a skinny peninsula with high-rise hotels, malls, and residential buildings fronting a wide swath of golden sand and the milky-blue Caribbean Sea. The main attraction is the beaches, which get packed on weekends with vacationing Colombian families, vendors, and masseuses. The beaches in no way compare to those of the Islas del Rosario and Barú, but they're close to the city center and easy to enjoy for an afternoon. At the southern end of the Bocagrande peninsula is the Laguito neighborhood, home to more

Centro

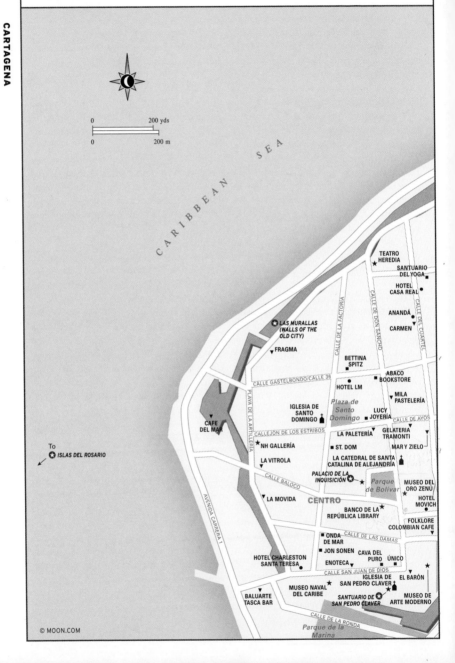

0   200 yds
0   200 m

CARIBBEAN SEA

TEATRO HEREDIA
SANTUARIO DEL YOGA
HOTEL CASA REAL
ANANDÁ
CARMEN

LAS MURALLAS (WALLS OF THE OLD CITY)
FRAGMA

CALLE DE LA FACTORÍA
CALLE DE DON SANCHO
CALLE DEL CUARTEL

BETTINA SPITZ
ABACO BOOKSTORE

CALLE GASTELBONDO/CALLE 36
HOTEL LM
MILA PASTELERÍA

PLAYA DE LA ARTILLERÍA
IGLESIA DE SANTO DOMINGO
Plaza de Santo Domingo
LUCY JOYERÍA
CALLE DE AYOS

CAFE DEL MAR
LA PALETERÍA
GELATERÍA TRAMONTI

CALLEJÓN DE LOS ESTRIBOS
NH GALLERÍA
ST. DOM
MAR Y ZIELO

To
ISLAS DEL ROSARIO

LA VITROLA
LA CATEDRAL DE SANTA CATALINA DE ALEJANDRÍA

CALLE BALOCO
PALACIO DE LA INQUISICIÓN
Parque de Bolívar
MUSEO DEL ORO ZENÚ

LA MOVIDA
CENTRO
HOTEL MOVICH

AVENIDA CARRERA 1
BANCO DE LA REPÚBLICA LIBRARY
FOLKLORE COLOMBIAN CAFE

ONDA DE MAR
CALLE DE LAS DAMAS

JON SONEN
CAVA DEL PURO
ÚNICO

HOTEL CHARLESTON SANTA TERESA
ENOTECA

CALLE SAN JUAN DE DIOS
IGLESIA DE SAN PEDRO CLAVER
EL BARÓN

BALUARTE TASCA BAR
MUSEO NAVAL DEL CARIBE
SANTUARIO DE SAN PEDRO CLAVER
MUSEO DE ARTE MODERNO

CALLE DE LA RONDA
Parque de la Marina

© MOON.COM

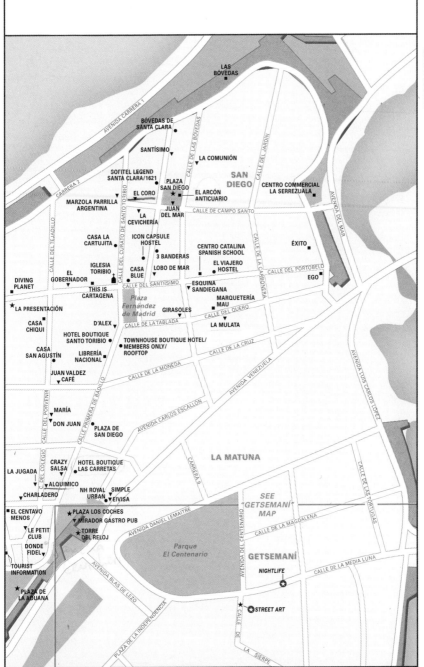

LAS
BÓVEDAS

BÓVEDAS DE
SANTA CLARA

AVENIDA CARRERA 1

SANTÍSIMO

CALLE DE LAS BÓVEDAS

LA COMUNIÓN

CALLE DEL JARDÍN

SOFITEL LEGEND
SANTA CLARA/1621

PLAZA
SAN DIEGO

EL CORO

EL ARCÓN
ANTICUARIO

SAN
DIEGO

CENTRO COMMERCIAL
LA SERREZUALA

CARRERA 2

MARZOLA PARRILLA
ARGENTINA

JUAN
DEL MAR

LA
CEVICHERÍA

CALLE DE CAMPO SANTO

AVENIDA DEL MAR

CALLE DEL CURATO DE SANTO TORIBIO

CASA LA
CARTUJITA

ICON CAPSULE
HOSTEL

CENTRO CATALINA
SPANISH SCHOOL

ÉXITO

CALLE DEL TEJADILLO

3 BANDERAS

LOBO DE MAR

EL VIAJERO
HOSTEL

CALLE DE LA CARBONERA

CALLE DEL PORTOBELO

DIVING
PLANET

EL
GOBERNADOR

IGLESIA
TORIBIO

CASA
BLUE

EGO

THIS IS
CARTAGENA

CALLE DEL SANTÍSIMO

ESQUINA
SANDIEGANA

LA PRESENTACIÓN

Plaza
Fernández
de Madrid

GIRASOLES

MARQUETERÍA
MAU

CASA
CHIQUI

D'ALEX

CALLE DE LA TABLADA

CALLE DEL QUERO

LA MULATA

HOTEL BOUTIQUE
SANTO TORIBIO

TOWNHOUSE BOUTIQUE HOTEL/
MEMBERS ONLY/
ROOFTOP

CALLE DE LA CRUZ

CASA
SAN AGUSTÍN

LIBRERÍA
NACIONAL

CALLE DE LA MONEDA

JUAN VALDEZ
CAFÉ

AVENIDA VENEZUELA

AVENIDA LUIS CARLOS LÓPEZ

CALLE DEL PORVENIR

MARÍA

CALLE PRIMERA DE BADILLO

DON JUAN

PLAZA DE
SAN DIEGO

AVENIDA CARLOS ESCALLÓN

LA MATUNA

C. DEL COLEGIO

CRAZY
SALSA

HOTEL BOUTIQUE
LAS CARRETAS

CARRERA 9

CALLE DE LAS TÓRTUGAS

LA JUGADA

ALQUIMICO

CHARLADERO

NH ROYAL
URBAN

SIMPLE
EIVISA

SEE
"GETSEMANÍ"
MAP

EL CENTAVO
MENOS

PLAZA LOS COCHES

MIRADOR GASTRO PUB

AVENIDA DANIEL LEMAITRE

CALLE DE LA MAGDALENA

LE PETIT
CLUB

TORRE
DEL RELOJ

DONDE
FIDEL

Parque
El Centenario

AVENIDA DEL CENTENARIO

CALLE DE LA MEDIA LUNA

GETSEMANÍ

TOURIST
INFORMATION

NIGHTLIFE

PLAZA DE
LA ADUANA

AVENIDA BLAS DE LEZO

CALLE DE

STREET ART

PLAZA DE LA INDEPENDENCIA

LA SIERPE

laid-back beaches that are popular with kite-surfers and other water sports enthusiasts. This is also where boats depart for the island of Tierrabomba and its much nicer, and still relatively undiscovered, white-sand beaches.

EL CABRERO

Just north of the Old City is the 19th-century district of El Cabrero. The neighborhood's sole attraction, besides beaches popular with locals, is the Casa Museo Rafael Núñez, once the home of conservative president Rafael Núñez, who governed from Cartagena.

SIGHTS
Centro

TOP EXPERIENCE

★ LAS MURALLAS

Referring to Cartagena's *murallas* (walls), Colombians endearingly call the city "El Corralito de Piedra" (little stone corral). One of the most salient features of the city, they provide epic views over Cartagena and the Caribbean Sea. A walk on the walls is a quintessential Cartagena experience, enjoyed by international visitors, Colombian honeymooners, and Cartagenan high school students alike. The best time for this is in the early evening hours around sunset, when the sky casts its fiery spell over the turquoise waters. Vendors sell cold beers along the wall at this time, and couples cuddle up to witness the impressive natural spectacle.

This is the largest series of fortifications in South America. The walls were built by the Spaniards after Sir Francis Drake sacked the city in 1568, in an effort to guard the gold and other goods they'd stolen from indigenous civilizations within Colombia. The project took almost two centuries to complete. The walls that can be seen today are mostly from the 17th and 18th centuries.

The most impressive section is the stretch that runs along the Old City parallel to the sea. This includes three *baluartes* (bulwarks, or ramparts) where Spaniards stood ready

to defend the city from attack. The massive **Baluartes de San Lucas y de Santa Catalina,** built in the very north of the city to repel attacks from land, are known as Las Tenazas because they're shaped like pincers. When the sea started depositing sediments and expanding the shore, thus enabling the enemy to maneuver south along the wall, the Spanish built a spike to halt them. This defensive structure, known as El Espigón de la Tenaza, lies at the far end of the seafront wall. About midway along the seafront wall is the equally impressive **Baluarte Santo Domingo,** now home to swank drinking hole **Café del Mar.** At the southern tip of the segment facing the sea, next to the Plaza de Santa Teresa, are the **Baluartes de San Ignacio y de San Francisco Javier,** also home to the **Baluarte Tasca-Bar,** a pleasant outdoor lounge.

★ SANTUARIO DE SAN PEDRO CLAVER

An outstanding example of colonial architectural majesty, the **Claustro de San Pedro Claver** (Plaza de San Pedro Claver No. 30-01, tel. 5/664-4991, www.sanpedroclaver.co, 8am-6pm Mon.-Fri., 8am-5pm Sat.-Sun., COP$14,000) is a massive former Jesuit monastery turned three-story museum. Saint Pedro Claver served here as a priest. The first person to be canonized as a saint in the New World, he fought for the rights of newly arrived enslaved Africans in Cartagena, and is said to have baptized hundreds of thousands of them as well as attended to their medical needs. In addition to encompassing a spacious, lush courtyard brimming with flowers and trees, the museum holds relics and art from the colonial era on the 1st floor, memorials to Saint Claver on the 2nd—including the Spartan little room where he lived and prayed—and an impressive collection of African and Afro-Colombian art on the 3rd.

1: colorful Callejón Angosto in Getsemaní;
2: Palacio de la Inquisición; 3: Iglesia de San Pedro Claver

Adjacent to the monastery is the towering **Iglesia de San Pedro Claver** (Plaza de San Pedro Claver No. 30-01, tel. 5/664-4991, masses 6:45am and 6pm Mon.-Sat., 7am, 10am, noon, and 6pm Sun.). Its majestic dome is one of the most prominent features of the ancient Cartagena skyline. Inside lies a beautiful marble altar, the final resting place for San Pedro Claver.

MUSEO DE ARTE MODERNO DE CARTAGENA DE INDIAS

Cartagena's main art museum, the **Museo de Arte Moderno de Cartagena de Indias** (Cl. 30 No. 4-08, Plaza de San Pedro Claver, tel. 5/664-5815, www.mamcartagena.org, 9am-noon and 3pm-7pm Mon.-Fri., 10am-1pm Sat., 4pm-9pm Sun., COP$10,000, Tues. free), is on the square in front of Plaza de San Pedro Claver, which contains several metallic sculptures by Cartagenero Edgardo Carmona that depict quotidian scenes of Cartagena life. The museum has a small permanent collection of works from 20th-century Colombian artists, including native sons Alejandro Obregón and Enrique Grau. The museum is in the old Customs House. For more detailed information on the museum and its collections, download Soundwalkrs, a free smartphone app.

MUSEO NAVAL DEL CARIBE

Adjoining the rear of the Santuario de San Pedro Claver is the **Museo Naval del Caribe** (Cl. San Juan de Dios No. 3-62, tel. 5/664-2440, www.museonavaldelcaribe.com, 10am-5:30pm daily, COP$16,000). This museum provides a history lesson of the area's earliest indigenous dwellers, continuing through the Spanish conquest and including a bit about the many (mostly English) pirates who tried to steal the Spaniards' gold loot. The 2nd floor has a lot of replicas of grand ships from the period and a history of the Colombian navy (you may be surprised to learn of its participation in the Korean War). There are few explanations in English. Part of the building dates to the 17th century and was a Jesuit convent; after the Jesuits were expelled by the king, the building was converted into a hospital. Pushing buttons in the submarine upstairs makes the price of admission worth it.

PARQUE DE BOLÍVAR

One of the city's most pleasant and lively squares is the **Parque de Bolívar,** which once served as a bullfighting ring. A statue of Simón Bolívar on horseback presides over the center of the lush park. Take a break on a bench under the shade of the rubber trees and enjoy a *tinto* (black coffee) from one of the vendors. *Palenquero* dancers and drummers frequently perform here in the afternoon.

★ PALACIO DE LA INQUISICIÓN

On the south side of the Parque de Bolívar is the **Palacio de la Inquisición** (Parque de Bolívar, tel. 5/664-4570, www.muhca.gov.co, 9am-6pm Mon.-Sat., 10am-4pm Sun., COP$21,000). This remarkable 18th-century construction, one of the grandest examples of colonial architecture in the city, was the headquarters of the Spanish Inquisition in Cartagena. The building housed the Tribunal del Santo Oficio, whose purpose was to exert control over the Indians, mestizos, and enslaved Africans not only in Nueva Granada but also in New World colonies in Central America, the Caribbean, and Venezuela. One of just three Palaces of Inquisition in the Americas (the others were in Lima and Mexico City), the tribunal was active from 1610 until the late 17th century.

The building's 1st floor is a museum displaying the weapons of torture employed by authorities as part of the Inquisition. In Cartagena as elsewhere, the most common punishable crime was "witchcraft," which could mean anything from practicing African religious rites to owning the wrong books, including science books that didn't align with church doctrine. Hundreds of supposed heretics were condemned here and dozens put to death. On the 2nd floor are exhibition spaces dedicated to the restoration of the building and to the history of Cartagena. Most explanations are written in Spanish; you may hire an English-speaking guide (COP$35,000 for a group up to five persons). On your way out, take a right and then another right onto Calle de la Inquisición and look for a small window on the palace wall. This was a secret spot where citizens of colonial Cartagena could anonymously report others for various and sundry heresies.

MUSEO DEL ORO ZENÚ

The **Museo del Oro Zenú** (Cra. 4 No. 33-26, Parque de Bolívar, tel. 5/660-0778, 9am-5pm Tues.-Sat., 9am-1pm Sun., free), on the east side of the Parque de Bolívar, exhibits gold jewelry and funerary objects from the Zenú indigenous people, who were the original dwellers of the Río Magdalena area and Río Sinú valley, to the southwest of Cartagena. It has excellent explanations in both English and Spanish. A smaller version of the Museo del Oro in Bogotá, this museum has a regional focus and is one of the few tributes to indigenous culture in Cartagena.

LA CATEDRAL DE SANTA CATALINA DE ALEJANDRÍA

Cartagena's most magnificent church, **La Catedral de Santa Catalina de Alejandría** (Cl. de los Santos de Piedra, Cra. 4, no phone, mass 6am, noon, and 6:15pm Mon.-Fri., 6:30pm Sat., 8am, 10am, 6pm, and 7pm Sun.) can be seen from just about anywhere in the city thanks to its ornate domed tower, which lights up with tropical colors at night. Built in 1577, it lies kitty-corner from the Parque de Bolívar and contains an 18th-century gilded altar and a marble pulpit.

Getsemaní
★ STREET ART

In recent years, Getsemaní has become a street art mecca, much like Bogotá's famed La Candelaria area. Key streets include **Calle de la Sierpe,** which is where the movement began when local artists from the CarTagEna Collective turned what was once a semi-industrial block used as a public bathroom into an endless mural, and **Avenida Pedregal.** Tiny **Callejón Angosto,** which is canopied by brightly colored umbrellas, is also lined with impressive street art. An annual **Aerosol Festival** (late Feb.), organized by the Champetú Collective, brings in street artists from all over Latin America to add more pieces. With the centuries-old residential neighborhood now facing rapid gentrification, many of the current works depict the faces of Getsemaní residents themselves.

street art in Getsemaní by Boni Olmoz

Getsemaní

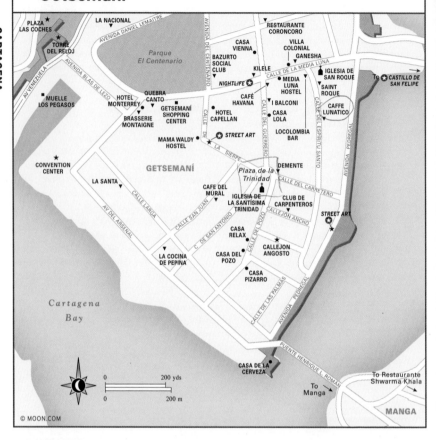

CHURCHES

There are two colonial-era churches in Getsemaní worth a peek. The first is the **Iglesia de la Santísima Trinidad** (Plaza de la Trinidad, tel. 5/664-2050, mass 6pm Mon.-Sat., 9am and 6pm Sun.), completed in the mid-17th century. This bright yellow church of three naves is modeled on the city's cathedral. The church is often open during the day, and visitors are welcome to sit on a pew in front of a massive fan and cool off. In the evenings the colorful Plaza de la Trinidad is a hub of activity.

In response to a deadly cholera outbreak that was ravaging Cartagena, church leaders committed to building a church dedicated to Saint Roch, protector of those afflicted with the plague. Construction on the simple **Iglesia de San Roque** (Cl. de la Media Luna and Cl. Espíritu Santo, tel. 5/664-2512, mass 7pm Mon.-Sat., 8:30am and 7pm Sun.) began in 1651.

PASEO DE LOS MÁRTIRES AND PARQUE DEL CENTENARIO

Paseo de los Mártires was once the main corridor that led from the Walled City to Getsemaní and today features nine marble statues of important historical figures. Adjacent to the corridor is the **Parque del**

Centenario, which was opened in 1911 in commemoration of Colombia's first century of independence. It's a pleasant place for a stroll, and you just might spot enormous iguanas, small monkeys, or even a sloth up in the trees. On the northern edge of the park is a series of stalls where vendors sell used books.

El Cabrero
CASA MUSEO RAFAEL NÚÑEZ

Just beyond the wall in the Cabrero neighborhood is the **Casa Museo Rafael Núñez** (Cl. Real del Cabrero No. 41-89, tel. 5/660-9058, 9am-5pm Tues.-Fri., 10am-4pm Sat.-Sun., free). This is the house of Rafael Núñez, the four-time former president of Colombia, author of the 1886 Colombian constitution, and author of the 11 verses of Colombia's national anthem. Núñez governed Colombia from this, his coastal home. The museum has memorabilia from his political life and is a beautiful example of 19th-century Cartagena architecture. Núñez's grave is in the Ermita de Nuestra Señora de las Mercedes across the street.

★ Castillo de San Felipe

The largest Spanish fort on the continent, the magnificent **Castillo de San Felipe** (Cerro de San Lázaro, east of Old City, tel. 5/656-6803, www.patrimoniodecartagena.com, 8am-6pm daily, COP$25,000) must have given pirates pause as they contemplated an attack on the city. While the walls around the city fended off maritime attacks, this fort was built atop the Cerro de San Lázaro to repel attacks by land at the Media Luna gate. Construction was begun in 1639 and completed more than a century later. Tunnels enabled soldiers to quickly move about without being noticed, and cells housed the occasional unlucky prisoner.

Today, visitors ramble through 890 meters (0.5 mi) of tunnels and secret passages (a flashlight will come in quite handy). Views from the highest points of the fort are magnificent. The best time to visit is late in the afternoon, when the intense sun abates. Audio tours (COP$10,000) are available. For some,

the view of the fort from a distance suffices, especially at nighttime when it's lit up.

If you want to do things up for a special celebration, you can rent out the entire *castillo* or space on the *murallas*. Contact the **Sociedad de Mejoras Públicas de Cartagena** (Castillo de San Felipe de Barajas, tel. 5/656-0590, www.fortificacionesdecartagena.com) for more information.

To get to the fort, take a cab (COP$6,000), a bus (COP$1,500) from Avenida Santander, or the TransCaribe (COP$2,000) from Avenida Venezuela.

La Popa

La Popa is a 150-meter-high (500-ft-high) hill east of Castillo de San Felipe, so named because of its resemblance to a ship's stern (*popa* in Spanish). La Popa is home to the **Convento Nuestra Señora de la Candelaria** (Cra. 20A 29D-16, tel. 5/666-0976, 9am-5:30pm daily, COP$11,000), which was built by Augustinian monks, reportedly on a pagan site of worship. The monastery has a courtyard abloom with flowers, a small chapel where faithful pray to the Virgen de la Candelaria, and memorabilia from Pope John Paul II's visit to the monastery in 1986. For many, the view of Cartagena is the biggest attraction. Cruise ship passengers arrive by busload at La Popa, so be prepared for crowds.

You can take a taxi there from the Old City for COP$50,000-60,000 round-trip. Arrange the price in advance and make sure the driver will wait for you. Many visitors combine a visit to La Popa with the Castillo de San Felipe, which is relatively nearby (although not within walking distance).

Mercado de Bazurto

Not for the faint of heart, a visit to the sprawling **Mercado de Bazurto** (Av. Pedro Heredia, 5am-4pm daily) is the best way to connect with workaday Cartagena. Be sure to peruse the seafood area on the waterfront periphery of this covered market, where women sell the catch of the day to restaurant owners. You'll also be amazed at all the different kinds of fruit on offer. Don't be afraid to barter a little and don't be shy: The hundreds of vendors generally enjoy interacting with foreign visitors. The market is at its liveliest in the morning, but it's also a great place to grab lunch; expect to spend a few hours here. Dress down and keep an eye on your valuables.

The market is in the Pie de la Popa neighborhood southeast of the Old City. The best way to get her is via taxi (COP$10,000). It's possible to take a bus (COP$2,200) from Avenida Santander and there is also a TransCaribe rapid bus station here.

Another way of visiting the market is as part of the **Cartagena Gastronomic Tour** (tel. 5/660-1492, cell tel. 315/655-4120, cevicheria@hotmail.com, COP$250,000 pp), which also makes stops at local eateries and is organized by La Cevichería and Bazurto Social Club. On the tour, you'll learn about the ingredients that make Caribbean cuisine special, particularly seafood and exotic fruits. You'll also meet the vendors who have worked their entire lives behind a stall at the market. Afterward you'll head to a beach house in the village of Manzanillo de Mar and have a gourmet lunch featuring lobster and other delicacies.

Sightseeing Tours

Beyond Colombia (cell tel. 312/441-3171, www.beyondcolombia.com) offers free walking tours of the Old City (10am and 4pm daily) and Getsemaní (10am daily), as well as food tours (4pm daily) that meet at the *Noli Me Tangere* statue in the middle of the Camellón de los Mártires plaza, just outside of the Torre del Reloj and the Old City, in front of the Muelle de los Pegasos. They're easy to find; look for their red umbrellas. Tours last about two hours and are led by locals, who request a COP$30,000 donation at the end; feel free to give what you think is appropriate.

Bursting with insider tips on the city and its environs, **This Is Cartagena** (Cl. Sargento Mayor, No. 6-107, Of. 104, cell tel. 318/516-7767, www.ticartagena.com, 9am-6pm Mon.-Fri.) offers unconventional tours of the city.

In addition to a top-notch walking tour of the Old City (US$50), the company also offers a tour devoted to the art scene (US$55), a bizarre-foods tour (US$85), a day of luxurious island-hopping on a yacht (US$750), and a drinking tour (US$75).

A fund-raising project for the nonprofit FEM (www.femcolombia.org), **Cartagena Insider** (Cl. del Quero No. 9-64, tel. 5/643-4185, www.insider.com.co) takes visitors beyond the boutique hotels and fancy restaurants of the Old City to experience the "real" Cartagena and its people. Tour options include a night of salsa, a day trip to La Boquilla fishing community, a walking tour of the Mercado de Bazurto, and a tour focusing on the *champeta* music culture unique to Cartagena. Proceeds go directly to the nonprofit's social programs in and around the city. Tours can also be arranged to communities such as Tuchín, Córdoba, Leticia (a town on Barú), Palmerito, and San Bacile de Palenque.

With an extensive array of interesting tours, **Alternative Travel Cartagena** (tel. 5/646-0701, www.alternativetravelcartagena.com) aims to take visitors to lesser-known areas in and around Cartagena for a unique experience. They are based in the fishing village of La Boquilla and offer horseback rides on the beach, cooking classes, and canoe rides through mangroves.

ENTERTAINMENT
★ Nightlife

Cartagena's nightlife rages seven nights a week, thanks to the steady river of tourists who pour into town. Bars tend to close at 2am or 3am weekdays, and some stay open until 5am on the weekends. Expect to pay a cover fee for larger discos and places with live music; those in groups can ask for a discount. The two most concentrated nightlife areas are around **Plaza de los Coches** in the Old City and **Calle Media Luna** in Getsemaní. The city's favorite music styles are Latin crossover rhythms, such as reggaetón and salsa, along with the Afrobeats of homegrown *champeta*.

Total Distance: 1.6 kilometers (1 mi)
Walking Time: 25-30 minutes
The best way to get to know Cartagena is to go for a morning stroll down its glorious balcony-lined streets, weaving your way from gorgeous plaza to plaza, and even getting lost a couple of times. This tour starts in the Centro and ends in San Diego.

1. Start at the **Plaza de los Coches** (west of Av. Venezuela, opposite Getsemaní), once the main entry point to the city. It is easily identifiable by the iconic 19th-century **Torre del Reloj** (clock tower) that tops the entrance through the wall. Inside stands a statue of Cartagena's founder, Pedro de Heredia. During the colonial period, this plaza was the site of the city's slave market. Today, the plaza is filled with watering holes catering to visitors. Along the main corridor is the **Portal de las Dulces,** a row of stands where Afro-Colombian women sell home-made sweets, often made from coconut and tamarind.

Torre del Reloj in the Plaza de los Coches

2. Immediately to the southwest is the large triangular **Plaza de la Aduana,** once the seat of power in colonial Cartagena. It's surrounded by stately colonial mansions. A statue of Christopher Columbus presides in the center. It has its fair share of ATMs and is where the main tourist office is located.

3. Adjacent to Plaza de la Aduana to the southwest is the **Plaza de San Pedro,** a small but charming square located in front of the imposing **Iglesia de San Pedro Claver** and its attached cloister.

4. Walk two blocks north on Calle de San Pedro and you'll arrive at the city's heart, the leafy **Parque de Bolívar,** a shady park with benches, fountains, and a statue of Simón Bolívar in the middle. Surrounding this lovely park are some of the most important buildings of the city, including **La Catedral de Santa Catalina de Alejandría** and the **Palacio de la Inquisición.**

5. Continue north on Calle de los Santos de Piedra for one block. Take the first left onto Calle de Ayos. One block west is the **Plaza de Santo Domingo,** in the heart of the former upper-class quarter. You will notice many superb two-story *casas altas* built by rich merchants. The plaza is dominated by the austere **Iglesia de Santo Domingo.** A rotund nude bronze sculpture by famous Colombian sculptor Fernando Botero is a centerpiece of this square. Live musical performances and many outdoor cafés liven up the popular plaza later in the day.

6. Walk north along Calle de Santo Domingo for a block, then turn right and head east for four blocks on Calle de la Mantilla until you reach Calle Segunda de Badillo. Turn left and half a block north is the large, green **Plaza Fernández de Madrid** in the San Diego district. On the northwest side is the charming **Iglesia de Santo Toribio de Mogrovejo,** with its magnificent wooden ceiling.

7. Head east on Calle del Santísimo for two blocks, then turn left on Calle Cochera del Hobo and go north just over a block to the **Plaza de San Diego,** which is surrounded by inviting restaurants. It's also where artisans sell handicrafts under the shade of a tree.

8. Walk north for one block on Calle de las Bóvedas, which will deposit you at the **Plaza de las Bóvedas** at the extreme northeast of the city. Once the location of a military storehouse, this is where you can browse handicrafts under the golden arched walls of the Galería de las Bóvedas.

Best Nightlife

- **Las Murallas:** Enjoy a drink from a bar or beer vendor on the walls surrounding Cartagena's Old City, overlooking the sparkling Caribbean Sea.

- **Plaza de la Trinidad:** Hang out with a drink and the locals on this happening plaza at the nexus of several hip, mural-lined streets in Getsemaní.

- **EL Coro:** Soak in the singular ambience of this swanky lounge located within a former monastery.

- **Alquímico:** Splurge on a masterfully crafted cocktail at this three-story colonial mansion turned tropical-cool lounge.

- **Rooftop:** Party at your own personal pool at this festive rooftop lounge.

- **La Caponera:** Dance on the sidewalk at this laid-back bohemian watering-hole.

cocktail at Alquímico

- **La Movida:** Mix and mingle on the garden patio of Cartagena's hippest disco.

- **Kilele:** Three levels and three flavors of party await at Getsemaní's largest dance club.

- **Bazurto Social Club:** Learn how to dance *champeta* during a free class at this friendly, bohemian club.

- **Donde Fidel:** Salsa dance the night away with devoted locals at this landmark bar.

More upscale places tend to play electronic music and top 40 hits mixed in with Latin beats.

LAS MURALLAS AND PLAZAS

With the Caribbean breeze kissing your face and the city and coast spread before you, ★ **enjoying a drink on *las murallas*** is an experience that shouldn't be missed. Sunset is especially divine, and that's when the real crowds gather. There are three official options for boozing on the wall. The most happening spot is the **Café del Mar** (Baluarte Santo Domingo, tel. 5/664-6515, 5pm-3am daily, no cover), on the wall just two blocks from the Plaza de Santo Domingo. A live DJ plays lounge-style electronic music, and it stays busy until late. It's a cool place, but it's not

great for mingling, as patrons are all seated in bulky furniture, and the drinks are pricey. There's also **Baluarte Tasca-Bar** (Cl. San Juan de Dios, tel. 5/660-0468, 5:30pm-2am daily, no cover), an open-air restaurant-bar on the wall across from the Plaza de Santa Teresa. It's chilled-out here, not trendy—but the drink prices are on the steep side, at COP$28,000 for a margarita. The third option is good for your budget: Buy a cold Águila beer from a roaming vendor (COP$4,000) and just hang out and enjoy the views.

Public drinking—legal throughout the city—is a popular sport all over Cartagena, and there are several other excellent spots to down a cold one in the open air. ★ **Plaza de la Trinidad** in Getsemaní is a great place to head after sunset to warm up for the evening. As the nexus of several hip, mural-lined streets, it's the beating heart and soul of the neighborhood and stays lively until late at night, although the action peters off after midnight or so. Cheap beers (COP$3,000) are sold by vendors, and street performers and dance groups, including *palenquero* dancers, perform from about 7pm to 10pm. Mingling with locals and other tourists is easy to do here. Several bars also front the plaza and offer sidewalk seating for those who prefer a more formal front-row seat. At the **Plaza de los Coches** under the Torre del Reloj, the people-watching just gets more interesting as the night goes on; pull up a bench, grab a giant mojito from street stand El Colombiano on the corner, and enjoy the nocturnal action.

BARS AND LOUNGES

If you're looking for atmosphere, head to ★ **El Coro** (Cl. del Torno No. 39-29, tel. 5/650-4700, 5pm-2am Sun.-Thurs., 5pm-3am Fri.-Sat., no cover) at the Hotel Sofitel Legend Santa Clara. At this posh bar in a former 17th-century convent, crisply dressed bartenders serve Caribbean cocktails to hotel guests and others while Latin jazz plays in the background. Of the larger convent complex, El Coro is located in the chorus area from where

the resident nuns sang while mass was celebrated in the adjacent chapel. Ask to see the crypt, which was an inspiration for Gabriel García Márquez as he wrote *Of Love and Other Demons.*

Three stories of tropical cool at their finest make ★ **Alquímico** (Cl. del Colegio No. 34-24, cell tel. 318/845-0433, www.alquimico.com, 6pm-2am Sun.-Thurs., 6pm-3am Fri.-Sat., no cover) the place for top-notch mixology in an inspiring setting. Housed in a restored colonial mansion, the 1st story wraps around a large central bar and is great for mingling, and the 2nd floor looks down on the first and is decked out with couches and tables that make for more intimate conversations. Up on the rooftop, dance tunes get the crowd bumping and grinding in the humid open air.

Townhouse Boutique Hotel (Cra 7. No. 36-88, cell tel. 304/355-1068, www.townhousecartagena.com) offers two unique watering holes. Downstairs, **Members Only** (9pm-1pm daily, no cover) is a piano bar that hosts live music, with a house jazz band as well as visiting performers, while up at the cocktail lounge ★ **Rooftop** (8am-1pm) several tables have their own mini-swimming pools, club music is played, and views over the

sunset at Café del Mar

illuminated domed churches of Cartagena simply cannot be beat; sometimes there's a cover here, but this varies seasonally.

In an unassuming corner of the Plaza de San Pedro Claver, **El Barón** (Cra. 4 No. 31-7, tel. 5/664-3105, 5pm-1am Sun.-Mon., noon-1am Tues., noon-2am Wed.-Sat.) is devoted to cocktail culture. The interior is all brass and rustic furnishings, but you can also sip the evening away out on the plaza, where the people-watching is fantastic. Allow the bartender to mix you a gin-basil smash—you can get a beer anytime. Tapas are also on offer.

Mirador Gastro Bar (Cra. 7, Plaza de Los Coches, tel. 5/664-6666, daily 6pm-2am, no cover), perched on the 5th-floor rooftop of a stately former warehouse overlooking Plaza de los Coches, is a great place for cocktails with stunning views of the Torre del Reloj and Cartagena waterfront. Videos of the latest Latin dance jams play in the background, and the cocktails are decently priced for the tourist center of town. Just across the Plaza de los Coches, **The Clock Pub** (Cl. 34 No. 7-33, Torre del Reloj, www.theclockpub.com/ctg. tel. 5/660-1310, 10am-2am daily, no cover) is your run-of-the-mill British-style pub transplanted to exotic realms, but it does stock some good-quality craft and international beers on tap. It also hosts live rock bands and a chill upstairs room that makes a great refuge when things get too crazy out on the plaza.

With sidewalk seats fronting charming Plaza de San Diego, **Cuba 1940** (Cl. Stuart No. 7-46, cell tel. 304/680-7301, 11am-midnight daily, no cover) is a classy Latin jazz joint decked out like an old-school Havana living room. Live bands play most nights of the week, and the friendly owners like to come around and chat with guests in between sets.

Local creatives and international travelers rub shoulders at ★ **La Caponera** (Cl. 24 No. 25-100, tel. 5/664-1372, 11am-3:30am daily), a funky and down-to-earth bar located across from the Getsemaní Convention Center, with a row of outdoor tables and inexpensive drinks. The place tends to get packed later in the evening, when the tight indoor dance floor spills out onto the sidewalk. Located just below The City Club, the city's top LGBT venue, there is considerable crossover between the two bars, and a friendly, open vibe in general.

For a chilled-out version of Café del Mar, check out **Casa de la Cerveza** (Cl. Aresenal No. 24, cell tel. 316/291-4644, www. casadelacerveza.com, 5pm-1am daily). It's located on top of the Baluarte el Reducto, an ancient battle station on the wall in Getsemaní. The outdoor beer garden here overlooks the bay and offers bed-style lounges for enjoying Colombian-brewed red, golden, or black beers on draft.

For a night out with locals, head to **Club de Carpinteros** (Cl. Ancho No. 10B, 2pm-3am Wed.-Sun.) in Getsemaní. This neighborhood watering hole is full of characters and has a small dance floor in the back room. On Sunday it throws a casual salsa party that brings out some of the city's most devoted fans and dancers.

Planeta Champeta (Cl. 35 No.10B-04, cell tel. 301/661-2385, noon-midnight daily), located in La Matuna right in front of Plazoleta Benkos Bioho, is popular with the hip creative class. Murals adorn the walls and local bands frequent the small house stage. Classic *champeta* is always on play during the week. It also hosts film screenings and other artistic events. Sometimes there's a cover for live music.

DISCOS AND CLUBS

★ **La Movida** (Cl. Baloco No. 2-14, cell tel. 310/636-4472, 9pm-4am Tues.-Sat., COP$30,000 cover) is the hippest disco in Cartagena at the moment, and for good reason. Located just across from the sea-fronting ancient walls in the Old City, the Euro-chic, gay-friendly disco has a large-ish indoor dance floor and lounge decked out with retro furnishings, and a two-level garden patio. Each space hosts its own DJ, playing everything from electronica to Latin club hits. It locks the doors after 3am and keeps the party going into the after-hours—you can leave,

Champeta for the People

A mix of fast footwork and twerking, *champeta* is a style of dance that was born in Cartagena decades ago, yet just recently has become an international sensation—greatly aided by Shakira's *champeta* performance for 2020's Super Bowl halftime show. Also known as *champeta Africana* because it has musical roots going back to Congolese culture—preserved in Colombia's San Basilio de Palanque, the first free African town in the Americas—the hypnotic rhythms are fun and sexy and embody a kind of *allegria* (happiness) that is infectious.

Champeta is based on harmonic rhythms played on a synthesizer, with a main singer backed by other instruments, including the guitar and drums. Although it was looked down upon by the upper classes as far too sexual for years, *champeta* is now considered a major Colombian musical style, and artists like Mr. Black and Kevin Florez have crossed over into pop music.

Originally known as *terapia* (therapy) because it was said to chase away the blues, *champeta* arose from Cartagena's underprivileged neighborhoods in the 1970s and 1980s and quickly spread to neighboring cities like Barranquilla. Much like U.S. hip-hop or Brazilian "funk," *champeta* channels the stories of the oppressed and cultivates street culture as joyous resistance.

The *champeta* culture of Cartagena revolves around huge street parties in the barrio and massive weekly concerts at venues like the softball stadium, but there are also a handful of nightlife spots in town where you can get a taste of this culture. The **Bazurto Social Club** hosts live *champeta* bands Wednesday-Saturday nights at midnight, with free *champeta* dance classes preceding at 10:30pm. Around the corner, **Kilele** features a live *champeta* band every night of the week on its 1st floor. Also nearby, **Planeta Champeta** is a small, artsy venue that hosts local and visiting bands on the weekends and plays classic *champeta* during the week.

For a deeper immersion into Cartagena's *champeta* culture, check out the **Champetú Collective,** an arts group that hosts regular *champeta* "pop-up" parties that typically celebrate album or single releases by local artists. The Champetú Collective also organizes the Aerosol Festival, a street art festival in Getsemaní, and other cultural events that focus on the street culture of Cartagena. Its Facebook page, @champetuoficial, is the best place to connect.

but you can't get back in. Also along the wall, **Fragma Club** (Cra. 2 No. 36-86, cell tel. 301/241-6747, 10pm-3am, COP$25,000 cover) is a typical high-end Colombian dance club with two cavernous dance floors, one playing electronic music and the other Latin crossover beats. It's a great place to go with friends and is very popular with visitors from cities like Bogotá and Medellín.

Right on the Plaza de los Coches, **Eivissa** (Cl. Portocarrero No. 7-33, cell tel. 301/623-2336, 9pm-4am daily, COP$20,000 cover) is a two-story club that's a favorite with international tourists—and the locals who want to meet them. Downstairs, a DJ spins top 40 and Latin beats, often accompanied by professional dancers, while up on the rooftop live bands play over sweeping views of the Torre del Reloj and the waterfront. Many hostels offer free passes to Eivissa, so

it's worth asking. Right around the corner, **La Jugada Club House** (Cra. 6 No. 34-25, cell tel. 317/713-1458, 5pm-4am daily, COP$30,000 cover) is a luxurious five-story historic mansion turned nightlife venue. It's decked out like something out of *The Great Gatsby* and has three outdoor terraces plus a rooftop *mirador*. Expect to pay through the nose for drinks and to be tightly held to the no sneakers/no T-shirts dress code at the door. Go to Alquímico across the street if things don't work out.

In Getsemaní, nightlife ground zero is Calle Media Luna. ★ **Kilele** (Cl. Media Luna No. 9-79, cell tel. 310/571-9945, 8pm-3am daily, COP$10,000 cover) hosts live *champeta* and Afrobeat bands on the 1st floor, a Latin crossover disco on the 2nd, and a world top 40 party on the rooftop, where dance circles form around new friends pretty quickly. It's packed every night of the week and draws both locals and visitors. Around the corner, ★ **Bazurto Social Club** (Cra. 9 No. 30-42, cell tel. 317/648-1183, www.bazurtosocialclub.com, 8pm-3am Wed.-Sat., COP$20,000 cover after 11pm Fri.-Sat.) offers free *champeta* dance classes at 10:30pm. Stick around until midnight to practice with the live house band, the Bazurto All Stars, and visiting performers. The friendly bohemian vibe here is great for mingling, so feel comfortable coming solo. Food is also served, with dishes such as shrimp empanadas and paella.

There is also a large cluster of nightclubs over by Calle del Arsenal, on the Getsemaní waterfront, that are popular with younger Colombians on vacation. **La Santa** (Cl. Larga 25 No. 8B-90, cell tel. 302/453-3732, 7pm-4am Tues.-Sat., 2pm-4am Sun., COP$25,000 cover) is the standout here; it's been voted best electronic club in the country several years in a row. The huge dance floor has two levels and is carefully tended to by an award-winning in-house DJ. The Sunday pool party at La Santa is a Cartagena partygoer institution.

For a Cartagena-style after-hours party, head to **Nexus** (Diagonal 21 No. 45-84, El Bosque, cell tel. 300/691-9719, 2am-10am daily). This large disco attracts an eclectic mix of vacationing Colombians, backpacking internationals, and women of the evening and pumps electronic and Latin beats until well after the sun rises. It's located about a 15-minute drive outside of the center, so take a taxi (preferably in a group) and don't pay more than COP$20,000 total.

SALSA

Colombia moves and grooves to the rhythm of salsa everywhere you go, and Cartagena is no exception. In fact, it's one of the country's salsa meccas and gave birth to Colombia's most famous salsa singer, Joe Arroyo. You will no doubt hear his greatest hit "Rebelión," a protest against enslavement and a tribute to Afro-Colombian history, all over town in taxis, supermarkets, and so on, during your stay. Dancing to salsa in Colombia is a bit different from in the United States or Europe, or even other salsa-smitten countries such as Cuba. The emphasis here is on musicality, not technique. Although Colombian salsa dancers are considered some of the best in the world, don't expect fancy turns unless the music expressly calls for it. Salsa is also often simply an accompaniment in dive bars to cold beers and intellectual conversations.

★ **Donde Fidel** (Plaza de los Coches, tel. 5/664-3127, noon-2am Sun.-Thurs., noon-3am Fri.-Sat., no cover) is a large, old-school salsa lovers' spot that spans three storefronts located right on Plaza de los Coches. The bar's name means "where Fidel is," and the walls here are covered with photos of owner Fidel posing with salsa stars from all over Latin America. Good times and cold beer can be found here every night of the week.

La Esquina Sandiegana (corner of Cl. del Santísimo and Cl. de los Púntales, no phone, 5pm-2am Sun.-Thurs., 5pm-3am Fri.-Sat., no cover) is perhaps the last local-style salsa hole-in-the-wall in the Old City. It's decorated with salsa posters, album covers, and photographs of salsa greats. Located in the San Diego neighborhood, it's as authentic as it gets.

Overlooking the gorgeous skyline of the Old City from a wraparound balcony, **Quiebra Canto** (Cra. 28B No. 25-110, tel. 5/664-1372, 7pm-2am Tues.-Thurs. and Sun., 7pm-4am Fri.-Sat., no cover) is the epitome of classy Colombian salsa joints. A Cartagena institution, live bands play here nightly, the walls are covered with photos of salsa legends, and the friendly regulars are always up for a dance. The massive Four Seasons hotel chain recently bought the entire block where Quiebra Canto is located, and the venue is now being integrated into the hotel. Nearby **Café Havana** (intersection of Cl. Media Luna and Cl. del Guerrero, cell tel. 314/556-3905 or 310/610-2324, www.cafehavanacartagena.com, 8:30pm-3am Thurs.-Sat., $30,000 cover) famously received an endorsement from Hillary Clinton on her trip to Colombia in 2012, when she was U.S. Secretary of State. This is a place for expensive rum drinks and all-night dancing backed by live orchestras, many of which travel from Cuba to perform here.

If you want to brush up on your salsa skills, stop by **Crazy Salsa** (Cra. 7 No. 34-23, cell tel. 300/561-9428, http://crazysalsa.net, 9am-9pm Mon.-Wed., 9am-3am Thurs.-Sat.). This Plaza de los Coches-area dance studio and salsa club offers private and group classes all day (COP$30,000 per hour) and at night hosts some of the city's best local salsa and *champeta* bands. For a more in-depth dive into Cartagena's dynamic salsa scene, contact Veronica Valdelamar Ramirez of **Crazy Dance Tours Cartagena** (cell tel. 313/826-7194, veronicavaldelamarramirez@gmail. com). A former professional dancer and Cartagena native, she can take you places far off the tourist trail and also offers private lessons.

GAY AND LESBIAN

Gay nightlife in Cartagena is growing, but hot spots come and go pretty quickly, making it hard to keep up. Crowds are friendly and the scene is mixed.

A landmark LGBTQ hangout, **Le Petit Club** (Cl. del Candilejo No. 32-34, tel. 5/664-3645, 5pm-2am Wed.-Sat.) has a pub-like atmosphere in the immediate post-work hours but transforms into a full-fledged disco come late night. Expect everything from Shakira to electronica on the small but packed dance floor. Sometimes there's a cover, but not usually.

The hottest gay disco of the moment is **The City Club** (Cra. 8B No. 24-16, cell tel. 305/466-2899, 9pm-4am Fri.-Sat., COP$10,000 cover Fri.-Sat.), located in Getsemaní near the convention center. Two dance floors, one playing electronic music and the other reggaetón, open onto balconies overlooking the street below. Because it's located above La Caponera bar, there's a mixing of crowds as some come down and then head back up again.

Festivals and Events

Cartagena feels like a celebration all the time, but it's especially true November-February, when an array of cultural events are featured. Pick up a copy of *Donde,* a free monthly newspaper with Cartagena event listings. You can find it at the airport and in big hotels.

ELECTRONIC MUSIC FESTIVALS

In early January every year, especially on the first weekend after New Year's Day, one or two multiday beachside electronic music festivals take place. Drawing a hip and sexy crowd from Bogotá, Medellín, and Cali, as well as international visitors escaping cold winters, the festival of the moment is **Storyland** (www. storyland.com.co). Tickets and information can also be found at Tu Boleta (www.tuboleta. com). Buy your tickets well in advance.

HAY FESTIVAL

The **Hay Festival** (www.hayfestival.com) is an important international festival that began in Wales nearly 30 years ago. It celebrates literature, music, environmental awareness, and community and is held in various cities across the world, including in Cartagena in late January. Bill Clinton has called it the "Woodstock of the mind." In addition to talks and concerts, the festival holds educational programs for youth in the neighborhoods of Cartagena. It also provides free or discounted tickets to students. Most of the events take place in the **Teatro Heredia** (Cl. de la Chichería No. 38-10, tel. 5/664-6023 or 5/664-9631). While the festival's name is pronounced as the English "hay," in Colombia it's often pronounced as the Spanish *"hay"* ("ai"). Hay Festival is thus a double entendre: *hay festival* in Spanish means yes, there is a festival!

FESTIVAL INTERNACIONAL DE MÚSICA

Over the course of a week in early to mid-January, the churches, plazas, and theaters of the Walled City become the setting for classical music concerts by musicians from all over the world during the **Festival Internacional**

de Música (International Music Festival, www.cartagenamusicfestival.com, tickets www.tuboleta.com). Most concerts sell out far in advance, but if you can't get tickets you might be able to catch a free performance in one of the churches or plazas in the Old City.

FESTIVAL INTERNACIONAL DE CINE DE CARTAGENA DE INDIAS

If you're in town during late February and are looking for an excuse to escape the heat, here it is: the **Festival Internacional de Cine de Cartagena de Indias** (International Film Festival, tel. 5/664-2345, www.ficcifestival. com). A tradition since the 1960s, this week-long film festival has an interesting program of documentaries, Colombian films, and shorts; a series of roundtable discussions with prominent actors and directors; and educational activities in neighborhoods throughout the city. The venues include historic buildings and plazas.

CARNAVAL OF INDEPENDENCIA

While the massive Carnaval over in Barranquilla gets lots of write-ups, many people don't realize that Cartagena was the original site of Colombia's Caribbean Carnaval celebrations. When that upstart two hours east took over as the coast's primary port and economic engine, the festival went with it. But Cartagena still throws the happening **Carnaval of Independencia** in the weeks leading up to November 11, the day the city declared its independence from Spain in 1811, eight years before the rest of the country did the same. During the day, brightly colored dancers accompany huge floats featuring live musical acts down Avenida Santander, which fronts the Caribbean Sea. At night, the streets are full of raucous parties, especially around the Plaza de los Coches in Centro and Calle Media Luna in Getsemaní. It's an amazing time to be in town; just watch your valuables when you head out into the revelry; the tight crowds create ideal situations for pickpockets.

CONCURSO NACIONAL DE BELLEZA

Beauty contests, especially the **Concurso Nacional de Belleza** (Miss Colombia Pageant, tel. 5/660-0779, www.srtacolombia. org), are a big deal in Colombia. The coronation of Señorita Colombia takes place every November and is the highlight of Cartagena's Independence Day celebrations. Aspirants for the title represent each of the departments of the country, in addition to some cities. Ladies from the Valle del Cauca and Atlántico have won the most titles (10 each) since the pageant began in the 1930s. In 2001, the first Miss Colombia of Afro-Colombian heritage was chosen: Vanessa Mendoza, who represented the Chocó department. Tickets to the main events—the swimsuit competition at the Cartagena Hilton and the coronation at the Centro de Convenciones—are hard to come by but not impossible to purchase.

RECREATION
Beaches

Cartagena boasts a seaside location and hosts wide swaths of city beaches—but most aren't going to blow your mind. The best are located on the Caribbean side of the **Bocagrande peninsula** and feature gray-sand beaches packed with Colombian families and plied by vendors and masseuses. Umbrella rentals are expected, and usually cost around COP$20,000 for the afternoon. At the far southwestern end is a gay-friendly section called **Playa Hollywood,** which also attracts those still partying from the night before. Beyond this point, the beach hangs a sharp left to the south and merges into the beaches of the Laguito neighborhood, where there are some waterfront restaurants and kitesurfing and windsurfing rentals.

From Laguito you can also get to the beaches on the nearby island of Tierrabomba, including **Punta Arena,** which has

1: boat from Cartagena to the Islas del Rosario; **2:** Punta Arena beach in Tierrabomba; **3:** beach on the Bocagrande peninsula

panoramic views over the modern high-rises of Cartagena; *colectivo* boats (COP$10,000) depart from in front of the Nuevo Hospital de Bocagrande. The water is clearer here than on the mainland and the crowds much thinner than at either Bocagrande or Playa Blanca, making this an excellent option for a close-in, quality beach break. Punta Arena is also home to several resorts that offer day passes (COP$20,000) that include use of beach chairs and restrooms. These include the upscale, holistically themed **Namaste Beach Club** (Punta Arena, cell tel. 300/678-0848, www.namastebeachclub.com, 9am-9pm daily), where you can lounge around on couch beds, drink smoothies on the sand, and even catch a yoga class. If you want to extend your time here, you can spend the night in a beach bungalow (COP$380,000 d). On the other side of Tierrabomba, **Playa Linda** is wilder and more natural, with a long stretch of sand fronting the clear Caribbean waters. If there are enough people interested you may be able to take a *colectivo* boat to this beach from Laguito; otherwise you may need to hire a private boat (COP$30,000).

For postcard-perfect white-sand beaches and palm trees, book a day tour or multiday excursion to **Barú** or the **Islas del Rosario.**

Diving

Diving Planet (Cl. Estanco del Aguardiente No. 5-09, tel. 5/660-0450, www.divingplanet.org, 8am-7pm Mon.-Sat.) offers classes and diving excursions to some 25 locations throughout the Parque Nacional Natural Corales del Rosario y San Bernardo. A two-day basic course costs US$535 and the advanced divers' training costs US$468. Discounts are offered for paying in advance online or in cash. Multiday PADI certification courses are also available, some of which include an overnight on the white beaches of the Islas del Rosario. Snorkeling excursions are also available (COP$190,000).

Sailing

It doesn't get much better than renting out

a 43-foot catamaran with a captain and crew and sailing around Cartagena and its nearby islands. **Veleros Colombia** (cell tel. 316/528-2413, www.veleroscolombia.com, COP$2,900,000/4 hours) can make that happen. It also rents out a variety of other sailboats for those who know the ropes. In addition, they offer sailing courses along the Caribbean coast and diving excursions in the Islas del Rosario and the Islas de San Bernardo; contact them for price details.

Biking

The best time to explore Cartagena by bike is early on a Sunday morning or on a Sunday or Monday evening when there is little activity and light traffic in the Old City. Many hostels and some hotels have bicycles for rent.

Bicitour Getsemaní (Cl. Don Sancho, Edificio Aqua Marina, cell tel. 300/357-1825, COP$7,000/2-hour rental) rents out bikes and offers guided tours of the Old City, Manga, and Bocagrande.

Kitesurfing and Windsurfing

About half an hour's drive northeast of Cartagena, along the beaches of the Manzanillo neighborhood, the Swiss-run **Pure Kitesurf** (Manzanillo, cell tel. 321/521-5110, www.purekitesurf.com) offers kitesurfing classes, with instruction available in Spanish, English, and German (US$60/hour). It also offers a six-day, all-inclusive "Kite Safari" tour of the Caribbean coast all the way to La Guajira for US$890.

Cartagena Kitesurf School (Cra. 1B No. 1-52, Laguito neighborhood, cell tel. 300/461-9947, www.kitesurfcartagena.com) offers a basic 10-hour course (COP$900,000) and a two-hour course (COP$250,000). If wind conditions are not good enough, the school will transport students to Puerto Velero, up the coast, where there's always a good breeze. While the school is located in the Laguito section of Bocagrande, most classes take place on the beaches of Las Americas.

Windsurfing and kitesurfing, as well as paddleboarding and surfing, classes and gear rental are also available through **Mokana Club** (Cra. 1 No. 1A-25, Laguito neighborhood, cell tel. 300/810-7502, www.mokanaclub.com, daily 9am-5pm daily). Windsurfing equipment runs COP$75,000-150,000 per hour, while kitesurfing equipment is COP$120,000 per hour.

Golf

The challenging 18-hole **TPC Cartagena at Karibana** (Manzanillo, cell tel. 317/516-1073, www.tpc.com/cartagena, greens fees US$95), about half an hour's drive east of the city, offers gorgeous views of the Caribbean—especially from the 13th hole, which is surrounded by the sea—and the Old City. This is the first Jack Nicklaus-designed course in South America. Karibana offers stay-and-play packages with several Cartagena-area hotels, in addition to being a resort hotel itself. Greens fees are discounted if you're a Karibana guest.

Yoga

Santuario del Yoga (Cl. El Estanco del Aguardiente No. 5, Centro, tel. 5/668-5338, cell tel. 313/649-3133 or 313/819-3114, 8am-9am and 5pm-6pm daily, COP$15,000) offers yoga classes in a small studio (that's also a shop/café) in the Centro. Some instructors are bilingual. On occasion they organize excursions (COP$120,000 pp) to the Volcán de Totumo that include canoeing through marshes, a yoga class, and a vegetarian lunch.

Vive Yoga (Cl. Ancha 44-10B, Getsemaní, cell tel. 304/528-9863, www.viveyogacartagena.com) leads a free yoga class in the Parque de la Marina on Wednesdays at 10am and will also come to your location for a private one-on-one (COP$35,000 per hour).

SHOPPING
Centro

The most historic place to pick up some Colombian handicrafts is **Las Bóvedas** (San Diego, extreme northeastern corner of the wall, 9am-6pm daily). Once a military storehouse, today it's the place to buy multicolored hammocks and all kinds of Colombian *artesanías* (handicrafts) of varying quality.

Cartagena is the kind of place just made for dressing up and walking around feeling like you're on a movie set. For men, nothing says Cartagena chic like a crisp linen shirt or a Cuban-style *guayabera*. The typical *guayabera* has two vertical embroidered stripes and four pockets, and can be worn to a wedding or special event, or even out to dinner at one of the elegant restaurants of the Old City. Tailor Edgar Gómez of **Ego** (Cl. de Portobello No. 10-92, tel. 5/668-6016, 9am-5pm Mon.-Fri.) purportedly once made guayaberas for Bill Gates and the king of Spain.

Along Calle Santo Domingo there are several boutiques of top Colombian designers focused on women's fashion. Bogotana **Bettina Spitz** (Cl. de la Mantilla No. 3-37, tel. 5/660-2160, www.bettinaspitz.com, 11am-1pm and 2pm-8pm daily) sells casual, beach, and formal clothes for women, as well as an array of accessories, shoes, and some men's items. **Onda de Mar** (Cl. de las Damas, tel. 5/668-5226, 9am-6pm daily) is a Colombian clothing brand that has everything you need for a day at the beach. **St. Dom** (Cl. de Santo Domingo No. 33-70, tel. 5/664-0197, 10am-8pm Mon.-Sat., noon-6pm Sun.) is a boutique that brings together Colombian designers of accessories, clothing, handbags, and jewelry. It has a beachfront location in Bocagrande as well (Cl. 2 No. 15-63, tel. 5/655-2542, 10am-6pm daily).

Antiques shops provide a glimpse into aristocratic living from the Cartagena of yesteryear. **El Arcón Anticuario** (Cl. del Camposanto No. 9-46, tel. 5/664-1197) showcases Colombian furniture from both the colonial and Republican eras. This is the spot to pick up your very own whimsical Cartagenan doorknocker or chandelier.

Casa Chiqui (Cl. de la Universidad No. 36-127, tel. 5/668-5429, www.casachiqui.com, 10am-6pm Mon.-Sat.) specializes in interesting interior design items, housewares, and furniture from around the world. While Asia, Africa, and the Middle East are represented, there are Colombian handicrafts, such as colorful Barranquillan Carnaval masks, woven handbags, and placemats made from palm leaves on display as well. At **La Cava del Puro** (Cl. de las Damas No. 3-106, tel. 5/664-9482, www.lacavadelpuro.com, 9am-8pm Mon.-Sat., 10am-8pm Sun.) they don't sell just any old stogie; here the cigars come from Havana and are of the best quality. Smoking is not only permitted here, but in fact promoted. Sometimes a little whiskey is served to perusing clients.

Abaco Libros (Cl. de la Mantilla, tel. 5/664-8290, 9am-9pm Mon.-Sat., 3pm-9pm Sun.) is a cozy bookshop and café with a variety of books on Cartagena, top Colombian novels, and a selection of magazines, classics, and best sellers in English. **Librería Nacional** (Cl. Segunda de Badillo No. 36-27, tel. 5/664-1448, 8:30am-12:30pm and 2pm-6:30pm Mon.-Fri., 8:30am-5pm Sat.) is a chain bookstore with shelves full of Colombian and Spanish-language books, and some books in English.

Once a bullfighting ring, **La Serrezuela** (Cra. 11 No. 39-21, www.plazalaserrezuela.com, 9am-11pm daily) is an architectural masterpiece of a shopping mall, with high-end boutiques circling the historic arena and cafés and restaurants opening onto several levels of terraces overlooking the city and seascapes. It's a great place to escape the afternoon heat and enjoy a Colombian coffee at local chains like Juan Valdez and Cafe Quindio in an elegant atmosphere with spectacular views. While here, also try to stop by **Artesanías de Colombia** (Local L-312, tel. 5/642-1785, 11am-9pm Sun.-Thurs., 11am-10pm Fri.-Sat.), a government-run shop that only stocks the highest-quality handmade crafts from across the country. Intricately woven palm-frond furniture and hats are available here, as well as colorful home decorations.

Getsemaní

Even more high-quality handicrafts are available at the Getsemaní outpost of **Artesanías de Colombia** (Centro de Convenciones, Local 5, tel. 5/660-9615, 10am-7pm Mon.-Sat.). The store specializes in masks from the Carnaval de Barranquilla, woven *mochilas* (handbags) from indigenous groups in the Sierra Nevada, and the colorful embroidery of *molas* from indigenous groups in the Darién Gap region near Panama.

The most atmospheric book-browsing experience in the city is on the northern edge of the Parque del Centenario in Getsemaní, home to several secondhand **book stalls.** You never know what you might find. Days and hours of operation are irregular, so just stroll by if you're in the area.

FOOD

Seafood reigns supreme in Cartagenan cuisine. Popular fish are *pargo rojo* (red snapper), *corvina* (sea bass), *dorado* (mahimahi), and *sierra* (swordfish). Shellfish include *langosta* (lobster), *langostinos* (prawns), and *chipi chipis* (tiny clams). These main dishes are often accompanied by delicious coconut rice and *patacones* (fried plantains). Caribbean *cocteles* (cocktails) of *camarones* (shrimp) are also wildly popular, and often mixed with *pulpo* (octopus) and *caracol* (conch). They make a perfect light, refreshing meal on a hot afternoon.

This Is Cartagena (www.ticartagena.com) offers a reservation service for many of the city's top restaurants.

Street Food

Street food is varied in Cartagena and quite inexpensive. There's no better refreshment than a cold *agua de coco* (coconut water), straight from the fruit itself. Street snacks, popular in the late morning or late afternoon, are called *fritos.* They include items like *arepa de huevo* (fried eggs in a corn arepa), *carimañola* (fried yuca-flour pastry with cheese and meat), and seafood empanadas. Fresh fruit, particularly *mango biche* (green mango served with salt and hot spices), can be a good break from the heavier *fritos.* For a sweet bite, head to the Portal de las Dulces, a traditional sweets market near the Torre del

Best Restaurants

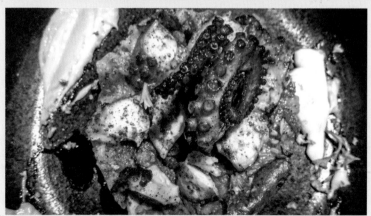
grilled octopus at Caffé Lunático

- **La Nacional:** Do street food like a local and grab some fresh shrimp and octopus *cocteles* and a fresh-squeezed juice.

- **Santísimo:** Dine at this Old City landmark restaurant where Cartagena classics go upscale.

- **Lobo de Mar:** Fall in love with the eclectic menu at this hip, locally owned dining hot spot.

- **Mar y Zielo:** Enjoy Peruvian-Caribbean cuisine on a rooftop terrace perched just beneath the city's most magnificent cathedral.

- **La Comunión:** Double your pleasure at this bicoastally influenced seafood restaurant.

- **Marzola Parrilla Argentina:** Bite into a perfectly marinated Argentine steak and pair it with glass of Mendoza wine.

- **Caffé Lunático:** Feast on Mediterranean-style dishes featuring locally caught seafood.

- **Cafe del Mural:** Sample the aromatic wares of Colombia's top coffee regions in an artistic space.

- **Restaurante Shwarma Khala:** Chow down on authentic Middle Eastern food at this hidden gem.

- **Kiosco el Bony:** Eat freshly caught fish at this old-school beachfront eatery run by a boxing champ.

Reloj, and try a *cocada*, made from coconut and raw sugar.

Stop by ★ **La Nacional** in the row of street *cevicherías* (Av. Venezuela and Cl. 34, 10am-6pm daily), just a block down and across the street from the Torre del Reloj in La Matuna, for excellent fresh *cocteles* from

friendly "Don Wicho." Sidewalk seating under the large trees makes for great people-watching here.

There are also still a few mom-and-pop restaurants featuring cheap set lunches for locals and backpackers who would balk at paying over COP$10,000 for their midday meal, especially on **Carrera 10** in Getsemaní between Calle Media Luna and La Matuna.

Centro
CARIBBEAN
Open since 1998, ★ **Santísimo** (Cl. del Torno No. 39-62, tel. 5/660-1531, www.elsantisimo.com, noon-11pm daily, COP$55,000) is one of Cartagena's original fine-dining restaurants and has elevated Caribbean cuisine to an art form. It remains popular and is a great place to indulge in thoughtful takes on Cartagena standards like *cazuela de mariscos* (seafood stew) in coconut milk. The decor has a religious theme, with candles and an austere interior design.

★ **Lobo de Mar** (Cl. del Santísimo No. 8-15, cell tel. 318/615-0434, 12:30pm-3pm and 7pm-11pm daily, COP$45,000) is a stylish restaurant owned by the same local team behind discos La Movida and La Jugada Club House. Well-prepared plates include mixed seafood paella and slow-cooked pork ribs, while the trendy bar up front attracts the cocktail-and-light-bites crowd. If you dine here, ask for a pass to one of the clubs.

Juan del Mar (Plaza de San Diego No. 8-12, tel. 5/664-2782, www.juandelmar.com, 12:30pm-1am daily, COP$38,000) is run by a former Colombian actor and model turned chef. His namesake restaurant does fresh Caribbean-style ceviche and traditional dishes like the *mofongo Caribeño*, a stewed meat and plantain dish that's popular from Cuba to Puerto Rico as well as here on the Colombian Caribbean coast. Right next door he also has a pizzeria and across the plaza is his Peruvian fusion joint. Since they all have outside seating, Plaza de San Diego might have to rename itself after him at some point.

Some of the freshest ceviche in town is served at **La Cevichería** (Cl. Stuart No. 7-14, tel. 5/660-1492, 1pm-10:30pm daily, COP$38,000). The restaurant has a creative menu, featuring options with mango and coconut. It's located on a quiet street with pleasant outdoor seating. Get a little taste of everything by ordering the "Miss-Cellanea"

ceviche sampler. You can also pick up a T-shirt at its little shop.

La Mulata (Cl. Quero No. 9-58, tel. 5/664-6222, noon-4pm Mon.-Sat., COP$18,000) specializes in Cartagenan cuisine. Its seafood dishes feature a perfect mound of coconut rice topped with a thin, crispy slice of fried plantain to add some height to the presentation. Decorated with names of regional dishes, the restaurant walls provide a vocabulary lesson on Caribbean cuisine. Try the coconut lemonade.

CARIBBEAN FUSION
Seafood meets the Andes at ★ **Mar y Zielo** (Cra. 5 34-63, cell tel. 317/391-1393, www.maryzielo.com, noon-4pm and 7pm-11pm Sun.-Thurs., noon-4pm and 7pm-midnight Fri.-Sat., COP$45,000), a fusion restaurant owned and managed by Peruvian chef Mariano Cerna. One of the most visually stunning restaurants in the entire city, it's located within the Casa de la Escribana, a historic mansion. Its elegantly decked-out dining room hosts live Latin music nightly as well as a rooftop terrace fantastically perched right under La Catedral de Santa Catalina de Alejandría, lit up at night. The food is as good as the ambience, with plates like the Caribbean *tiradito* (Peruvian-style sashimi) smothered in *leche de tigre* (the lime-and-fish juice left over from ceviche) and a pumpkin puree, securing the restaurant's reputation as one of the best Colombian-Peruvian marriages on the continent.

The Pacific and Caribbean coasts of Colombia unite at ★ **La Comunión** (Cl. de las Bóvedas No. 39-116, tel. 5/645-5301, noon-10:30pm daily, COP$36,000), which is housed in a cheerfully decorated space. Chef Charlie Otero spent years researching the two coastlines to come up with this unique menu that features items like black tamales filled with octopus and squid and a salad made from *chontaduro,* a savory palm fruit said to have aphrodisiac powers.

Fabulous **Carmen** (Cl. de Santísimo, Cl. 38 No. 8-19, tel. 5/664-5116, www.

carmencartagena.com, noon-3pm and 6pm-11pm Mon.-Tues., noon-11pm Wed.-Sun.) blends Caribbean with Asian and Middle Eastern cuisine, offering a five-course tasting menu (COP$159,000) that includes wine hand-selected by a Cordon Bleu-certified chef trained in San Francisco, California. An à la carte menu (COP$65,000) is also available. Impeccable service and an unforgettable meal await. Seating is indoors or out on the patio. Reservations are necessary.

For pork ribs in hoisin sauce or a lobster sandwich, visit **María** (Cl. del Colegio No. 34-60, tel. 5/660-5380, www.mariacartagena.com, noon-3pm and 6:30pm-11pm Mon.-Fri., 6:30pm-11:30pm Sat., COP$42,000), a restaurant with nods to Asian cuisine. It's a cheerful, bright space, and the only place in town where you can dine under the glow of a chandelier of ceramic pineapples.

The **1621** (Hotel Sofitel Legend Santa Clara, Cl. del Curato, tel. 5/650-4741, noon-11pm daily, COP$45,000) combines French and Caribbean cuisine in the elegant and spacious lush central garden courtyard of a classic hotel that was once a 17th-century convent. Desserts are sumptuous, a perfect match for the ambience. Don't miss the extensive wine collection.

El Gobernador by Rausch (Cl. del Sargento Mayor No. 6-87, tel. 5/642-4100, www.bastionluxuryhotel.com, noon-3pm and 7pm-11pm daily, COP$45,000) in the Bastion Luxury Hotel is a fancy Mediterranean-Caribbean fusion restaurant with serious chandeliers. Favorites on the menu include scallops with pork belly and duck in corozo sauce. For dessert, try the piña colada mousse. The restaurant also has a bistro with an ample outside patio in the La Serrezuela shopping center.

SEAFOOD AND STEAK

The mischievous smiles of tango crooners like Carlos Gardel watch over diners at ★ **Marzola Parrilla Argentina** (Cra. 7 No. 38, tel. 5/660-2403, noon-midnight daily, COP$48,000). The small menu focuses on just the essentials: a trio of thick, juicy steaks done Buenos Aires-style and two high-quality bottles of wine from the Mendoza region of Argentina. The house-made chimichurri sauce comes in both classic green and paprika-infused red; be sure to ask for both.

Cartagena-born chef Juan Felipe Camacho's **Don Juan** (Cl. del Colegio No. 34-60, tel. 5/664-3857, www.donjuancartagena.com, 12:30pm-3pm and 7:30pm-11pm daily,

cazuela de mariscos at Kiosco el Bony

COP$48,000) offers a sophisticated but unpretentious take on local seafood, steak, and pasta specialties in a simple and elegant bistro-style setting. Try the tangy grilled sea bass on lemon risotto.

Transport yourself to the Havana of yesteryear at **La Vitrola** (Cl. Baloco, Cl. 33 No. 2-01, tel. 5/664-8243, noon-3pm and 7pm-midnight daily, COP$35,000), an always-elegant, always-packed restaurant that specializes in Caribbean seafood, such as the popular tuna steak with avocado and mango, as well as pasta dishes. Immaculately dressed bartenders are a blur of constant motion as they mix innumerable mojitos. La Vitrola is pricey, but the atmosphere, with live Cuban music in the evenings, makes it worthwhile. Reservations must be made well in advance.

CASUAL DINING

El Balcón (Cl. Tumbamuertos No. 38-85, cell tel. 300/336-3876, noon-midnight daily, COP$22,000) in Plaza de San Diego is a friendly place with a view from its 2nd-story wraparound balcony. Get here in the early evening and enjoy a sundowner cocktail as you listen to lounge music or have a light meal with a refreshing gazpacho or their shrimp "sexviche."

Casual and cute, **Collage Charladero** (Cl. Roman No. 5-47, tel. 5/660-7672, www.collagecharladero.com, noon-midnight Mon.-Sat., noon-5pm Sun., COP$22,000) serves sandwiches, burgers, falafels, fresh juices (watermelon with lime and mint), and refreshing sangria in a clean and cool environment close to all the historic sites.

Simple (Hotel NH, Plaza de los Coches, tel. 5/645-5051, www.simplecartagena.com, 7am-10:30pm daily, COP$36,000) has Scandinavian interior design and an interesting menu with items like crab tacos and coconut prawns. It also serves fresh pastries at breakfast.

Plaza Majagua (Plaza Fernández de Madrid, cell tel. 315/323-0001, noon-2am daily, COP$15,000) offers amazing seating right on leafy Plaza Fernández de Madrid, as well as daily lunch specials that are surprisingly well done. At night, come for the two-for-one hamburger and cocktail happy hour.

ITALIAN

Twinkling lights and fountains create ambience on the patio of **Enoteca** (Cl. San Juan de Dios No. 3-39, tel. 5/664-3806, www.enoteca.com.co, noon-11:30pm daily, COP$30,000), a Cartagena pizza and pasta institution. The pizzas are better than the pasta. If you want air-conditioning more than atmosphere, grab a table inside.

VEGETARIAN

The inexpensive set lunches at vegetarian **Girasoles** (Cl. de los Puntales No. 37-01, tel. 5/660-2625, 11am-4pm daily, COP$12,900) are a salvation for many vegetarian visitors. The usual lunch includes a vegetable soup to start, followed by a main protein dish accompanied by rice and vegetables. This informal lunch counter has many regular customers and usually publishes the day's menu on its Facebook page.

BAKERIES AND CAFÉS

One of the best bakery-cafés in town is swanky **Mila Pastelería** (Cl. de la Iglesia No. 35-76, tel. 5/664-4607, www.mila.com.co, 9am-10pm Mon.-Sat., 10am-9pm Sun., COP$17,000), a bright place for sandwiches, tempting desserts, and a late breakfast (served until 11am) for those who slept in too late at the hotel.

Beans from top coffee regions in Colombia are freshly ground and brewed at **Folklore Colombian Cafe** (Cl. 32 No. 4-17, tel. 5/668-5057, www.folklorecolombiancafe.com, 7:30am-8:30pm daily, COP$8,000). A quiet oasis just off Plaza de la Aduana, it also serves an impressive house-made triple-layer ganache chocolate cake.

SWEETS

A homemade ice cream popsicle from **La Paleterría** (Cl. de Ayos No. 3-86, 11am-11pm daily, COP$10,000) makes a late-afternoon stroll around the steamy city much more enjoyable.

Run by two Italian brothers, one of whom actually graduated from a gelato-making university, **Gelateria Tramonti** (Cl. 35 No. 480, tel. 5/664-9354, 9am-1am daily, COP$8,000) offers sensual treats that you won't soon forget. Flavors include fruit juice-sweetened local delights like *maracuya* (passionfruit) and *zapote,* a creamy delight that's much like a sweet avocado, as well as a dark chocolate (80 percent cacao) that will leave you buzzing from a natural high.

Getsemaní
CARIBBEAN

Restaurante Coroncoro (Cra. 10 No. 39-22, cell tel. 314/541-0393, 7:30am-10pm daily, COP$16,000) has been serving up freshly caught *mojarra* (local whitefish), *posta negra* (a beef dish featuring a molasses-based marinade), and other Cartagenan classics to locals since the 1970s and has the best budget lunch special (COP$10,000) in town. Everything here has that homemade taste like it came right out of grandma's kitchen.

At **La Cocina de Pepina** (Callejón Vargas, Cl. 25 No. 9A-06, Local 2, tel. 5/664-2944, noon-4pm and 6pm-10pm Tues.-Sat., noon-4pm Sun.-Mon., COP$28,000), typical dishes from across the Caribbean coast are thoughtfully reinvented. The *mote de queso,* a thick soup made of salty Costeño cheese and yams, gets rave reviews. It's a cozy place in an alley near Calle del Arsenal.

Unpretentious **Casa de Socorro** (Cl. Larga No. 8B-112, cell tel. 315/718-6666, noon-midnight Tues.-Sat., COP$35,000) may surprise you with its Cartagenan specialties, ceviche, and *limonada de coco* (coconut lemonade). The loyal clientele of locals speaks for itself.

SEAFOOD

At cozy ★ **Caffé Lunático** (Cl. Espíritu Santo No. 29-184, tel. 5/660-1735, www.caffelunatico.com, 11am-10:30pm daily, COP$32,000) freshly caught local Caribbean

seafood is masterfully utilized in classic Spanish tapas and Mediterranean fusion plates. Giant paellas and *fideuás* (Spanish noodles) bursting with shellfish are meant to be shared and make an excellent and decently priced gourmet dinner. The restaurant's bottomless mimosa brunch special (COP$52,000) includes a three-course meal and is available daily.

Marea by Rausch (Centro de Convenciones, Cl. 24 No. 8A-344, tel. 5/654-4205, www.mareabyrausch.com, noon-3pm and 7pm-10pm Tues.-Sat., 4pm-10pm Sun., COP$65,000) is an ultra-chic seafood restaurant that is the brainchild of the Rausches, two brother chefs from Bogotá. Specialties include tuna tartare and prawns in a coconut and saffron sauce. This restaurant has excellent views of the bay and the Torre del Reloj.

TAPAS

The Plaza de la Trinidad is the beating heart of happening Getsemaní, and it's home to some swanky spots perfect for a small meal and a couple of drinks. Cool **Demente** (Plaza de la Trinidad, cell tel. 311/831-9839, www.demente.com.co, 4pm-2am Mon.-Sat., COP$28,000) specializes in cocktails and tapas. It's an open-air spot with a retractable roof, where the music is funky, the cocktails are chic, and the cigars are Cuban. On the back patio is a beer garden complete with twinkling lights, serving wood-oven pizza and craft beer. It's a fun place for an evening of small plates and drinks.

INDIAN

For a little curry with your shrimp, try **Ganesha** (Cl. Media Luna No. 10-81, cell tel. 301/767-7294, noon-3pm and 6:30pm-11pm Tues.-Sun., COP$35,000), an Indian restaurant with an extensive menu and many vegetarian options.

DUTCH-INDONESIAN FUSION

Delightful **Saint Roque** (Cl. Espíritu Santo No. 29-214, cell tel. 317/226-8039, 5pm-midnight Mon.-Sat., COP$28,000) serves

Dutch-Indonesian cuisine in an up-and-coming area of Getsemaní. Try the *gado-gado* vegetarian salad with peanut sauce, and choose a candlelit table on the sidewalk.

FRENCH

Brasserie Montaigne (Cra. 8B No. 25-103, tel. 5/650-3030, noon-3pm and 6pm-11pm daily, COP$34,000) is a classic French restaurant in the Hotel Monterrey. Cordon bleu and crème brûlée are classics on the menu.

BAKERIES AND CAFÉS

For a real Colombian coffee-tasting experience hit up ★ **Cafe del Mural** (Cl. San Juan No. 25-60, cell tel. 321/288-9323, 3pm-8pm daily). With outside garden seating under a street mural and an artsy indoor area, this bohemian Getsemaní institution also offers a wide variety of brewing methods to choose from and hosts regular coffee tastings and classes.

Manga

Authentic Middle Eastern specialties await at ★ **Restaurante Shwarma Khala** (Cl. 26 No. 18, tel. 5/660-5382, 10am-9pm daily, COP$14,000), a true hidden gem that is both inexpensive and top quality. From falafel and shawarma wraps to full plates featuring Middle Eastern delights, this is the place to get your hummus fix without breaking the budget.

With a terrace overlooking the bay, **Verona** (Cra. 20 No. 24-22, tel. 5/670-0416, noon-11pm Mon.-Fri., 6pm-11pm Sat.-Sun., COP$26,000) serves delicious thin-crust pizzas, offers a salad bar, and caters to locals in the Manga neighborhood. After dinner, be sure to stroll the pleasant promenade along the water.

The **Club de Pesca** (Fuerte de San Sebastián del Pastelillo, tel. 5/660-4594, noon-11pm daily, COP$59,000) is a Cartagena classic in the old San Sebastián del Pastelillo fort, with magnificent views to the bay. It's a favorite spot for wedding banquets, and some guests arrive in yachts. Try the *jaiba gratinada* (crab au gratin).

Bocagrande

A Cartagena institution since the 1980s and right on the beach at Playa Hollywood, ★ **Kiosco el Bony** (Playa Hollywood, Cra. 1, 8am-10pm daily, COP$28,000) serves freshly caught fish in a variety of styles as well as classic ceviches and *cocteles*. Run by ex-boxing champ Bonifacio Ávila Berrío (El Bony), the restaurant does a house special *cazuela de mariscos* (seafood stew) that's packed with shellfish and secret spices to recharge body and soul. Bony's has both indoor and outdoor dining rooms with views over the packed beach.

Elegant **Arabe Internacional** (Cra. 3 No. 8-83, tel. 5/665-4365, www.restaurantearabeinternacional.com, noon-3:30pm and 7pm-10pm Mon.-Fri., noon-10pm Sat.-Sun., COP$28,000) has been serving authentic Middle Eastern cuisine since 1965. It's a popular place for the Cartagena business crowd.

Tabetai (Av. San Martín No. 5-145, tel. 5/647-9861, noon-11pm daily, COP$28,000) specializes in Japanese cuisine, specifically sushi. It has fun happy hours most afternoons, often with specials on mojitos and DJs on the weekend.

Riquisimo BBQ (Cra. 1 No. 1A-148, tel. 5/655-0861, 7:30am-midnight daily, COP$18,000) looks like a coffee shop, but serves typical Cartagenan fare in addition to sandwiches and fixed-price lunches. The generously portioned breakfasts are a specialty.

ACCOMMODATIONS

As the top tourist destination in Colombia, Cartagena boasts a large and diverse hotel sector. Centro and Getsemaní are the top neighborhoods for small, high-end boutique hotels, often occupying well-restored colonial-era homes; many feature rooftop terraces and swimming pools, which go together quite nicely. Being pampered at one of these luxury

Best Accommodations

- **Icon Capsule Hostel:** Get your own private dorm "capsule" at Centro's best hostel.

- **3 Banderas:** Stay in a classic colonial house turned hotel in a perfect location in Centro.

- **Casa San Agustín:** Drink your tea with views from the terrace at this world-renowned historic mansion-hotel.

- **Hotel Charleston Santa Theresa:** Stay near the seawall of the Old City and take in Caribbean views from the rooftop pool at this five-star historic property.

- **Sofitel Legend Santa Clara:** Enjoy tropical splendor in a monastery turned luxury hotel.

- **Townhouse Boutique Hotel:** Party in your personal swimming pool at the rooftop bar of this modern hotel.

- **Media Luna Hostel:** Gain an immediate global network of amigos at Cartagena's largest party hostel.

- **Casa del Pozo:** Relax poolside in the garden patio of this small and charming "boutique hostel."

- **Casa Pizzaro:** Slip away from the crowds at this lush hideaway tucked into a quiet Getsemaní neighborhood.

- **Hotel Caribe:** Stay on the waterfront at this historic Bocagrande hotel with resident parrots and deer and its own beach club.

options—even for just a few nights—will be a highlight of your visit.

Hostels proliferate in the city, especially in Getsemaní. The vast majority offer private rooms with air-conditioning, but these tend to go fast, so plan to reserve at least a few weeks in advance. Some hostel dorm rooms don't have air-conditioning.

Bocagrande, with its high-rise hotels and condos, is more popular with Colombian families than with international visitors. Staying here means proximity to Bocagrande's beaches and several shopping malls. For something even more chilled-out try historic Manga or the beachside areas of Crespo and Marbella, just east of the Old City.

For most international visitors, hotels should not charge IVA (sales tax). Inquire about IVA when you make your reservation, and again when you're checking in, to be sure you aren't improperly charged. (For more information on the regulations behind IVA, see the *Essentials* chapter.)

Centro
UNDER COP$200,000

The ★ **Icon Capsule Hostel** (Cra. 8 No. 38-27, tel. 5/679-5772, COP$45,000 dorm, COP$200,000 d) has a perfect location in the Old City, just a block from Plaza de San Diego in one direction and Plaza Fernández de Madrid in the other. The historic colonial mansion has been renovated and includes a small outdoor pool on the 1st-floor patio as well as a hot tub on the rooftop terrace bar. Dorms here are private capsules with individual lights, outlets, and curtains for privacy Around the corner, the Uruguayan hostel chain **El Viajero** (Cl. Siete Infantes No. 9-45, tel. 5/660-2598, www.elviajerohostels.com, COP$50,000 dorm, COP$230,000 d) has air-conditioned dorm rooms of various sizes. A handful of private rooms are located across the street in a more subdued environment. A decent breakfast is included in the room rate. Guests enjoy socializing at the bar.

Hotel Casa Real (Cl. del Cuartel No. 36-122, tel. 5/664-7089, www.casarealhotel.com.co, COP$180,000 d) has two rooftop terraces, adequate rooms with antiques from old Cartagena, and a central location.

COP$200,000-400,000

A midrange option with a guesthouse feel is ★ 3 Banderas (Cl. Cochera del Hobo No. 38-66, tel. 5/660-0160, www.hotel3banderas.com, COP$297,000 d). This hotel is housed in a 200-year-old building with two interior patios and a rooftop terrace with a tiny pool. Some of the 24 rooms are small, but it's generally a good value. Request one of the rooms with a small balcony.

Previously a hostel, Casa Blue (Plaza Fernández de Madrid, Cl. del Curato No. 38-08, tel. 5/668-6501, COP$260,000 d) is within the Walled City just a few blocks from the Plaza de Santo Domingo. The rooms are private and the hotel markets itself to a budget-conscious business crowd. Its location on a popular plaza means you should expect some noise in the evenings.

A friendly staff is what sets Hotel Boutique Las Carretas (Cl. de las Carretas No. 34-28, tel. 5/660-4853, COP$309,000 d) apart. Rooms are spacious and some have balconies with a street view. On the rooftop you'll find a small pool. The building itself is an architectural mishmash, and the interior design is more folksy than sophisticated.

COP$400,000-800,000

You can't really go wrong at the NH Urban Royal (Plaza de los Coches No. 34-10, tel. 5/645-5050, www.nh-hotels.com, COP$532,000 d), one of two locations of the NH Hotels chain in the city. Rooms are equipped with basics, and most offer nice views of the always-busy Plaza de los Coches. The rooftop pool is a welcome sight after a long day—the view is quite something, too—and the included breakfast is ample.

With just eight rooms, a pleasant rooftop terrace, and a delicious breakfast, Hotel Boutique Santo Toribio (Cl. Segunda del

Badillo No. 36-87, cell tel. 317/893-6464, www.hotelsantotoribio.com, COP$450,000 d) checks off all the boxes for a comfortable stay in the city. Lounge music adds an air of chicness. Bikes are available for rent.

The two-story colonial-era Casa la Cartujita (Cl. del Curato No. 38-53, tel. 5/660-5248, www.casalacartujita.com, COP$675,000 d) has seven bright-white minimalist rooms and a lovely terrace, Jacuzzi, dipping pool, and pleasant reading room. Rent the entire house and you'll have a personal chef at your service.

Good taste reigns at Anandá (Cl. del Cuartel No. 36-77, tel. 5/664-4452, COP$750,000 d), whose name means "maximum state of happiness" in Hindi. It's certainly close to the truth at this gorgeous, meticulously restored 16th-century home. There are 23 rooms of three different styles and a pool, Jacuzzi, and daybeds on the rooftop. Anandá is home to the restaurant Carmen.

The two-story Bóvedas de Santa Clara (Cl. del Torno No. 39-114, tel. 5/650-4464, www.bovedasdesantaclara.com, COP$760,000 d) has only 18 rooms, some of which are extremely spacious, some with views of the water. Guests can use the Sofitel Legend Santa Clara spa and facilities, located in a massive former monastery right across the street. The hotel staff can organize day trips to the Hotel San Pedro Majagua in Islas del Rosario. Breakfast is served.

OVER COP$800,000

The result of a meticulous restoration of three adjacent 17th-century houses, the ★ Casa San Agustín (Cl. de la Universidad No. 36-44, tel. 5/681-0000, www.hotelcasasanagustin.com, COP$1,960,000 d) is easily one of the most luxurious addresses in Cartagena, if not all of Colombia. Among the amenities are an inviting pool on the main floor, complimentary afternoon tea in the library, a terrace with

---

1: Hotel Charleston Santa Teresa; 2: pool at Media Luna Hostel

a fabulous view, spacious rooms with exposed wood-beamed ceilings, a cozy bar, and the original stone walls. This hotel is a member of Leading Hotels of the World.

The 89-room ★ **Hotel Charleston Santa Teresa** (Plaza de Santa Teresa, tel. 5/664-9494, www.hotelcharlestonsantateresa. com, COP$1,247,000 d) is steps away from the wall and just below the Baluarte Tasca-Bar. It was built in the 17th century as a convent for Carmelita nuns. In the 1980s it was converted into a hotel. There are two wings to this historic hotel, a colonial one and a Republican-era one dating from the early 20th century. Rooms are nothing short of luxurious, with accommodations in the colonial wing a notch above the more modern ones. The two inner courtyards are lovely, with astounding and ever-changing floral displays, and the front courtyard is so large it is almost its own plaza. Concierges can arrange any excursion you'd like. The hotel's many amenities—four restaurants (one run by renowned chef Harry Sasson), a rooftop pool, a spa, and a gym—ensure a relaxing stay. Another iconic Old City classic, also housed in a former convent, is in San Diego: The 122-room ★ **Sofitel Legend Santa Clara** (Cl. del Torno No. 39-29, tel. 5/650-4700, www.sofitel.com, COP$1,243,000 d) is synonymous with class and luxury, though it once served as a monastery for nuns. The stunning central colonial courtyard features tropical plants, a fountain, and modern sculptures, all dotted with tables where guests wine and dine. The gorgeous chapel is available for weddings. Be sure to request a tour of the hotel from a staff member to see remnants of the convent. Make time for drinks at the on-site bar El Coro. The pool area is large; during low season, nonguests can obtain day passes.

Party animals will love the rooftop bar of the ★ **Townhouse Boutique Hotel** (Cra. 7 No. 36-88 tel. 5/664-9100, www. townhousecartagena.com, COP$1,203,000 d), where champagne is served at private swimming pools and the electronic music pumps out over views of the historic skyline. A jazz piano bar is located on the ground floor, which attracts an artsy crowd, and rooms are each individually decorated by local Colombian artists. Townhouse also runs the Blue Apple Beach House on the island of Tierrabomba, just 30 minutes away by boat. Guests can visit for the day for free or stay the night there at discounted rates.

Comfortable and boasting a fabulous location—just around the corner from Parque de Bolívar and La Catedral de Santa Catalina de Alejandría—**Hotel Movich** (Cl. Velez Danies No. 4-39, tel. 5/660-0133, www.movichhotels. com, COP$1,130,000 d) offers good value despite its high price tag. Light floods its spacious rooms, and the rooftop terrace has a refreshing pool with a 360-degree view of the Old City. A 15-minute massage is included with your stay.

Getsemaní
UNDER COP$200,000

The Shangri-la of backpacker accommodations in Cartagena is the famous ★ **Media Luna Hostel** (Cl. de la Media Luna No. 10-46, tel. 5/664-3423, www.medialunahostel.com, COP$40,000 dorm, COP$180,000 d). Located on the edge of Getsemaní, it's a high-energy place with socializing (and flirting) centered on the medium-sized pool in the courtyard. If you're looking to break out of your shell, this may be the place. It has a capacity of more than 100 guests, with just a couple of private rooms (book early for those). The staff organizes lots of activities and bikes are available to rent. Then there's the bar, which is only open on Wednesday nights for the famous Visa por un Sueño party that is open to the public. Media Luna also runs a beachfront hostel on the end of Barú.

★ **Casa del Pozo** (Cra. 10B No. 5-95, 5/679-9066, COP$40,000 dorm, COP$114,00 d) is a "boutique hostel" that opens out onto Plazuela del Pozo, where tables fill with diners from surrounding restaurants come sundown. With an outdoor swimming pool, a comfy book-filled common area, and a street-front café that serves breakfast and lunch, this is one of the nicer backpacker options in town. Dorms are private capsule style, with individual outlets, lighting, and curtains.

Just a block up from bustling Plaza de la Trinidad, **Mama Waldy** (C. de la Sierpe No. 29-03, 5/678-5225, COP$30,000 dorm, COP$90,000 d) is a small hostel that feels a bit like a home away from home, A living room with a flat-screen TV opens onto a garden courtyard where breakfast is served. A bar and Jacuzzi on the rooftop terrace are open to the public and get packed around sunset.

COP$200,000-400,000

★ **Casa Pizarro** (Cra. 10B No. 2556, 5/6436867, www.hotelcasapizarro.com, COP$349,000 d) is almost hidden from street view behind the massive trees fronting it; it's a true sanctuary in the middle of frenetic Cartagena. Many rooms in this lovingly restored colonial mansion have private walled garden patios, some with hot tubs as well as comfy outdoor sofas and beds. A long, narrow pool occupies the ground-floor courtyard while the rooftop hosts a lounge restaurant and sundeck.

Casa Relax (Calle del Pozo No. 25-105, cell tel. 310/443-1505, www.cartagenarelax.com, COP$270,000 d) feels like a hostel for adults without the discomfort of dorm accommodations. Here you can make use of the kitchen, have a cocktail by the groovy pool, and socialize a bit. There are 12 rooms.

Low-key **Casa Villa Colonial** (Cl. de la Media Luna No. 10-89, tel. 5/664-5421, www.casavillacolonial.com.co, COP$250,000 d) is a midrange option for those interested in staying close to the Old City. Rooms are basic, with wood furniture and tiled floors. Its rooftop terrace has a pool.

Hotel Monterrey (Cra. 8B No. 25-100, tel. 5/650-3030, www.hotelmonterrey.com. co, COP$350,000 d) is a classic hotel with a huge rooftop terrace that houses a small pool, perfect for soaking up views of the Old City. It's on a busy street across from the convention center, but traffic noise isn't an

issue. Breakfast is served in a cute interior courtyard.

COP$400,000-800,000

Style is the thing at **Casa Lola** (Cl. del Guerrero No. 29-108, tel. 5/664-1538, www.casalola.com.co, COP$495,000 d), designed and managed by a Spanish couple who were some of the first hoteliers in Getsemaní. The hotel, spread over two buildings (one colonial and one Republican-era), has 10 rooms featuring furniture and art from all over the world. Its location near Café Havana means there may be street noise on weekend nights.

The most luxurious option in Getsemaní is the **Hotel Capellán** (Cl. de La Sierpe No. 29-52, 5/660-9562, www.hotelcapellandegetsemani.com, COP$792,000 d). A poolside bar graces the rooftop terrace, an on-site spa offers pampering treatments, and a top-floor duplex suite might be just right for families or a group of friends. Period details abound but the rooms are mostly minimalist and modern.

Bocagrande
UNDER COP$200,000

Relaxed **New Hostal Las Velas** (Cl. 1B No. 1-52, cell tel. 300/831-0159, www.hostallasvelas.com, COP$35,000 dorm, COP$100,000 d) is just steps from the beach in the Laguito neighborhood and draws travelers who can't get enough kitesurfing, surfing, and windsurfing. This medium-sized house has one dorm room with eight beds and two private rooms (one with an en suite bathroom). The rooms don't have much flair, but this is a friendly spot in an area not frequented by tourists.

Small **Barahona 446** (Cra. 2 No. 4-46, tel. 5/665-6144, www.hotelesbarahona. com, COP$197,000 d) is an arty, tropically themed bargain in the middle of Bocagrande, about a five-minute walk from the beach. The rooms are decent, but don't expect a view. Light sleepers may want to use earplugs, as noise from common areas can be a nuisance.

COP$200,000-400,000

Bocagrande's most classic digs are to be found at the ★ **Hotel Caribe** (Cra. 1 No. 2-87, tel. 5/650-1160, www.hotelcaribe.com, COP$298,000 d). The historic Spanish-style complex, comprising three large buildings, is right across from Playa Hollywood, and has a beach club exclusively for guests. The hotel's nicest feature is the lush garden complete with resident parrots and deer. The 360 medium-sized rooms have views of the sea or the garden. Most visitors enjoy lounging by the pools and drinking a fruity cocktail.

INFORMATION AND SERVICES

Tourist Information

In addition to locations at the airport and at the cruise ship terminal, there are city-run **tourist information kiosks** (no phone, 9am-noon and 1pm-6pm Mon.-Sat., 9am-5pm Sun.) near the Torre del Reloj and an air-conditioned main office in the historic **Casa de Marquez Plaza de la Aduana** (tel. 5/660-1583, 9am-noon and 1pm-6pm Mon.-Sat., 9am-5pm Sun.).

Emergency and Medical Services

In case of an emergency, call the **police** at 112. For medical emergencies, call an **ambulance** by dialing 125 or head to **Hospital Universitario** (Cl. 29 No. 50-50, tel. 5/669-7308, 24 hours daily).

Spanish-Language Courses

Cartagena offers many opportunities to take group and individual Spanish classes. Many hostels have local Spanish tutors or can recommend a school or private teacher. You may want to try out a class before committing to several days' instruction.

One recommended school is **Lengua Nativa Spanish School** (cell tel. 304/573-1027, individual class US$15). **Nueva Lengua** (Callejon Ancho No. 10B-52, Getsemaní, tel. 5/660-1736) has a solid track record, with

locations in various cities. A 15-hour week of classes costs US$200.

Centro Catalina (Cl. Siete Infantes No. 9-21, San Diego, cell tel. 310/761-2157, www.centrocatalina.com) offers small-group classes in a house in the San Diego district.

Volunteering

The **Fundación La Vecina** (La Boquilla, www.fundacionlavecina.com) helps low-income children living in La Boquilla. It was started by a Dutch woman, Nathalie Rietman. The foundation has short-term positions open during school vacations (January, July, and December), in addition to long-term (three months and up) opportunities.

The **Fundación Juan Felipe Gómez** (Cl. 31 No. 91-80, Ternera, tel. 5/661-0937, www.juanfe.org) is the brainchild of Catalina Escobar, a Colombian businesswoman who was nominated as CNN Hero of the Year in 2012 for her tireless efforts to help at-risk teenage mothers. Both short- and long-term volunteers are invited to share their skills with the young women at this impressive center. You can take a public bus or a taxi (20 minutes) from the Centro to the *fundación*.

Founded by Colombian pop singer Shakira in the late 1990s, the Barefoot Foundation, aka **Fundación Pies Descalzos** (Pie de la Popa, www.fundacionpiesdescalzos.com), builds schools, including the stunning Colegio Lomas del Peyé to the northeast of town, which it also operates. See the website for volunteer opportunities as well as fund-raising needs.

Cartagena Paws (www.cartagenapaws.com) rescues abandoned dogs, and can always use kind dog walkers.

The **Fundación por la Educación Multidimensional** (FEM, Cl. del Quero No. 9-64, Centro, tel. 5/643-4185, www.femcolombia.org) strives to make an impact on budding entrepreneurs by pairing them with volunteers who have expertise in business, architecture, community development, and other vocations. FEM generally seeks longer commitments of multiple weeks from its volunteers, but some short-term opportunities are occasionally offered.

TRANSPORTATION
Getting There
AIR
Cartagena's **Rafael Núñez International Airport** (CTG, tel. 5/656-9202, www.sacsa.com.co) is located to the east of the city, about a 12-minute cab ride from Cartagena. Taxis from the airport to the Old City are reliable and regulated. The current fixed rate is COP$15,000.

Delta (www.delta.com) has nonstop service to Cartagena, offering flights from Atlanta. **JetBlue** (www.jetblue.com) and **Avianca** (www.avianca.com) operate flights between New York-JFK and Cartagena. Nonstop flights from Florida are offered by **Spirit Airlines** (www.spirit.com) via Fort Lauderdale; Avianca has a nonstop out of Miami. **Copa Airlines** (www.copaair.com) serves Cartagena from its hub in Panama City, Panama. Charter carrier **Air Transat** (www.airtransat.com) flies nonstop from Montreal to Cartagena December-March.

The main national carriers, Avianca and **LATAM Airlines** (www.latam.com), operate many flights each day to Cartagena from various Colombian cities. **VivaColombia** (www.vivacolombia.co) often offers inexpensive fares between Cartagena and Medellín, Bogotá, Cali, and Pereira. **ADA** (www.ada-aero.com) serves the city with flights from Medellín, Montería, and Cúcuta. **EasyFly** (www.easyfly.com.co) has a nonstop from Bucaramanga. The new Cali-based airline **GCA Air,** (www.gcaair.com) offers direct, low-cost daily flights between Cali and Cartagena, connecting the two Afro-Colombian capitals.

BUS
Regular bus service connects Cartagena with all major and coastal cities. The **Terminal de Transportes** (Diag. 56 No. 57-236, tel. 5/663-0454) is a 20- to 30-minute cab ride from the Centro. Expect to pay about COP$30,000 for the trip.

The Terminal de Transportes offers bus service to Bogotá, Medellín, Cali, and other interior cities. However, if you are making your way along the coast, it's quicker and easier to get to Santa Marta or Barranquilla by taking one of the fast *busetas* (large vans) that regularly serve the main Caribbean cities. **Marsol** (Cra. 2A No. 43-11, tel. 5/656-0302, www.transportesmarsol.net) and **Berlinas** (Cl. 46C No. 3-80, tel. 5/693-0006, www.berlinasdelfonce.com) are the top choices and have pickup sites near the Centro in the Marbella neighborhood. Marsol even offers door-to-door service (*puerta-puerta*). The last *buseta* leaves Cartagena around 8pm. It's a decent option to travel after dark—the roads are good and it's safe—as the roadside scenery isn't that impressive, there's less traffic, and you may as well spend the remaining daylight hours enjoying a mojito in the Old City.

CRUISE SHIP
Cartagena is a major port of call for cruise ships from across the globe, bringing around 350,000 visitors each year. The entry into the Bahía de Cartagena is a dramatic one, as the ships pass through ruins of old Spanish forts.

The city is a living museum, and the best way to get to know it is by walking its narrow streets, getting lost, and finding one's way again. Be sure to bring some sun protection and water—the sticky midday heat can be sizzling. If you take an organized walking tour, you will likely be hounded by hawkers selling Colombian souvenirs.

Take a cab from the port to the Torre del Reloj, one of the main entrances to historic Cartagena. Pop into a museum and a grandiose colonial-era church, enjoy a delicious meal at one of the many fine restaurants, and cap it all off with a walk and a drink on the *muralla* (wall) facing the Caribbean Sea.

CAR OR MOTORCYCLE
Consider renting a car or motorcycle for overland travel. Hertz and National, as well as local companies, have pickup and drop-off locations at the airport. This could be a good

option if you are planning on taking your time getting to know the Caribbean coast or are continuing onward to Colombia's interior. The main road to Barranquilla is mostly four lanes, but shrinks to two lanes closer to Santa Marta.

Getting Around

Walking is the best way to get around Centro, Getsemaní, and La Matuna. Thanks to its narrow streets, scarce parking, and heavy traffic, the Centro is not particularly car friendly.

TAXI AND RIDE-HAILING APP

For short hops between neighborhoods, cabs are quick and easy. Taxis here do not have meters, so it's possible you won't get the local rate. Before hopping in a cab, ask a local or two the standard rate. Or just use **Easy Taxi** (http://cabify.com), an app run by Cabify; it connects you with a taxi and allows you to see the fare upfront. From the Old City to Bocagrande, expect to pay around COP$10,000. A ride to the airport will cost COP$20,000, and a trip to the beaches at Las Americas will be COP$15,000. Tipping is not customary. **Uber** (www.uber.com) was banned in Colombia in 2019 and in 2020 is in a lawsuit against the Colombian government, so may or may not be in operation.

BUS

It may seem overwhelming at first, but taking a public bus is a cheap way to get around. To hop on a bus to Bocagrande from the Old City, walk down to Avenida Santander along the sea and flag down just about any bus you see (or look for a sign in the window that reads "Bocagrande"). The ride will set you back COP$2,200. There are a few options for getting off: As you board, tell the bus driver where you would like to be let off; belt out *"¡Parada!"* as you approach your destination; or discreetly exit behind someone else. On the main road (Carrera 11) just to the east of the walls, facing the Monumento India Catalina, is a nonstop parade of buses loading and unloading. From here you can get to the Castillo de San Felipe, the Mercado de Bazurto, or the bus terminal, for the same low price of COP$2,200.

TRANSCARIBE

The **TransCaribe bus system** (www.transcaribe.gov.co) employs organized stations (rather than standard bus stops). It caters mostly to residents but may be useful for visitors interested in traveling out of the Centro to the city's southern neighborhoods. Some of the major stops are at Muelle de la Bodeguita, La Matuna, Chambacú (Castillo de San Felipe), and Mercado de Bazurto.

The bright orange bus stations are located along Avenida Venezuela, a thoroughfare between the Centro and La Matuna that extends into the southern neighborhoods. Expect to pay COP$2,000 for the comfortable ride.

Vicinity of Cartagena

VOLCÁN DEL TOTUMO

One of the most popular day trips from Cartagena is **Volcán Del Totumo,** a mud volcano that offers an opportunity for you to indulge in a natural day spa. Guests climb a stairway up the cone, which is 15 meters (49 ft) high, and then slide into the crater at the top for a mud bath. The mud has a pudding-like consistency and is reputed to have medicinal properties. Locals at the top offer on-site massages (donation based, typically COP$5,000-10,000) while you float in the goop. Afterward, let the mud dry on you for a bit in the sun before you take a shower and you'll feel like a newborn child. The location of the Volcán Del Totumo, about an hour by road north of the city on the shores of a large lake, Ciénaga del Totumo, makes getting there by tour the best option. Most Cartagena hotels offer packaged day trips to this attraction for around COP$50,000, which includes round-trip transportation and entrance to the volcano. They usually pick you up from your hotel around 9am and have you back around 3:30pm. Lakeside restaurants offer fish lunches for around COP$20,000. Locals also sell bags and bottles of the mud that you can take with you.

BOCACHICA

Bocachica, which means "Small Mouth," is one of two entrances to the Bahía de Cartagena. It is at the southern end of the bay. The other, much wider entrance is Bocagrande ("Big Mouth"), more familiar as the peninsula southwest of the Old City. In 1640, when three galleons sank at Bocagrande and blocked that passage, the Spaniards decided to fortify the more easily defensible Bocachica.

The **Fuerte de San Fernando** (Isla Tierrabomba, tel. 5/655-0211 or 5/655-0277, www.patrimoniodecartagena.com, 8am-6pm daily, COP$9,000) and **Batería de San José** are two forts at either side of Bocachica, the first line of defense. The Fuerte de San Fernando, at the southern tip of the island of Tierrabomba, is a particularly impressive example of 18th-century military architecture. It is very well preserved and you can still see the barracks, kitchen, storerooms, and chapel enclosed within the massive fortifications. The low-lying Batería de San José, located on a small island just south of Tierrabomba, is a much more modest affair, and can be visited with a ticket for Fuerte de San Fernando.

The only way to get to Bocachica is by one of the *lanchas* (fast boats, COP$15,000) that depart from the Muelle Turístico de la Bodeguita, the tourist port in Cartagena near the Torre del Reloj. The 45-minute trip through the bay provides interesting views of Cartagena and the port. The waits between departures can be long, so bring sunscreen and something to do.

In Bocachica, there are a few small, informal restaurants where you can eat fried fish, coconut rice, and *patacones* (fried plantains) and drink a cold beer.

PLAYA BLANCA AND BARÚ

South of Cartagena is the elongated island of **Barú,** which is separated from the mainland by the Canal del Dique, an artificial waterway built in 1650 to connect Cartagena with the Río Magdalena. Barú is home to several nice beaches, but **Playa Blanca** is by far the most popular, and is the easiest to get to. Lapped by bright blue turquoise water, the beach is lined with restaurants and hostels run by locals. Downsides are that it gets very crowded, and vendors are constant. Be careful of masseuses who begin massaging you without permission—if you don't ask them to stop right away, they'll ask for money.

A bit farther south along the peninsula from Playa Blanca, **Playa Tranquilo** is a slightly more laid-back version. You can walk there in about 30 minutes or take a *mototaxi* (COP$5,000) from Playa Blanca.

Barú is also home to the **Aviario Nacional de Colombia** (Km 14.5, cell tel. 322/552-9134, www.aviarionacional.co, 9am-5pm daily, COP$60,000). For those interested in seeing up close the incredible diversity of Colombia's birds—the greatest diversity in the world—this is mecca. The aviary is home to nearly 200 different species of birds endemic to Colombia, including the scarlet ibis and harpy eagle, and its 22 exhibits cover different ecosystems including mangrove forests, tropical rainforests, and desert.

Food and Accommodations

To enjoy fresh seafood and fabulous cocktails under the sun, **Pescador de Colores** (Km. 3 past Pasacaballos Bridge, Barú, cell tel. 315/394-2374, www.elpescadordecolores.com, 11:30am-5:30pm Wed.-Mon., COP$40,000) is the place to be on Barú. This swanky beach

The Unconquerable Town of San Basilio de Palenque

Cartagena was one of the main slave ports in Spanish America during the colonial era, and enslaved people who escaped created free communities, known as *palenques.* The largest, oldest, and most famous of these is the inland town of San Basilio, just 50 kilometers (31 mi) southeast of Cartagena yet a world apart.

Founded in the 16th century by **Benkos Biohó,** an African king turned escaped slave, it soon became a refuge for other enslaved people who escaped from Cartagena. After years of skirmishes with the Spanish, the outlaw town signed a peace treaty with the governor of Cartagena in 1605 and won its right to exist. Although Biohó was betrayed by the Spanish in 1621—he was captured and executed—San Basilio de Palenque remained unconquered and was finally declared free by royal decree of the king of Spain in 1691. This makes San Basilio de Palenque the **first free African town in all the Americas,** a historical distinction that was honored by **UNESCO** in 2005 with its placement on the Representative List of the Intangible Cultural Heritage of Humanity.

statue of San Pedro Claver with Benkos Biohó by Enrique Grau

As a free and independent city, San Basilio de Palenque nurtured many of the African traditions that were stamped out in other diaspora hot spots. Over the centuries, this little Africa would exert a major influence on Cartagena; after Colombia banned slavery in 1851, many *palenqueros* retuned to Cartagena and infused it with their African-influenced culture and music. *Palenqueros* to this day are an integral part of the city's cultural fabric. You'll see dancers performing to drum-driven music around the city and brightly dressed women selling fruits and posing for photos.

GETTING THERE

Day tours to San Basilio de Palenque run only on Sundays, and although these trips are sold all over town, it's best to go with a company that has a connection to the community. The best of these is **TuCultura** (Cra. 10C No. 25-51, Getsemaní, tel. 5/6436662, www.tucultura.co), a nonprofit cultural tourism organization founded in 2009 by Merly Beltrán Vargas with the mission to use tourism to promote the culture and traditional art forms of Cartagena. Its daylong tour (COP$150,000) includes round-trip transportation from your hotel at 8am, lunch at a typical restaurant, visits to major historical sites in San Basilio de Palenque, and an expert tour guide, before returning to Cartagena around 5pm.

lounge specializes in Euro-Caribbean cuisine, but the biggest attraction is hanging out on a beach bed.

Playa Blanca is lined with simply styled accommodations with on-site restaurants, most charging about COP$150,000- 200,000 in high season. Most of these hotels double as beachfront restaurants serving the day crowds. The food offered on Playa Blanca is all the same overpriced tourist fare, but most

visitors will have lunch included in the price of the day tour. If not included, expect to pay around COP$30,000 for a fresh fish lunch—try negotiating for the use of the beach facilities for the rest of the day if you eat at a venue.

Best known for its location in Cartagena, **Media Luna Hostel** (Playa Bobo, Barú, cell tel. 313/536-3146, www.medialunahostel. com, COP$50,000 dorm) also owns a chill beachside hostel at the southern tip Barú, far from the frenzy of Playa Blanca. It consists of five two-story thatched-roof *cabañas* fronting the beach. Each *cabaña* has four beds and a bathroom and can be either a private room or a dorm, depending on your preference. The hostel takes care of round-trip transportation (COP$60,000) from its Getsemaní location, where pickup is at 9am daily, or you can opt for a backpacker-friendly all-inclusive deal that comes with meals (COP$150,000) in addition to accommodations.

Aura Hotel Barú (Ensenada del Cholón, Km. 26, Barú, cell tel. 314/506-6520, www.aurahotelbaru.com, COP$800,000 d) is a relaxing beach resort nestled among the mangroves on the quiet side of the Cholón lagoon. There are three cabins with multiple rooms each for rent; the older ones with thatched roofs have more charm. All 16 or so of them are comfortable, but the Wi-Fi is iffy. A visit here usually includes lounging on the beach in front of the hotel or at Playa Azul, a small, uninhabited island with a nice beach that's just a quick boat ride away. For those staying more than a day, the food can get a little repetitive (lots of fried fish and coconut rice). You can also take a day trip here (COP$238,000), which includes transportation, lunch, and an excursion to Playa Azul; pickup is from your hotel at 8am.

Getting There

The most common way to get to Playa Blanca is by bus on a day tour ($50,000, 8am daily). These tours pick you up at your hotel in Cartagena and have you back by 5pm or 6pm and usually include a basic lunch on the beach. Some tour companies combine visits to Playa Blanca with some of the closer Islas del Rosario, especially Cholón, where semi-submerged bars serve overpriced cocktails and yachts pull up and blast music.

You can also get to Barú from Cartagena on public transit. This involves taking the bus (COP$2,200) from Calle 30 and Carrera 17, which is just over the bridge from Getsemaní near the Castillo de San Felipe, to Pasacaballos in Barú. This ride is about an hour. At Pasacaballos, you'll find *moto-taxis* waiting to take you to Playa Blanca or the aviary (COP$8,000), or beyond to Playa Tranquilo (COP$15,000).

Another option is contacting Alvaro Maldonaldo (cell tel. 321/360-3693), a friendly local with a beat-up but trustworthy car who will take an entire group from Pasacaballos to Playa Blanca for COP$20,000 and give you a chuckle-filled insider tour along the way.

★ ISLAS DEL ROSARIO

Part of the Parque Nacional Natural Corales del Rosario y San Bernardo, the 25-plus small coral islands comprising the **Islas del Rosario,** about 25 kilometers (15.5 mi) southwest of Cartagena and just offshore of Barú, are a marine wonderland. They encompass spectacular white-sand beaches and crystalline Caribbean waters, and feel remote even though they're just an hour's boat ride from the city. While many of the smaller islands are private, and home to Colombian celebrities like Shakira and Carlos Vives—who each own their own island—much of this paradise is open to the public and makes by far the best day trip or overnight escape from Cartagena.

Hotels and small resorts offer both day passes and lodging options on several of the islands. The standard price for a day trip, typically departing at 8am and returning by 5pm and available from any tour agency in town or at the port of Muelle Turístico de la Bodeguita, is around COP$180,000 and includes round-trip boat transportation, lunch, and use of all hotel or resort facilities. Many of these hotels offer kayak, snorkeling equipment, and Jet Ski rentals to visitors, and most have onsite bars. Spending the night on the islands is also highly recommended, but this should be worked out with your accommodations ahead of time so that transportation can be arranged outside of the standard day tour.

Isla Grande is the largest of the islands, and has the most options for visitation,

whether you're day-tripping or overnighting. Some tours island-hop, but it's better to spend the day lounging in one beautiful spot rather than bouncing around from island to island.

Food and Accommodations

Most day-trippers have lunch included in their tours, and most overnight visitors eat at their accommodations. There are also some very informal local eateries on the island.

★ **Gente de Mar** (Cartagena office: Cl. Gastelbondo, No. 103, Isla Grande, tel. 5/674-2553, www.gentedemar.co, COP$480,000 d) is situated right near several picture-perfect cove beaches, and brightly colored parrots roost in the almond trees. It's a true tropical paradise. Rooms open onto an outdoor seating area next to the on-site restaurant and bar. **Hotel San Pedro de Majagua** (Cartagena office: Cl. del Torno No. 39-114, Isla Grande, tel. 5/650-4464, www.hotelmajagua.com, COP$479,000 d) offers suites with private hammock-strung patios overlooking the sea. Food is included in both hotels' rates.

EcoHotel Las Palmeras (Isla Grande, cell tel. 314/584-7358, COP$40,000 dorm, COP$85,000 d) is run by the native islander community, descendants of enslaved people who escaped and settled Isla Grande centuries ago and who live by fishing the calm waters just offshore. It's economical and also a culturally fascinating option, but it requires a bit more independent exploration. Located inland, it's just minutes from beaches by either walking or cycling; bikes are available for rent here (COP$20,000 per day). Local-style meals, usually fried fish and plantains, are available at the hotel and run about COP$20,000.

★ **Isla Bendita** (cell tel. 300/425-0902, www.benditabeach.com, COP$850,000 d), otherwise known as "Bendita Beach," is on a small private island that's open to day-trippers as well as those interested in all-inclusive overnight stays. The resort has a half-dozen simple beach cabañas fronting

1: beach at Gente de Mar on Isla Grande; 2: Iglesia de Santa Bárbara in Mompox

the sapphire-hued sea. Canopy beds line the main beach, which sports a long sandbar that heads out into the exceptionally calm, shallow waters—perfect for wading or snorkeling in. On the back side of the island, more beds are hidden among the coastal forest canopy overlooking the sea, some providing a romantic level of privacy. The on-site restaurant serves exceptionally well-prepared freshly caught items, and the beachfront bar whips up some massive piña coladas.

★ MOMPOX

Mompox was founded in 1540 on the eastern edge of a large island between two branches of the Río Magdalena (the Brazo de Loba and the Brazo Mompox). This lovely town was an opulent center of trade, connecting the interior of the country with Cartagena during the colonial era. But then the mighty river changed its course in the late 18th century, and Mompox's port became instantly obsolete.

Now lost in time, Mompox is what Cartagena looked like before it became a tourist destination. It retains a yesteryear charm that's unlikely to change soon—especially considering it's southeast of Cartagena by a multi-hour journey. In 1995, due to its architectural importance, the town was declared a UNESCO World Heritage Site. The attraction of Mompox today is strolling along the waterfront, admiring the impressive and colorfully painted colonial mansions decorated with intricate iron latticework, and stopping to sip a coffee or fresh juice in a rocking chair overlooking the river. Monkeys frolic in the trees here and hummingbirds dart about. If there has to be just one city in Colombia that perfectly typifies "magic realism," Mompox is it.

Mompox has a number of plazas. From south to north are **Plaza de Santa Bárbara, Plaza de la Concepción** (also known as Plaza Mayor), and **Plaza de San Francisco,** lined by a wide _malecón_ that runs along the river. Other squares include **Plaza de la Libertad,** in front of the city hall, and **Plaza Bolívar,** a leafy square where fresh

Mompox

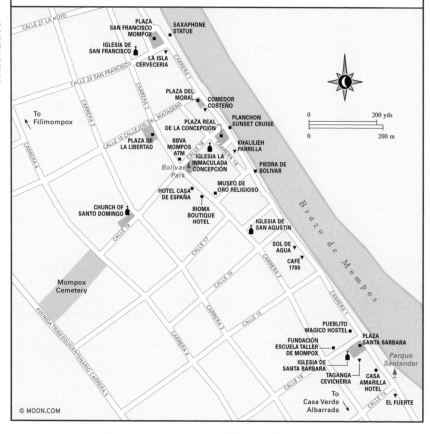

juices are served. Three main streets run parallel to the river: Calle de la Albarrada (which corresponds to Carrera 1) facing the river; the Calle Real del Medio, Mompox's main street, one block west of the river; and the Calle de Atrás (literally, the "street behind"). All three are lined with impressive whitewashed colonial houses now home to shops, restaurants, hotels, and cafés.

Despite its geographical obscurity, Mompox is an important cultural city for Colombia. Many of the country's top *cumbia* bands come from this enchanted town, including Totó La Momposina, the most famous singer of the genre in the world. Her classic

"El Pescador" is sung by traveling musicians all over Latin America and has been reinterpreted by many top recording artists. It's an homage to fishers, the likes of whom you may see walking up from the Río Magdalena loaded with meter-long catfish any given morning in Mompox to this day.

Sights

There are two historic churches worth visiting in Mompox. The riverfront **Iglesia de Santa Bárbara** (Cl. de la Albarrada and Cl. 14, mass 6pm Fri.-Sun.) was built in 1630. The facade is painted a striking yellow, with colorful floral decorations. It has an unusual baroque octagonal tower with a balcony wrapping around it. Inside is a magnificent gilded altar. The church extends from the Plaza de Santa Bárbara to the Plaza de San Francisco. The second noteworthy church is the **Iglesia de San Agustín** (Cl. Real del Medio and Cl. de la Albarrada, mass 4pm daily), which houses the Santo Sepulcro, a gilded reproduction of Christ's tomb. The churches are only open during mass times. Guests of the **Casa Amarilla** (Cl. de la Albarrada No. 13-59, tel. 5/685-6326 or cell tel. 301/362-7065, www. lacasaamaraillamompos.com) can make a request with the hotel to take a quick peek inside the churches.

The only museum in town, which keeps irregular hours, is the **Museo Cultural de Arte Religioso** (Cl. Real del Medio No. 17-07, tel. 5/685-6074, 9am-noon and 3pm-4pm Tues. and Thurs.-Fri., 9am-noon Sat.-Mon., COP$2,000). It's home to displays of gold- and silverwork from the colonial era. Mompox silver- and goldsmiths made a name for themselves with their intricate filigree jewelry.

Another interesting sight is the **Piedra de Bolívar** (Cl. de la Albarrada and Cl. 17), a river-facing monument with a stone slab that lists all the visits Simón Bolívar made to Mompox.

Mompox's atmospheric 19th-century **Cementerio Municipal** (Cl. 18 and Cra. 4, 8am-noon and 2pm-5pm daily, free) is well worth a detour. The cemetery houses the tombs of Afro-Colombian poet Candelario Obeso and General Hermógenes Maza, who fought beside Simón Bolívar. The cemetery is also known for the resident cats that frolic among the graves.

Festivals and Events

Carnaval (usually late Feb. or early Mar.) in Mompox is a mostly local affair, but it's a lot of fun if you're in town for it. Things start revving up with pre-Carnaval weekend celebrations a month or so before the main event all along the riverfront. On the weekend leading up to Ash Wednesday on the Catholic calendar, *cumbia* dancers take over the streets during the day

and impromptu drinking fests bring in the dawn along the riverfront. Watch out for the kids throwing flour around, a local tradition.

Semana Santa (Holy Week), which occurs during late March or April, is the most important celebration in Mompox. Visitors from all over Colombia converge on the town to watch its religious processions and attend concerts. You'll have to book months in advance to get a hotel room during that time. The **Mompox Jazz Festival** (early Oct.) has become the biggest show in town, with performances by international artists such as Tito Puente selling out far in advance. Many performances take place right on the waterfront at the Plaza San de Francisco, which is home to a statue of a giant saxophone.

Shopping

Mompox is known in Colombia for its intricate gold filigree jewelry. Look for the **Joyería Filimompox** (Cl. 23 No. 3-23, tel. 5/685-6604 or cell tel. 313/548-2322, hours vary), where the staff will explain their craft to you during your visit to their workshop. The shop accepts credit cards.

At the **Escuela Taller de Artes y Oficios de Santa Cruz de Mompox** (Claustro de San Agustín, Cl. 16 No. 1A-57, tel. 5/685-5204, hours vary), young people learn traditional handicrafts. Visitors are welcome to drop by and watch these artisans at work. There's an interior courtyard that's an inviting place to linger.

Food

Right on the riverfront, ★ **Cafe 1700** (Cra 1 No. 15-55, cell tel. 313/533-7840, 10am-8pm Tues.-Sun., COP$5,000) offers espressos and house pastries in the spacious living room of the Legado de la Marquesa, an opulent colonial mansion (that can also be entirely rented out for family vacations). It's hard to move off the porch here, as the oversized rocking chairs and sound of the river lull you into a feeling of pure tranquility.

The **Comedor Costeño** (Cl. de la Albarrada No. 18-45, tel. 5/685-5263,

7am-5pm daily, COP$15,000) serves *comida típica* (Colombian fare), including the tender local beef specialty, *posto puyada momposina*, on a wooden terrace overlooking the Magdalena River.

On Plaza de Santa Bárbara, try **Taganga Cevicheria** (Plaza Santa Barbara, cell tel. 300/762-9355, 5pm-10pm daily, COP$18,000). Grab a shrimp-and-octopus-stuffed *patacón* (fried plantain) and enjoy the people-watching. On the Plaza de la Concepción, **Khalilieh** (Cra. 1A No. 17A-54, tel. 5/685-5978, noon-9pm daily, COP$14,000) serves Lebanese food and grilled meats. On Plaza de San Francisco, **La Isla Cerveceria** (Cra. 1 No. 19-139, 3pm-11pm daily, COP$8,000) offers beers from Minca's excellent Cerveceria Nevada on draft, plus small plates meant for sharing.

Belgian-run **El Fuerte** (Cra. 1 No. 12-163, tel. 5/685-6762, 6pm-9pm Fri.-Sun., COP$22,000) is one of the best dining options in town. It's mostly Italian cuisine, and the pizza and pasta are done right.

During high season, inquire about the *planchon* **sunset cruise** (three hours, COP$30,000), where passengers enjoy a drink on the river, floating on a wooden barge. For more information, contact Carmen Garrido (cell tel. 310/606-4632) or check in at the floating dock just below Plaza de la Concepción.

Accommodations

It's all about location at ★ **Pueblito Magico Hostel** (Cra. 1 No. 14-37, cell tel. 302/443-3530, COP$30,000 dorm, COP$80,000 d). The small, artsy hostel opens onto Plaza de Santa Bárbara and has its own outdoor seating where sipping coffee and people-watching can easily take up the better part of the day. A multilingual book library, retro-style bikes for rent, and friendly and knowledgeable staff make this a popular option among international travelers.

The ★ **Casa Amarilla** (Cl. de la Albarrada No. 13-59, tel. 5/685-6326 or cell tel. 301/362-7065, www.lacasaamarillamompos.com, COP$160,000 d), owned by British travel writer Richard McCall, author of *Was Gabo an Irishman?*, is another excellent choice. Standard rooms here open onto a pleasant garden patio and include use of a large book-filled living room. After a careful restoration, the Casa Amarilla added a luxurious colonial house, the Casa de la Concepción (COP$1,850,000), which has four bedrooms and two interior patio gardens; the 2nd-story balcony provides a lovely view to the plaza below. Best of all, it has a pool.

Bioma Hotel Boutique (Cl. Real del Medio No. 18-59, tel. 5/685-6733 or cell tel. 315/308-6365, www.bioma.co, COP$190,000 d) may be one of the most comfortable options in town, as it offers 12 air-conditioned rooms, a dipping pool, and good food.

At **Sol de Agua** (Cra 1 No.15-101, cell tel. 313/571-2688, COP$120,000 d), guest rooms open onto a pleasant courtyard that leads to a riverfront café. It serves an excellent cup of joe made from coffee beans from a farm in the Sierra Nevada and has outdoor seating at which to enjoy it. The family-run establishment also bakes excellent cakes and muffins and offers bicycles for rent.

Casa España (Cl. Real del Medio, tel. 5/685-5373 or cell tel. 313/513-6946, www.hotelcasaespanamompox.com, COP$180,000 d) is a guesthouse with 16 basic rooms, most with two double beds, and an interior courtyard with plenty of rocking chairs in which to relax.

Getting There

Most visitors arrive in Mompox from Cartagena. There is one direct bus that leaves from Cartagena's **Terminal de Transportes** (Diag. 57 No. 24-236, tel. 5/663-0454) at 6:30am daily. The ride takes eight hours and costs COP$50,000. More comfortable is a door-to-door service with a company like **Toto Express** (cell tel. 310/707-0838, COP$75,000), which takes six hours.

Santa Marta and La Guajira

Nature lovers will find heaven on earth on the stretch of coastline from Santa Marta to the Guajira region. Landscapes not usually associated with the Caribbean— from the snowcapped peaks of the Sierra Nevada to the dramatic red desert bluffs of Cabo de la Vela—make this an extraordinarily dynamic region, even in a country famed for its record-setting biodiversity.

Parque Nacional Natural Tayrona, the country's most visited national park, is perhaps the crown jewel of the area, a tropical wilderness of rugged coastal mountains and hidden cove beaches. Backpacker hangouts like beachfront Taganga, mountainous Minca, and rainforest-cradled Palomino all beckon with equal intensity yet are entirely unique in character and offerings. Sunbathing, hiking, scuba

Highlights

Look for ★ to find recommended sights, activities, dining, and lodging.

★ **Celebrate at Carnaval de Barranquilla:** Join the street crowds for one of the most colorful and raucous festivals on the continent (page 84).

★ **Hang Out in Caribbean Bohemia:** With a spectacular setting on the coast, the friendly fishing village of **Taganga** lures hippie backpackers and sunseekers of all ages and nationalities with its laid-back vibes (page 96).

★ **Retreat to Mountainous Minca:** Hike to waterfalls, visit a coffee farm, or just hang in a hammock in this hip town in the Sierra Nevada (page 99).

★ **Explore Parque Nacional Natural Tayrona:** Camp overnight and enjoy the beaches and trails along the wilderness coastline of Colombia's most popular natural area (page 102).

★ **Trek to the Lost City:** Embark on the multiday hike through the rainforest-covered Sierra Nevada to **Ciudad Perdida,** the ancient ruins of a complex society (page 112).

★ **See Flamingos in the Wild:** At the **Santuario de Fauna y Flora Los Flamencos,** you can spot hundreds of the birds in a lush wetland reserve (page 121).

★ **Kitesurf or Windsurf in Cabo de la Vela:** Backed by the Alta Guajira desert, this is a magical landscape against which to practice these water sports (page 123).

★ **Journey to the Northernmost Point in South America:** Traversable only by 4x4, the wild desert landscape of **Punta Gallinas** is a symphony of oranges, ochres, and browns that abuts unspoiled beaches and dunes (page 126).

diving, and surfing are all popular activities in the region.

The area is also one of Colombia's indigenous heartlands, with the stoic Kogi people of the Sierra Nevada in their priestly white robes standing in vivid contrast to the brightly adorned and gregarious Wayúu, who call the Guajira their home.

Santa Marta is the natural urban base for the area, offering surprisingly hip dining and nightlife options, but hidden treasures also await in under-hyped cities like Riohacha, where Caribbean breezes keep temperatures down and a fascinating multiculturalism typifies life.

Come February, the coast revs up its engines for Carnaval, a party centered on Barranquilla—located halfway between Cartagena and Santa Marta—but with celebrations all along the coastline.

PLANNING YOUR TIME

You need at least 5-7 days to even scratch the surface of this multifaceted stretch of the Colombian coastline. If you base yourself in Santa Marta, this gives you time to visit Taganga and Minca, and spend a night or two in Parque Nacional Natural Tayrona. Add about five days more each if you'd like to trek to Ciudad Perdida or head to the Alta Guajira.

While Santa Marta is a common and convenient base for adventures in the region, others may prefer to base themselves in the low-priced boho beachfront paradises of Taganga or Palomino. Minca is more of an escape from the coast than a base for exploring it, which may appeal to some.

Public transportation is good throughout the region until you reach the Alta Guajira, where most people join organized tours to see the area's sights.

High tourist season (Dec.-Jan.) hits the coast hard as urbanites flee Bogotá, Medellín,

and other large cities of the interior for their annual beach breaks. Prices double in places like Santa Marta and Palomino. If possible, avoid visiting Parque Nacional Natural Tayrona during these months, as well as during Semana Santa (Holy Week), and, to a lesser extent, the summer school holidays mid-June-mid-July.

April-November, the Santa Marta area experiences its wet season, which can make hiking in the Sierra Nevada difficult and put a literal damper on camping in PNN Tayrona. In the arid Guajira, tropical storms hit sporadically in June and July, and in September-November the official rainy season often puts the brakes on travel into the desert.

If you're planning to attend the Carnaval de Barranquilla, make your hotel and flight reservations early—several months in advance is best.

Safety

Travelers to this part of the Caribbean coast will receive many mixed messages in regard to cannabis. The Sierra Nevada is one of Colombia's traditional cannabis-growing areas, much of it run by the Kogi people and other indigenous groups. Cannabis culture is present throughout the region, sold openly in shops and smoked on the beach, and part of the area's history in developing into a backpacker mecca. That said, recreational cannabis has been decriminalized but not yet legalized in Colombia—although congress drafted legislation in 2019 to do so, and the country is expected to become the leading producer in this new world market. Until legalized, however, note that corrupt police may try to take advantage of this confusion around cannabis, shaking down unsuspecting travelers and soliciting bribes under threat of arrest, especially in Santa Marta and Taganga.

Previous: shrine to Mary overlooking the coast in La Guajira; coffee berries in Minca; dancers at the Carnaval de Barranquilla.

Santa Marta and La Guajira

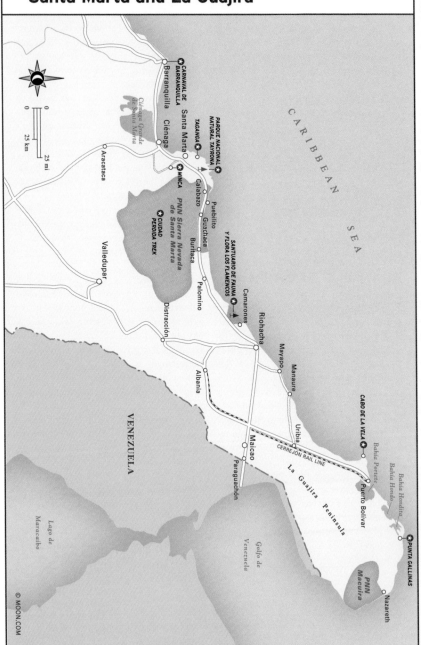

CARNAVAL DE BARRANQUILLA

Barranquilla

Ciénaga Grande de Santa Marta

Ciénaga

Santa Marta

TAGANGA

PARQUE NACIONAL NATURAL TAYRONA

Aracataca

MINCA

Calabazo

Pueblito

Guachaca

PNN Sierra Nevada de Santa Marta

CIUDAD PERDIDA TREK

Buritaca

Valledupar

Palomino

SANTUARIO DE FAUNA Y FLORA LOS FLAMENCOS

Camarones

Distracción

Riohacha

Mayapo

Manaure

Albania

CABO DE LA VELA

CARIBBEAN SEA

Bahía Portete

Uribia

Maicao

CERREJÓN RAIL LINE

Paraguachón

La Guajira Peninsula

Puerto Bolívar

Bahía Honda

Bahía Hondita

VENEZUELA

Lago de Maracaibo

Golfo de Venezuela

PNN Macuira

PUNTA GALLINAS

Nazareth

0   25 km

0   25 mi

© MOON.COM

Santa Marta and Vicinity

With a charming historic district, great hotel and restaurant options, and proximity to beaches and mountains, Santa Marta is a major tourist destination. Steamy Barranquilla gets very little tourism—outside of the world-renowned Carnaval de Barranquilla.

BARRANQUILLA

Colombia's fourth-largest city (pop. 1.6 million) is known for its busy port, which has spurred its growth into the economic engine of the Caribbean area. But besides business travel, it's primarily visited for the bacchanalian Carnaval de Barranquilla. This, one of the most famous celebrations in Colombia, is a time of music, dancing in the streets, and revelry. Usually occurring in February, it lasts only about five days, but the city pulses with anticipation for days (if not weeks) in advance.

Barranquilla is not a colonial city, but vestiges of its early-20th-century importance can be seen in El Prado district. The city offers a handful of attractions, including the Museo del Caribe and the quirky Bocas de Ceniza, a spit of land that divides the Río Magdalena from the Caribbean Sea. A wealth of comfortable hotel and restaurant options may be the trick for weary travelers returning from the jungle or beach.

Aside from Carnaval, however, there's not a whole lot to lure visitors to Barranquilla. The city has one of the highest inequality levels in Colombia, making petty theft and robbery a nuisance here, and caution should be maintained if walking around the historic center and Barrio Abajo areas, which are adjacent to the El Prado district, especially at night.

Sights

Two museums lend insight into Barranquilla's people and culture. The first, **Casa del Carnaval** (Cra. 54 No. 49B-39, tel. 5/319-7616, 9am-5:30pm Mon.-Fri, 9am-noon Sat., COP$5,000), is Carnaval headquarters, and its Sala Carnaval Elsa Caridi provides an interactive introduction to the annual event. After a visit here, you'll come to understand the many components of the celebration, including the different musical styles: *cumbia, mapalé, chandé,* and *son.* While at first blush it may seem that the Carnaval de Barranquilla is just a big party, there is more to it than meets the eye. Behind every costume, parade, and dance there is a story. Knowledgeable guides will share this story and their genuine enthusiasm for the festival at this well-done museum.

The other top museum is **Museo del Caribe** (Cl. 36 No. 46-66, tel. 5/372-0582, www.culturacaribe.org, 8am-5pm Mon.-Fri., 9am-6pm Sat.-Sun., COP$14,000, COP$19,000 with guide), one of the finest museums in the country, with a focus on Costeño (Caribbean coast) culture. There is a room dedicated to Gabriel García Márquez, in which characters from the author's books come alive; the exhibit may be hard to follow if your Spanish is less than fluent. There are slide shows on Caribbean ecosystems and exhibits on the people of the Caribbean, including a fascinating video series on the region's many indigenous tribes. Of particular interest is a room that examines immigration to the coast, from enslaved Africans to "Turcos," meaning those mostly coming from Syria, Lebanon, and Palestine. The museum has a small restaurant with reasonably priced meals on the plaza in front.

On the restored **Plaza San Nicolás** (between Clls. 32-33 and Cras. 41-42) is the neo-Gothic **Iglesia San Nicolás Tolentino** (Cra. 42 No. 33-45, tel. 5/340-2247), which took about 300 years to build. It's usually open, with mass occurring several times a week. Be wary of pickpockets in this part of the city.

Barranquilla

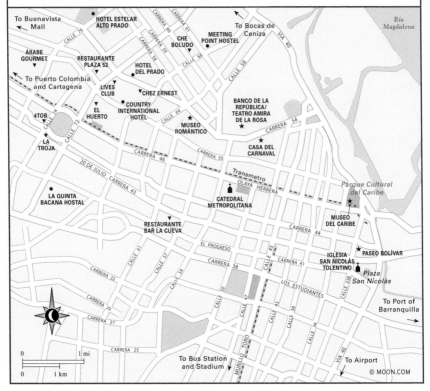

Entertainment and Events

★ CARNAVAL DE BARRANQUILLA

For most Colombians, Barranquilla is synonymous with Carnaval, and they boast that the city's celebration is the world's biggest after that held in Rio (although folks from New Orleans or Trinidad and Tobago may balk at this claim). During the four days prior to Ash Wednesday, in late February or early March, the **Carnaval de Barranquilla** (www.carnavaldebarranquilla.org) is full of Costeño pageantry, with costumes, music, dancing, parades, and drinking. Designated a World Masterpiece of the Oral and Intangible

Heritage of Humanity by UNESCO, the Carnaval actually began in Cartagena; but when Barranquilla took over as the coast's most economically important city, Carnaval went with it. And because Barranquilla attracted new residents from all over the Caribbean with its industrial port jobs, many of their small-town Carnaval traditions came with them. For this reason, Barranquilla's Carnaval is more an expression of traditional Costeño culture than anything specifically related to the city itself.

Prior to the official festivities of Carnaval, there are *verbenas,* which are parties open to the public in different parts of the city. To get an invite to one, ask a local or two. Carnaval officially begins on a Saturday, but on the Friday night one week before, the celebration

La Guacherna (Cra. 44 and Cl. 70) awakens the city with parades and concerts.

The Saturday before Ash Wednesday is the main event. That's the day of the **Batalla de las Flores** (Battle of the Flowers) parade. It's when floats carrying beauty queens, dancers, and members of the general public in *comparsas* (groups) in elaborate costumes make their way down Calle 40 under the sizzling Barranquilla sun. This event dates back to 1903, when it began as a celebration of the end of the Guerra de los Mil Días (Thousand Days' War). Participation in the parades is serious business here, involving planning, practice, money, and, sometimes, connections. However, there is one *comparsa* during the Batalla de las Flores in which just about anyone can participate, and it's one of the most popular: the "Disfrázate como Quieras"—go however you like. Anybody in a costume, from the silly to the sexy, can participate. Check out the Disfrázate como Quieras Facebook page to find out how you can join in the fun.

On Sunday, during the **Gran Parada de Tradición y Folclor,** groups of dancers perform on Calle 40 to the hypnotic music of Carnaval—a mix of African, indigenous, and European sounds. On Monday there is another parade, the **Gran Parada de Comparsas.** Starting in the late afternoon, a massive concert attracts more than 30 musical groups, who compete for the award of Congo del Oro.

On Tuesday, after four days of music and dancing, things wind down with the parade **Joselito Se Va con las Cenizas** (Cra. 54 and Cl. 59). This is when Joselito, a fictitious Barranquillero, "dies" after four days of rumba, and his "body" is carried through the streets as bystanders weep. Joselito is sometimes played by an actor, and other times is a mannequin.

Watch all the action of the parades from the *palcos* (bleachers) that line Calle 40, the only way to spectate. Keep in mind that the parades take place in the middle of the day, meaning lots of sun and heat. Tickets for the *palcos* (COP$180,000-330,000) and the official opening night concert (COP$60,000-8,000,000), which features top Latin music acts from around the world, can be ordered online at **Tu Boleta** (www.tuboleta.com). If you're looking for tickets at the last minute, your hotel may be able to assist you.

As fun as the processions are to watch during the day, the real participatory action of Carnaval happens at night. On the Friday, Saturday, and Sunday night before Ash

dancers in the Carnaval de Barranquilla

Wednesday, the **Baila la Calle** ("dance the streets") brings hordes of people, including many still-costumed dancers from the processions, into the historic streets of Barrio Abajo for all-night dance parties. Different corner *tiendas* (stores) become de facto bars and the pavement outside makes for impromptu dance floors, creating a raucous fiesta that just might be a highlight of the festival—after all, the ancient roots of Carnaval were about different classes mixing it up in revelry rather than sitting and watching from the bleachers.

Every night of Carnaval also features a **Carnavalada,** or after-party, that takes place in the Parque Cultural del Caribe, right in front of the Museo del Caribe. Starting at about 10pm and running until the sun comes up, these free concerts bring in bands from across Colombia as well as international acts from Cuba, Venezuela, Mexico, and more. Everything from classic salsa to electronica-backed *cumbia* keeps the party rocking, while a row of bars serve ice-cold beers, bottles of rum, and *aguardiente,* Colombia's national drink.

With regard to Carnaval, it's said that *"Quien lo vive es quien lo goza"* ("Whoever experiences it is who enjoys it"). But to do that, it's crucial to get hotel and flight reservations early—ideally a few months in advance.

NIGHTLIFE

As a major Colombian city, Barranquilla has endless nightlife options. One of the unique ones is ★ **La Troja** (Cra. 44 No. 72-263, cell tel. 301/348-2029, www.latroja.org, 4pm-3:30am Fri., 1pm-3:30am Sat.-Sun., COP$10,000 cover during Carnaval). This old-school corner salsa bar opened in 1963 and has become such a Barranquilla nightlife institution that they now close off the entire street in front of the bar so that people can dance in the open air. During Carnaval, La Troja is one of the unofficial after-party destinations each night, and a few entire blocks are fenced off. Just a half block away from La Troja, **4toB** (Cl. 74 No. 44-37, cell tel. 312/422-6078, 5pm-2am Sun. and Thurs., 5pm-3:30am

Fri.-Sat., no cover) is a hip, local watering hole where creative types like to hang out over classic rock and live DJs spinning electronic music. It's a great place to meet some new Colombian friends.

Food

Regional standouts include *butifara soledena,* which is a beef and pork sausage normally served with *bollo de yuca,* a boiled ball of yuca. Another meaty dish, popular during Carnaval, is *sancocho de guandú,* a stew of beef, yuca, yams, plantains, and vegetables. For breakfast on the go, Barranquilleros grab an *arepa de huevo* (an egg in a cornmeal arepa that is then fried). Many restaurants are clustered around Carrera 52 between Calles 70 and 100.

The ★ **Restaurante Bar La Cueva** (Cra. 43 No. 59-03, tel. 5/340-9813, www.fundacionlacueva.org, noon-3pm and 6pm-10pm Mon.-Thurs., noon-3pm and 6pm-midnight Fri.-Sat., COP$40,000) has history and lots of character. It was the hangout of Gabriel García Márquez and artists such as Alejandro Obregón in the 1960s. Elephant tracks, memorabilia, and photos make it seem like a museum, but it's still a restaurant, and a popular one at that. The specialty here is seafood. There's live music on Friday and Saturday evenings. Be sure to check out the Obregón work *La Mulata de Obregón,* complete with a bullet hole thanks to a drunken friend of the artist. Reservations are essential on weekend evenings.

El Huerto (Cra. 52 No. 70-139, tel. 5/368-7171, 8am-7pm Mon.-Sat., 10am-3pm Sun., COP$12,000) offers an inexpensive and healthy all-vegetarian break from the norm with breakfast and a daily set lunch menu. There is also a small store that sells baked goods and health food products such as quinoa and granola.

Accommodations

Because of its status as a business destination, Barranquilla has a number of hotel options, while hostels are fewer are farther between.

Colombia's Caribbean Carnaval Experience

Carnaval is widely celebrated across the Caribbean region of the Americas, and coastal Colombia is no exception. It's the only region in the country that celebrates the pre-Lenten Carnaval based on the Catholic calendar. With roots in ancient European bacchanalian festivities, Carnaval rose to importance in medieval times as a festival during which the repressed classes celebrated the fertility of spring as well as mocked those in power. Carnaval provided a once-a-year vehicle for people at the bottom of the social ladder to take over the streets and turn things upside down, perhaps a reason why this traditional celebration became so popular in areas of the Americas that were focal points of the transatlantic slave trade: Rio de Janeiro, New Orleans, and, originally, Cartagena.

Carnaval

In Colombia, many of the subversive and anti-authoritarian traits of Carnaval have been incorporated into folkloric traditions that are played out without much explanation. Be prepared to see costumed devils making threatening gestures at the crowd, people in blackface making grotesque facial expressions meant to shock people into giving money, and other rituals whose roots have been semi-obscured by the passage of time. The one strong current that runs through all modern Carnaval celebrations, however, is their complete takeover of the streets by people of all classes, a revolution by way of joy-making—that must be enacted every year in order to renew the world.

If you're visiting the Caribbean region of Colombia during Carnaval season—the days leading up to Ash Wednesday on the Catholic calendar (typically late Feb. or early Mar.)—consider joining the festivities; many towns are in party mode for nearly a month or more prior. Although most people associate Carnaval in Colombia only with the massive celebration in Barranquilla, the UNESCO-recognized mega-bash, several other towns on the Caribbean coast also throw Carnavals well worth seeking out, including Cartagena in the off-season.

- Cartagena hosted the big Carnaval on the coast before Barranquilla stole its thunder as the region's economic engine. But the ancient city now throws an interesting Carnaval. Its Carnaval of Independencia (page 52) celebrates the city's independence from Spain in November, in the week before the 11th. For those who won't be on the coast during regular Carnaval season, this is a chance to experience the street dancers, floats, and all-night revelry that typifies the festival.

- Mompox (page 77), Colombia's capital of *cumbia,* hosts live musical groups and parades along its historic streets during Carnaval season. This is a fun, local festival that keeps the riverfront buzzing with action late into the night.

- Santa Marta (page 91) throws its own small-scale Carnaval that centers on the historic residential neighborhoods right outside of the city center near the port. Handmade floats take over the streets and kids throw flour and *spuma* (shaving cream) at each other.

- Dibulla, located just a couple towns down the coast and about 20 minutes (shared taxi COP$5,000) east of Palomino (page 107), is known for hosting a festive Carnaval that draws a diverse crowd. After the day processions of folkloric dancers have finished, the party heads to Punta de los Remedios, a beachside community where a large stage hosts live bands.

- Riohacha (page 118) hosts a major Carnaval that rocks the pretty seaside city for weeks. One of the oldest Carnavals in Colombia, it's steeped in local traditions and culture and features beauty pageants—crowning a festival queen and, more recently, an LGBT queen—as well as tons of music on the beach.

Rates at chain hotels can significantly drop on weekends. During Carnaval, prices skyrocket and hotels sell out months in advance.

★ **Hotel Estelar Alto Prado** (Cl. 76 No. 56-29, tel. 5/336-0000, COP$292,000 d) is a modern, comfortable, and stylish address in Barranquilla. This is where the Argentinian national soccer club stays when they face off against Colombia.

Friendly and low-key, the **Meeting Point Hostel** (Cra. 61 No. 68-100, tel. 5/318-2599, www.themeetingpoint.hostel.com, COP$28,000 dorm, COP$95,000 d) caters to international travelers and also has a pizzeria out front. The neighborhood is quiet and green, about a 15-minute walk from El Prado. Cozy and colorful **La Quinta Bacana Hostal** (Cl. 71 No. 39-195, tel. 5/304 637-9129, COP$35,000 dorm, COP$80,000 d) is another backpacker-friendly choice. It's close to several malls and supermarkets, and has a shared kitchen as well as both indoor and outdoor common areas.

Transportation

GETTING THERE

Terminal Metropolitana de Transportes (Km. 1.5 Prolongación Cl. Murillo, tel. 5/323-0034, www.ttbag.com.co), which is about 15 minutes from downtown, connects Barranquilla to all points in Colombia with regular bus services. For Santa Marta or Cartagena it's more convenient to take a fast van service. From their terminals in town, both **Berlinastur** (Cl. 96 No. 46-36, tel. 5/385-0030, www.berlinastur.com) and **MarSol** (Cl. 93 No. 47-13 Local 4, tel. 5/357-6209) make the daily journey to Santa Marta (2 hours, COP$25,000) and Cartagena (1.5 hours, COP$20,000) from early in the morning until around 6pm. They are fast and reliable and usually take credit cards. There's no need to reserve a seat.

Barranquilla's **Aeropuerto Internacional Ernesto Cortissoz** (Soledad, www.baq.aero) offers excellent connections with all major cities in Colombia and a handful of nonstop international flights as well.

The airport is south of the city in Soledad. Taxi rides cost about COP$20,000 from the airport to downtown.

Avianca (www.avianca.com) flies nonstop to Barranquilla from Miami, Bogotá, Cali, and Medellín. **LATAM Airlines** (www.latam.com) has flights from Bogotá. **Copa Airlines** (www.copaair.com) has nonstop flights from San Andrés and Panama City. **VivaColombia** (www.vivacolombia.co) flies direct from both Bogotá and Medellín, and **EasyFly** (www.easyfly.com.co) has nonstop flights from Bucaramanga, Valledupar, and Montería.

GETTING AROUND

Barranquilla is not a pedestrian-friendly city. Unmetered taxi cabs are the most convenient way to get around. Ask a local how much you should expect to pay before stepping into a cab. You should rarely pay more than COP$15,000 to get to in-town locations. The taxi-hailing app **Easy Taxi** (http://cabify.com) is available here, and allows you to see the fare upfront. **Uber** (www.uber.com) has operated here in the past but was banned in 2019; as of 2020 it's in litigation against the government of Colombia, so double-check to see if its services are available at your time of travel.

Transmetro (www.transmetro.gov.co, 5am-11pm Mon.-Sat., 6am-10pm Sun., COP$2,200) is the city's rapid bus system, which runs along two main avenues: Avenida Murillo (also known as Calle 45) and Avenida Olaya Herrera (also known as Carrera 46). There are stations in front of the Museo del Caribe, the cathedral, and the stadium.

SANTA MARTA

Founded in 1525, Santa Marta is Colombia's oldest city. Although its architectural glory seems paltry next to grandiose Cartagena, the city's pleasant pedestrian-only streets and historic plazas exude a tropical cool and friendly local vibe not found anywhere else on the coast. It's also the launching pad for visits to the nearby Sierra Nevada—including

Santa Marta

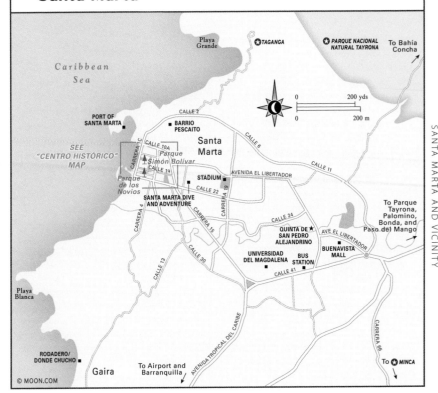

Parque Nacional Natural Tayrona and Ciudad Perdida—the lush mountain coffee town of Minca, and chilled-out Taganga, making it a logical base for the entire region.

The **Centro Histórico** extends from the busy Calle 22 (Avenida Santa Rita) in the south to the Avenida del Ferrocarril in the north, and from the same Avenida del Ferrocarril in the east to the *malecón* (Carrera 1C/Avenida Rodrigo de Bastidas) to the west. The focal point of the Centro is the Parque de los Novios (Carreras 2A-3 and Calles 19-20). This is a lovely park with pedestrian streets (Calle 19 and Carrera 3) intersecting on its eastern side. Most sights are within a smaller range of streets from Carrera 5 to the water and between Calles 20 and 14.

The **Rodadero district,** also known as

Colombia's Miami Beach, is lined with beachfront condos and hotels. It's located just southwest of town, but local buses continuously ply the stretch between the Centro Histórico and Rodadero.

Sights
CENTRO HISTÓRICO

The compact Centro Histórico in Santa Marta feels like a living museum thanks to its mix of colonial and Republican-era architecture. All major sights, save for the Quinta de San Pedro Alejandrino, are located here and can be visited in one day. The best way to get around the Centro Histórico is on foot. A recommended **walking tour** (cell tel. 301/485-9222, free) of historic Santa Marta is offered by local Eduardo Riveira. Tips are welcome, and the walks usually take place at 10am on most weekdays.

The **Parque de los Novios** (Cras. 2A-3 and Clls. 19-20) is a symbol of the city's rejuvenation. The pedestrian streets around the park make a pleasant place for a stroll and a meal. Restaurants line the park's periphery, and on the Calle 20 side of the park is the grandiose neoclassical **Palacio de Justicia,** Santa Marta's main courthouse.

The **Catedral de Santa Marta** or **Basílica Menor** (Cr. 5 No. 16-30, tel. 5/421-2434, masses at noon and 6pm Mon.-Sat., 7am, 10am, noon, and 6pm Sun.) took around 30 years to build and was completed in 1794, toward the end of Spanish reign in Nueva Granada, as colonial Colombia was called. It is one of the oldest cathedrals in Latin America. The city's founder, Rodrigo de Bastidas, is buried there, and Simón Bolívar lay in rest there before his body was moved to Caracas.

The **Plaza de Bolívar** (Cras. 1-2 and Clls. 14-15) has a statue of Simón Bolívar on horseback, ready to destroy the oppressors. The **Banco de la República** (Cl. 14 No. 1C-37, tel. 5/421-0251, www.banrep.gov.co, 8:30am-6pm Mon.-Fri., 9am-1pm Sat., free) often has art exhibits and also has a peaceful public library on its 3rd floor.

The **Museo del Oro Tairona** (Cl. 14 No. 1C-37, tel. 5/421-0251, www.banrepcultural.org, 9am-5pm Tues.-Sat., 10am-3pm Sat., free) is in the historic **Casa de la Aduana,** perhaps the oldest customs house in the Americas, dating back to 1531. A smaller version of the famous Museo del Oro in Bogotá, this facility focuses on the Tayrona people, who were the native settlers of the region and forebears of the Kogis, Arhuacos, Kankuamos, and Wiwas who live in the Sierra Nevada. There are ceramic and gold artifacts on display, and a description of the Ciudad Perdida archaeological site. The second level of the museum is devoted to the history of the city of Santa Marta and the diverse populations that reside in the region.

Along the waterfront is the **Paseo de Bastidas** (Cra. 1) boardwalk (called the *malecón*). Locals flock here at sunset to down a cold one over views of the port, the sailboats moored at the Marina Santa Marta, and Isla Morro.

QUINTA DE SAN PEDRO ALEJANDRINO

Simón José Antonio de la Santísima Trinidad Bolívar y Palacios, better known as Simón Bolívar, was instrumental in bringing independence to several countries in Latin America, including Venezuela, Colombia, Ecuador, Peru, and Bolivia. While awaiting exile to Europe, he passed away at the age of 47 in Santa Marta at the **Quinta de San Pedro Alejandrino** (Mamatoco, tel. 5/433-2995, www.museobolivariano.org.co, 9am-4:30pm daily, COP$22,000). This country estate is now a museum where visitors can see the bedroom in which Bolívar died in 1830. A modern wing houses the Museo Bolivariano de Arte Contemporáneo.

Young guides will offer to take you around the complex for about COP$2,000, but you're probably better off on your own. The *quinta* is set in a manicured botanical garden. There is a small snack bar and gift shop on the grounds.

Recreation

There are some terrific diving spots quite close to Santa Marta. **Santa Marta Dive and Adventure** (Cl. 17 No. 2-43, tel. 5/422-6370, www.santamartadiveandadventure.com.co) is a reputable agency that offers dive tours and courses with some English-speaking instructors. Dive sites are off the coast of Parque Nacional Natural Tayrona, at two shipwrecks near Santa Marta, and offshore from the town of Taganga. A three-day course goes for COP$650,000, a half-day course is COP$200,000, and a diving excursion for certified divers costs COP$160,000.

Entertainment and Events

The **Parque de los Novios** is the center of nocturnal action in Santa Marta, where tourists and locals mix it up over beers bought from street vendors. Kitty-corner from the

Centro Histórico

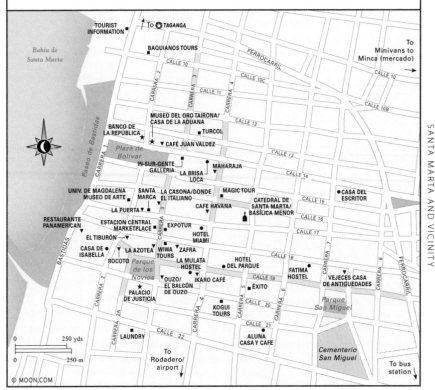

TOURIST INFORMATION
To TAGANGA
Bahía de Santa Marta
BAQUIANOS TOURS
FERROCARRIL
To Minivans to Minca (mercado)
CALLE 10
CALLE 10
CALLE 11
CALLE 10C
CALLE 10B
CARRERA 2
CARRERA 3
CARRERA 4
CALLE 12
MUSEO DEL ORO TAIRONA/ CASA DE LA ADUANA
TURCOL
BANCO DE LA REPÚBLICA
Paseo de Bastidas
CAFÉ JUAN VALDEZ
Plaza de Bolívar
CALLE 13
IN-SUR-GENTE GALLERIA
MAHARAJA
LA BRISA LOCA
CALLE 14
CARRERA 2
UNIV. DE MAGDALENA MUSEO DE ARTE
SANTA MARCA
LA CASONA/DONDE EL ITALIANO
MAGIC TOUR
CALLE 15
CASA DEL ESCRITOR
LA PUERTA
CAFE HAVANA
CATEDRAL DE SANTA MARTA/ BASÍLICA MENOR
CALLE 16
RESTAURANTE PANAMERICAN
ESTACION CENTRAL MARKETPLACE
EXPOTUR
HOTEL MIAMI
CALLE 17
EL TIBURÓN
CARRERA 7
CASA DE ISABELLA
LA AZOTEA
WIWA TOURS
ZAFRA
CALLE 18
ROCOTO
Parque de los Novios
LA MULATA HOSTEL
HOTEL DEL PARQUE
FATIMA HOSTEL
CARRERA 8
FERROCARRIL
OUZO/ EL BALCÓN DE OUZO
IKARO CAFÉ
CALLE 19
ÉXITO
VEJECES CASA DE ANTIGUEDADES
BASTIDAS
PALACIO DE JUSTICIA
CARRERA 5
CALLE 20
Parque San Miguel
KOGUI TOURS
CARRERA 2A
CARRERA 4
CALLE 21
CARRERA 6
CALLE 22
LAUNDRY
ALUNA CASA Y CAFE
Cementerio San Miguel
0   250 yds
0   250 m
To Rodadero/ airport
To bus station
© MOON.COM

park are several popular bars with outdoor seating, making for excellent people-watching. **Marley Bar Reggae Rock '80's** (Cra. 3 No. 19-13, cell tel. 301/318-7662, 3pm-2am daily) is the coolest of the bunch, with some vintage decor, a decent happy hour (two-for-one cocktails 3pm-8pm), and friendly table service. Just a half block away **La Azotea** (Cra. 3 No. 19-25, cell tel. 300/349-6248, www.laazotea. co, 6pm-2am daily) is a big dance club where different DJs rock the house most nights of the week and the sweaty dance floor stays packed till closing time. Sometimes there's a cover, but cost varies.

Opening onto the plaza in front of the Catedral de Santa Marta is ★ **Cafe Havana** (Cra. 4 No. 16-42, no phone, 5pm-2am Wed.-Sat., no cover), which has indoor and outdoor

seating and hosts live salsa bands. Dancers sometimes spill out into the plaza, pulling passersby into the fiesta.

If you're in the area and interested in a lower-key version of Carnaval than Barranquilla's, you can enjoy festivities right in Santa Marta. Held in the seaside neighborhood of Pescaito, Santa Marta's **Carnaval** is a local affair that features floats and musical groups taking over the streets on the weekends and weekdays leading up to Ash Wednesday on the Catholic calendar, usually late February or early March. Throughout the festival kids throw flour and shaving cream at each other, and sometimes on unsuspecting visitors—overreacting negatively is sure way to get more thrown on you! On Fat Tuesday, the residents reenact a "battle of flowers" that commemorates the death of José Ariza, also known as Joselito Carnaval; this mythical figure from Barranquilla is said to have died from excessive drinking during Carnaval so that everyone else could keep on partying.

Shopping

For funky gifts made by local designers, such as T-shirts and art, check out the small shop **Santa Marca** (Cl. 17 No. 2-45, tel. 5/423-5862, 10am-7pm Mon.-Sat.).

Go back in time in **Vejeces Casa de Antiguedades** (Cl. 18 No. 7A-64, cell tel. 300/305-3324, 9am-5pm Mon.-Sat.), a quaint Centro shop jam-packed with interesting stuff. While there are some pre-Columbian pieces for sale, note that it is illegal to take these abroad.

Stock up on coffee and chocolate at **Estación Central Market Place** (Cl. 17 No. 2-56, tel. 5/422-2411, http://estacioncentralmarket.com, 10am-8pm Monday-Sat.), an organic/sustainable food shop that showcases local products. It also has a small café in the back.

El Tiburón (Cra. 2 18-09, tel. 5/421-4301, 10am-6pm daily) makes shocking use of every square inch of its space in the Centro to display Colombian handicrafts and kitsch, and by no small miracle shop employees seem to know where everything is.

In-Sur-Gente Casa Galería Cultural (Cl. 14 No. 3-28, cell tel. 311/683-0081, noon-9pm Mon.-Sat.) is a large, crumbling historic mansion that houses a T-shirt shop, as well as a performance space. It's worth stopping by just to check out the murals on the walls.

Food

Most of Santa Marta's finest restaurants can be found in the Centro Histórico or on the waterfront around the *malecón*. For a delightful ambience, seek out restaurants on pedestrianized streets such as Carretera 3 between Calles 15 and 16 (Callejón del Correo), Calle 19 between Carreteras 3 and 5, and on the Parque de los Novios. The Rodadero area is known for its seafood joints, but many are overpriced.

CENTRO HISTÓRICO

★ **Ouzo** (Cra. 3 No. 19-29, tel. 5/423-0658, www.ouzosantamarta.com, noon-10:30pm Mon.-Thurs., noon-11pm Fri.-Sat., COP$40,000) is co-owned by the brothers behind La Brisa Loca hostel and consistently ranks as one of the top fine-dining restaurants in Santa Marta. Specializing in Mediterranean fare, Ouzo has brought some serious class to the Parque de los Novios, onto which it opens. Order a plate of sizzling seafood or pasta accompanied by a glass of white wine. **El Balcón de Ouzo** (same hours as restaurant) serves tapas and pizza on the rooftop terrace of Ouzo. It's one of the best spots in Santa Marta for a sundowner.

Curry lovers will celebrate the offerings at the Rajasthani chef-run ★ **Maharaja** (Cra. 4 No. 14-34, cell tel. 315/246-1905, 11am-9pm Mon.-Sat., COP$13,000). One of the most authentic Indian joints in the entire country, its veggie and meat set lunches are a great deal and the full dinner menu includes a fiery vindaloo.

With lush living walls, comfy sofa beds, and outdoor seating on bustling pedestrian-only Calle 19, ★ **Ikaro Café** (Cl. 19 No. 3-60, cell tel. 310/407-8533, www.ikarocafe.com, 8am-9pm daily, COP$16,000) is easily the coolest and coziest café in the Centro Histórico. It serves organic coffee produced on its own farm in the Sierra Nevada, Thai-Colombian fusion plates, and bomb raw chocolate tarts, as well as the full line of artisan beers from Minca's Nevada Cerveceria.

La Casona Restaurante Pizzeria (Cra. 3 No. 16-26, cell tel. 316/429-1131, 5pm-10pm Mon.-Sat., COP$35,000) is a cheerful restaurant where even the standard pasta arrabiata tastes exquisite. The diverse menu offers Caribbean cuisine (with an Italian flair) in addition to traditional pasta dishes.

Locals rave about the steaks at **Zafra** (Cl. 18 No. 3-38, tel. 5/420-9443, 5pm-9pm Mon.-Sat., COP$30,000). Served on a shady

---

1: Museo del Oro Tairona; **2:** view of Catedral de Santa Marta from La Casa del Farol hotel

1

2

garden patio, the steaks come in different styles, many based on traditional Colombian sauces and ingredients. Chef Yurani migrated to Santa Marta from Bogotá, where she ran the kitchen at one of the capital's top-rated restaurants.

RODADERO

★ **Donde Chucho** (Cl. 6 No. 2-61, tel. 5/422-1752, 11am-11pm Mon.-Thurs., 11am-midnight Fri.-Sat., 11am-10pm Sun., COP$35,000) is the classic Santa Marta seafood joint, so popular it has branches in Bogotá. The original restaurant (there is another location in the Centro) is a casual open-air place filled with photos of Chucho, the owner and chef, posing with Colombian beauty queens, sports stars, and politicians. It's hard to believe that Chucho began this seafood empire with a humble wooden ceviche stand in Rodadero in the 1990s.

For delicious seafood, pasta, and wine in a minimalist setting, try **DiVino** (Cl. 6 No. 1-26, tel. 5/421-3735, noon-11pm daily, COP$30,000), one of the top restaurants in Rodadero.

The terrace of **Pepe Mar** (Cra. 1 No. 6-05, tel. 5/422-2503, noon-10pm daily, COP$30,000) is the best place for people-watching in all of Rodadero. Try the fried red snapper with coconut rice and a *patacón* (fried plantain) or two. Casual attire, like tank tops and bathing suits, is okay here.

Accommodations

The Centro Histórico offers everything from comfortable hostels to posh boutique hotels, making it a great base. Rodadero is packed with high-rise hotels, many of which are all-inclusive and mostly catering to vacationing Colombian families.

Some prefer to stay in the relaxed beach village of Taganga just north of town, and visit Santa Marta for its restaurants in the evenings.

UNDER COP$200,000

While many hostels in Santa Marta vie for the title of "party hostel," ★ **La Brisa Loca** (Cl. 14 No. 3-58, Centro Histórico, tel. 5/431-6121, www.labrisaloca.com, COP$50,000 dorm, COP$160,000 d) occupies the top spot and has no serious competition. This revamped colonial mansion has a small pool in the main courtyard that's surrounded by three floors of private rooms and large mixed dormitories (6-10 beds). On the 2nd floor is a bar with balconies over the street that, thanks to daily drink specials, gets jammed with backpackers and locals alike, especially on weekends. Take your cocktail upstairs to the swank rooftop lounge and enjoy *la brisa loca* ("the crazy breeze") along with music from a DJ.

★ **Aluna Casa y Cafe** (Cl. 21 No. 5-27, Centro Histórico, tel. 5/432-4916, www.alunahotel.com, COP$30,000 dorm with fan, COP$100,000 d with a/c) is a small, quiet hostel with a mix of dorms and private rooms, all of which are immaculately maintained. The owner also runs an ecological farm, Finca Entre Rios, in the quiet mountainside community of Paso del Mango (about 15 km/9.3 mi outside of Santa Marta, *colectivo* taxi COP$10,000), where guests can walk to waterfalls and hike to Minca. It's also possible to stay overnight at the farm. The hostel's café serves breakfast and snacks.

Tucked down a residential street, ★ **Casa del Escritor** (Cr. 7 No. 14-11, Centro Histórico, tel. 321/522-854, COP$89,000-139,000 d) offers private rooms with shared or private bathrooms in a eclectically furnished and book-filled modern home away from home. Most rooms have both hammocks and sofas to create a living room space and all are fitted with a desk made for writing.

Located just a block outside the Centro Histórico, **Fatima Hostel** (Cl. 18 No. 05-66, cell tel. 321/755-9049 www.fatimahostels.com, COP$25,000 dorm, COP$75,000 d) is the beach outpost of a popular Colombian-run landmark hostel in Bogotá; it has the same street art aesthetic, but in tropical hues.

Eco-Lodgings in the Jungle

Visiting an eco-lodge in Colombia is one of the best experiences the country offers. Paso del Mango is an eco-village comprising lodges and nature reserves that share a commitment to preserving the land.

The best place to stay in Paso del Mango is the shockingly deluxe Finca Carpe Diem (tel. 5/420-9610, www. fincacarpediem.com, COP$17,000 hammock, COP$35,000 dorm, COP$180,000 luxury cabin), which is perched on the cusp of the jungle. This Belgian-run lodge is also a working farm and a 50-hectare natural reserve, and is home to a tree-planting project. There's a refreshing natural pool, beekeeping classes, and a restaurant on-site, which offers a variety of options in a friendly atmosphere.

It's also possible to stay at the Finca Entre Rios (tel. 5/432-4916, www. fincaentrerios.com, COP$100,000 pp), run by the owner of Aluna Casa y Cafe in Santa Marta. Accommodations are in two different farmhouses, and prices include three meals a day. The farm is a permaculture project aimed at reforesting the surrounding area, including the planting of many cacao and fruit trees, and long-term volunteer stays are also possible.

To get to Paso del Mango, take a taxi to the village of Bonda (COP$10,000) from Santa Marta. From the soccer field, take a *mototaxi* (COP$8,000) along the scenic road up to the mountains.

Fatima gives guests a free drink voucher on check-in; redeem it in the spacious hammock-lined rooftop bar, which also boasts a hot tub.

Mulata Hostel (Cl.19 No. 3-32, Centro Histórico, tel. 5/420-7305, COP$30,000 dorm, COP$60,000 s, COP$90,000 d) enjoys an action-fronting location right on pedestrian-only Calle 19, with bars, restaurants, and Parque de los Novios a stone's throw away. The lively hostel hosts regular yoga and salsa classes as well as live music on the weekends, and an on-site bar serves the pleasant inner patio and a handful of sidewalk tables. Bike rentals are available.

Hotel Miami (Cl. 17 No. 3-96, Centro Histórico tel. 5/420-6847, www. hotelmiamism.com, COP$65,000 d) is an elegant 1920s-era hotel located near the Catedral de Santa Marta. Rooms are basic and come with flat-screen TVs, but the hotel's common areas feature lots of period charm.

The Hotel del Parque (Cl. 19 No. 4-45, Centro Histórico, tel. 5/420-7508, COP$110,000 d) is located on the busy principal pedestrian-only street of Calle 19. Supremely low-key, this hotel has just a handful of air-conditioned rooms but is very well maintained, and, best of all, it's fairly priced. There's complimentary coffee.

COP$200,000-400,000

The 10-room ★ Casa de Isabella (Callejón del Río, Cra. 2 No. 19-20, Centro Histórico, tel. 5/431-2082 or cell tel. 301/466-5656, www. casaisabella.com, COP$245,000 d) is a tastefully revamped Republican-era house with nods to both colonial and Republican styles, and it surrounds a tamarind tree that's over 200 years old. The top-floor suites have fantastic private terraces and hot tubs.

La Casa del Farol (Cl. 18 No. 3-115, Centro Histórico, tel. 5/423-1572, www. lacasadelfarol.com, COP$200,000 d) was one of the first boutique hotels in the city. It's in an 18th-century house and has six rooms that are named for different cities of the world. The tiny wading pool on the rooftop affords a nice view of the city.

For a beachfront option in Rododero, check out Tamacá Beach Resort Hotel (Cra. 2 No. 11A-98, Rodadero, tel. 5/422-7015, www. tamaca.com.co, COP$270,000 d). It has 81 rooms with all the usual amenities and a fantastic pool area overlooking the water. The hotel has two towers, with the beach-side tower preferred by most.

Information and Services

In addition to a stand at the airport, there is a PIT (Punto de Información Turística, Cra.

SANTA MARTA AND LA GUAJIRA
SANTA MARTA AND VICINITY

1 No. 10A-12, tel. 5/438-2587, 9am-noon and 2pm-6pm Mon.-Fri., 9am-1pm Sat.) tourist information booth along the waterfront.

Lavandería El Paraíso (Cl. 22 No. 2A-46, tel. 5/431-2466, cell tel. 315/681-1651, 9am-6pm Mon.-Fri., 9am-1pm Sat.) will wash your clothes and have them ready for pickup by the next day.

Transportation

Santa Marta is easily accessed by land and air from all major cities in Colombia.

There is hourly bus service to Cartagena (5 hrs, COP$26,000), Barranquilla (2 hrs, COP$12,000), and Riohacha (3 hours, COP$18,000) from downtown Santa Marta (along Cra 5). Many buses to nearby destinations like Minca leave from the market area (Cra. 11 and Cl. 11) in the Centro Histórico. Long-haul buses for destinations such as Bogotá, Medellín, and Bucaramanga depart from the **Terminal de Transportes** (Cl. 41 No. 31-17, tel. 5/430-2040) outside of town (Taxi COP$15,000).

Taxis to Taganga cost around COP$12,000 and *colectivo* buses are around COP$2,000. These can be found on the waterfront near Parque Simón Bolívar, along Carrera 5, or at the market at Carrera 11 and Calle 11.

The **Aeropuerto Internacional Simón Bolívar** (Km. 16.5 Troncal del Caribe) is 16 kilometers (10 mi) west of the Centro Histórico. Taxis to the Centro Histórico from the airport cost around COP$20,000. Domestic carriers **Avianca** (www.avianca.com), **LATAM Airlines** (www.latam.com), **VivaColombia** (www.vivacolombia.co), and **EasyFly** (www.easyfly.com.co) connect Santa Marta with the major cities of Colombia. **Copa Airlines** (www.copaair.com) has nonstop flights from its hub in Panama City, Panama.

TOP EXPERIENCE

★ TAGANGA

Taganga is a popular beachfront community that's tucked into a picturesque cove-like bay along the curving mountainous coastline just north of Santa Marta. In the 1970s, this sleepy fishing village was discovered by hippies looking for an escape from urban life, and it soon became a backpacker haven. After gaining an infamous reputation for excessive partying in the mid-2010s, Taganga has chilled out a bit—the hard-core party scene has moved to Palomino—and is now one of the most relaxing places on the coast to spend a couple of days or weeks. On any given day you'll brush shoulders with Colombian families, beach bum expats, diving fanatics, traveling musicians, fishers, and sunseekers of all ages and nationalities.

Recreation
DIVING AND SNORKELING
The warm waters (24-28°C/75-82°F) off of Taganga provide some good diving and snorkeling opportunities. Diving excursions take you into the waters off of Parque Nacional Natural Tayrona to the northeast, to Isla Morro off the coast of Santa Marta, or to a shipwreck near the beaches of Rodadero. The best months for diving here are July-September.

Tayrona Dive Center (Cra. 1C No. 18A-22, tel. 5/421-5349, cell tel. 318/305-9589, www.tayronadivecenter.com, 8am-noon and 2pm-6pm daily) is an organized agency that offers PADI certification courses (COP$750,000) over a period of three days with six dives each day, a one-day mini-course (COP$180,000), and diving excursions for those with experience. It also has a hotel (COP$80,000 d) at the same location with six rooms, five with views of the water. Rooms have a safe-deposit box and big refrigerators. The hotel is exclusively for divers during high season (mid-Dec.-mid-Jan., Holy Week, and mid-June-mid-July).

Oceano Scuba (Cra. 2 No. 17-46, tel. 5/421-9004, cell tel. 316/534-1834, www.oceanoscuba.com.co, 8am-noon and 2pm-6pm daily) offers an array of diving activities, from a one-day beginner's course (COP$240,000) to an open-water PADI certification course (COP$900,000) that lasts three days. Night dives (COP$110,000)—during which you might come across eels—and snorkeling (COP$65,000) are also on offer.

Poseidon Dive Center (Cl. 18 No 1-69, tel. 5/421-9224, www.poseidondivecenter.com, 9am-6pm daily) is a PADI 5-star certified dive center that has English-speaking instructors. It offers dozens of courses, like an open-water diving class (COP$1,300,000), and tours, such as a 10-dive package (COP$1,120,000).

BEACHES

Partially lined by a boardwalk that's packed with restaurants, Taganga's city beach is a long, crescent swath of golden sands cradled by a picturesque mountainous cove. Fishing boats dock off the northern side of the beach, but a large section of the sands on the southern side is reserved for swimmers and attracts an eclectic mix of visitors both day and night. It's a magical place to take in the sunset, and people lounge around talking, drinking, and mingling late into the night.

Playa Grande is just north of town around the next cove. It has a more natural setting and is also quite spectacular come sunset, which bathes the mountainous cliffs in orange. It costs COP$10,000 round-trip to get there by boat from the boardwalk; there are always fishers waiting, or you can walk a pretty little mountain path to the beach in about 20 minutes. The trail is clearly marked on the northern end of the city beach, and passes by several detours to tiny cove beaches tucked into the rocky coastline, where more solitude can be found than at either the town beach or Playa Grande.

Boats from Taganga's beach can also take you to some of the nearby beaches within **Parque Nacional Natural Tayrona,** to the northeast of town, although note that park staff prefer travelers to visit the park by land, and, during the windy months of December-February, boat transportation can be rough, bordering on dangerous. The closest of the park's beaches is **Playa Concha** (COP$80,000 round-trip), which sits prettily within the large Bahía Concha and offers calm, clear waters to splash in. Just around

the next bend in the coastline is **Playa Cristal** (COP$110,000 round-trip), which sits under a jungle-covered arm of the mountainside. This expansive wilderness beach, backed by verdant tropical mountains, is also called Playa del Muerto (Beach of the Dead) because it was an important ceremony center to the ancient Tayrona civilization. Although all visitors to the park are supposed to pay an entrance fee, these beaches are exempt most of the time; whether this is official or not is still in question.

Food

★ **Babaganoush Restaurante y Bar** (Cra. 1C No. 18-22, 3rd fl. above Taganga Dive Center, cell tel. 318/868-1476, 1pm-11:30pm Wed.-Mon., COP$26,000) is an excellent Dutch-run restaurant and bar with amazing views. It's a true crowd-pleaser, with a diverse menu of falafel, seafood, steak, and even a shout-out to Southeast Asia. Go in the evening for the atmosphere, and drinks. The daily happy hour (5pm-7pm)—which converges with sunset—is hard to pass up.

Direct from Atlanta comes ★ **Taco Beach Bar and Grille** (Cra. 1 No. 18-49, tel. 5/423-3912, noon-8pm daily, COP$25,000). With Tex-Mex delights, happy hours, and sand beneath your feet, this spot is all that you need in a beach bar.

Tucked away on a side street a block or two from the beach, **Pachamama** (Cl. 16 No. 1C-18, tel. 5/421-9486 or cell tel. 318/393-9291, noon-11pm daily, COP$28,000) has a sophisticated menu that includes Argentinian steaks, ceviche, pasta, and refreshing cocktails, all skillfully prepared by the French chef. Live music often accompanies dinner.

Café Bonsai (Cl. 13 No. 1-07, tel. 5/421-9495, www.cafebonsai.com, 8am-5pm Mon.-Sat., COP$12,000) is a cute place for coffee, freshly baked breads and pastries, and sandwiches and other lunch items.

For late-night eats or general munchies stop by **Jimmy en tu Fiesta** (Cra. 2 No. 11-1, 5pm-midnight Mon.-Sat., COP$10,000), a hole-in-the-wall where cheap but delicious

home-cooked carne asada and fried chicken have gained a strong local following.

Accommodations

On the southern end of the beach, ★ **Hospedaje El Shadday** (Cra. 1 No. 18-161, tel. 5/421-9232, COP$160,000 d) is a locally owned boutique hotel with three stories of pleasant, private rooms, many with large French windows opening onto panoramic views of the bay. There's also a communal rooftop terrace, and snorkeling gear, kayaks, and beach chairs are available for rent.

Located a 15-minute walk up the hill from the beach, ★ **La Casa de Felipe** (Cra. 5A No. 19-13, tel. 5/421-9120, www.lacasadefelipe. com, COP$35,000 dorm, COP$80,000 d) is a spacious and comfortable hostel with extensive gardens strung with hammocks, a swimming pool, and an on-site restaurant that serves nice crepes and salads. Right across the street, **Casa Gypsy** (Cl. 19 No. 5-40, cell tel. 300/527-1344, COP$25,000 dorm, COP$72,000 d) is a colorfully painted hostel run by a young Colombian-French couple. A bar on the rooftop terrace offers great pizza and is a comfy place to chill in a hammock overlooking town.

If you want backpacker prices without a backpacker scene, check out the centrally located and popular **Hostal Pelikan** (Cra. 2 No. 17-04, tel. 5/421-9057 or cell tel. 316/756-1312, COP$30,000 dorm, COP$75,000 d), a decent place to stay with a nice terrace for your morning coffee. Breakfast is an additional cost.

For a local vibe, check into **Nativo Hostel** (Cl. 17 No. 2-42, cell tel. 304/384-7800, COP$35,000 s, COP$45,000 d), where a local family rents out inexpensive rooms and serves great fresh fish lunches (COP$10,000) on a sidewalk patio.

Probably the most luxurious option in Taganga is the **Hotel Bahía Taganga**

1: the fishing village of Taganga; 2: peaceful Minca, in the Sierra Nevada; 3: Colombian coffee at Finca La Victoria in Minca; 4: view from the pool at Hostal Sierra Minca

(Cl. 8 No. 1B-35, tel. 5/421-0653 or cell tel. 310/216-9120, www.hotelbahiataganga.com, COP$260,000 d), on the northern side of the bay. Head to the terrace pool in the late afternoon and watch the sun slip behind the mountains.

Transportation

Taganga is easily reached from Santa Marta and from points east, such as the Parque Nacional Natural Tayrona and Palomino. Minibuses and buses ply both routes daily.

From Santa Marta's Centro Histórico, you can take a *colectivo* minibus to Taganga for about COP$2,000. Taxis from the center of Santa Marta cost around COP$12,000, more from the bus terminal or airport. The ride from Santa Marta to Taganga takes about 20 minutes. Once in Taganga, you can walk everywhere you need to go.

TOP EXPERIENCE

★ MINCA

Minca offers a change of pace, and altitude, from the beaches and seductive Caribbean cities that typify most of the coastline. At an elevation of 660 meters (2,165 ft) and located partway up the Sierra Nevada, the forest-covered mountains surrounding this small town beckon. Hiking to waterfalls and vista points, bird-watching, and enjoying the high-quality coffee and chocolate grown here are the highlights of a visit to Minca, all over a bird's-eye view of Santa Marta, just 45 minutes away. The bohemian vibe of the town itself is addictive, and travelers often end up staying much longer than they expected. Many accommodations are dispersed around the mountains in unique locations; you may want to visit and stay at several before leaving.

Recreation

In and around Minca there are no safety issues, and you can hike up the mountain on your own without a guide. *Mototaxis* also make popping from one destination to another relatively easy.

The Sierra Nevada de Santa Marta is a renowned coffee-growing region. The **Finca La Victoria** (no phone, 9am-4pm daily, COP$15,000) is a historic family-run coffee farm that you can visit for a small fee. It is between Pozo Azul and Los Pinos, a moderately vigorous 1.5-hour walk south of town, or you can take a 10-minute *mototaxi* ride (COP$8,000). The farm uses an astonishing hydroelectric system and machinery dating back over 100 years. After the tour, try the house-made chocolate banana bread with a coffee at the small on-site café. While you're at the café, grab some of Minca's homebrewed beer—including Happy Coca, which is macerated in coca leaves and gives you a small lift—made by **Cerveceria Nevada,** located right on the Finca La Victoria and run by one of the family members. The working brewery isn't open to the public, but you can take a six-pack with you.

HIKING

Minca is a paradise for hikers. Nearby are several gentle hikes along tranquil mountain roads and paths to spectacular waterfalls with swimming holes of either freezing-cold or wonderfully refreshing water—depending on the thickness of your skin. Three popular waterfalls are within easy walking distance from Minca: Cascada Oigo del Mundo (25 min.), Pozo Azul (45 min.), and the Cascadas Marinka (1.5 hrs.). All are clearly marked from town. Maps of the Minca area are also readily available at most hotels and cafés; pick one up before you set out on a trek.

BIRD-WATCHING

High in the Sierra Nevada, two hours from Minca at an elevation of around 2,400 meters (7,875 ft), the **Reserva El Dorado** (www.proaves.org) is one of the finest bird-watching reserves in the country. The area is home to 19 endemic species, including the Santa Marta antpitta, Santa Marta parakeet, Santa Marta bush tyrant, blossom crown, and screech owls. Anybody can stay at El Dorado, even the non-birding crowd. For reservations

(COP$569,000 3 nights all-incl.), contact **EcoTurs** in Bogotá (Cra. 20 No. 36-61, tel. 1/287-6592, info@ecoturs.org) or **Aviatur** (tel. 1/587-5181, www.aviaturecoturismo. com), also in Bogotá. There are 10 rooms and five huts modeled after traditional Kogi houses, as well as great food, and, crucially, hot showers.

You can also join a group tour with **Jungle Joe** (cell tel. 317/308-5270, www. junglejoeminca.com, 6am daily, COP$40,000) for 3-4 hours of bird-watching in the immediate area around Minca, binoculars and guidebook included. Jungle Joe (Joe Ortiz), originally from Barranquilla, also runs coffee, rafting and other specialized tours out of his office in the center of Minca across from the police station, which is where tours meet.

Food

There are some good eateries in Minca, including more vegetarian restaurants per capita than possibly anywhere else in Colombia. Several hostels also host excellent restaurants that are open to the public. Standouts include **Hostal Casa Loma** (50 m above the church, cell tel. 313/808-6134 or 321/224-6632, www. casalomaminca.com) and **Hostel Mirador** (200 m from town entrance, cell tel. 311/671-3456 or 318/368-1611).

The excellent Middle Eastern food at ★ **Arabesca Minca** (Cl. 3a at Cra. 5a, cell tel. 315/322-0964, www.arabesca-minca. business.site, 11am-10pm daily, COP$15,000) is crafted by a Lebanese chef and served on a spacious mural-lined garden patio. The falafel is to die for and the menu features a vegan/vegetarian section.

★ **Tienda Café de Minca** (diagonal from police station, cell tel. 312/638-5353, 8:30am-8pm daily, COP$12,000) serves pastries, breakfast, lunch, coffee, beer, and wine. A good place to find out what's going on in town—it's full of tacked-up notices about local events and run by a friendly family—this café is the informal visitors center of Minca in many ways. It also has a store stocked with locally grown and produced coffee beans, dark chocolate, and health products, as well as pieces by local artists. The café has a nice wraparound balcony facing the street and occasionally hosts live music on weekends.

Lazy Cat (across from Tienda Julimar, cell tel. 313/506-5227, noon-9pm daily, COP$15,000) offers a filling meal of pasta or burgers, plus fruit smoothies and beers from the Cerveceria Nevada, on both a back patio and a street-front bar area. It's in the center of town on the main street.

Dining at **Ei Mox Muica** (300 m from town entrance, cell tel. 311/699-6718, 10am-9pm daily, COP$18,000) is like being invited to a friend's house. It only has two tables, which overlook a lush garden. The menu includes a variety of pasta, salads, crepes, and wines. They are into locally produced chocolate here—it might even make an appearance in your pasta.

There is currently a showdown for best bakery going on in Minca. **La Miga Panadería** (Cl. 5A, next to Caja Mágica Internet, cell tel. 313/537-2218, 8am-6pm daily, COP$5,000), with its sidewalk patio, freshly brewed local organic coffee, and house-made *pan de chocolate,* is a sure bet.

Accommodations
MINCA
★ **Hostal Casa Loma** (50 m uphill from a small church, cell tel. 313/808-6134, www.casalomaminca.com, COP$30,000 dorm, COP$90,000 d) is on a hilltop with an impressive vantage over Santa Marta. It's a friendly place where delicious food (often vegetarian) is served and you can mingle with other travelers. Cabins, such as the Casa Selva and Casa Luna farther up on the hillside, are quieter than the rooms near the main social area, providing the ultimate jungle experience. Camping (COP$20,000) is also available. To get to Hostal Casa Loma, climb a winding path just behind the church. Casa Loma offers yoga classes (COP$20,000) and massages (COP$55,000), and shows two films a week in an outdoor setting.

Oscar's Hostal Finca La Fortuna (400 m from town entrance near casino area, cell tel. 313/534-4500, www.oscarsplace.com.co, COP$20,000 hammock, COP$30,000 dorm, COP$50,000 d) consists of simple and luxurious cabins dramatically set on a bluff with extraordinary views of Santa Marta and the surrounding countryside. Oscar's is completely off the grid, with solar panels providing electricity and rainwater collection and a well accounting for all water. The sunsets here, particularly from mid-June until mid-December, are "living art," as owner Oscar puts it. At times Oscar's can have a party atmosphere.

Hostel Mirador (200 m from town entrance, cell tel. 311/671-3456 or 318/368-1611, http://miradorminca.wordpress.com, COP$35,000 dorm, COP$90,000 d) is an enchanting hostel with a great view, warm hosts, and delicious meals. The hostel has two private rooms and a dorm room with three beds, as well as a lush and art-filled garden with chairs and hammocks set up for watching the sunset. The lovely dining area is open-air and open to the public nightly; meals cost around COP$25,000.

Hotel Minca (near town entrance, cell tel. 321/204-1965, www.hotelminca.com, COP$140,000 d), once a convent, was one of the first hotels in Minca. There are 14 spacious yet basic rooms in this old-fashioned building that boasts broad verandas with hammocks. There's a nature path on the grounds, and numerous hummingbird feeders along the open-air dining area ensure a breakfast-time show.

IN THE MOUNTAINS OUTSIDE OF MINCA
★ **Hostal Sierra Minca** (cell tel. 313/587-7677, COP$35,000 dorm, COP$100,000 d) has a fantastic mountainous location with an outdoor pool boasting views over the entire Minca area. Several multi-person hammocks—holding up to 10 people—are built into the mountainside, suspending you over the lush valley below. A poolside bar serves all the classics, while an on-site restaurant serves dinner by reservation. From the hostel, you

can hike 30 minutes up to Los Pinos, where you'll gain views into the interior of the Sierra Nevada and out to Barranquilla to the west. You can get to the hostel via a three-hour up-hill hike, but most people hire a *mototaxi* from Minca (COP$20,000).

Consistently rated one of the top hostels in Colombia, ★ **Casa Viejas** (cell tel. 321/523-7613, www.casasviejasminca.com, COP$50,000 dorm, COP$280,000 d) is nestled into the mountainside a 20-minute walk above Finca La Victoria and Cerveceria Nevada. Guests have access to the 500-hectare reserve and coffee farm, an infinity pool, yoga classes, and an on-site restaurant where health-conscious breakfasts, lunches, and dinners are served. Hammocks offering million-dollar views abound. A *mototaxi* from town runs about COP$10,000-15,000.

Ecological farm and ecolodge **Mundo Nuevo** (cell tel. 300/360-4212, www.mundonuevo.com.co, COP$20,000 hammock, COP$30,000 dorm, COP$90,000 d) is located up a steep mountain road to the northwest of Minca—a *mototaxi* from Minca costs COP$20,000—and sports dizzying views out over both it and Santa Marta. The permaculture farm produces coffee, chocolate, and honey as well as produce that makes its way into the vegetarian meals served at the lodge. Mundo Nuevo has also opened its land to local indigenous Wiwa people, who have built a handful of huts that they use as a stop-over rest point as they travel up and down the Sierra Nevada on foot. From Mundo Nuevo you can hike down to Pozo Azul (1.5 hours).

Information and Services

Bring plenty of cash with you to Minca: There are no ATMs here, but there is a Banco de Bogotá cash transfer office at **The Embassy Center** (10am-8pm daily) in the center of town next to the Caja Mágica Internet.

Transportation

Minca is easily reached from Santa Marta. *Taxis colectivos* (shared taxis) depart from Santa Marta on a regular basis from the market (Cra. 11 and Cl. 11). These cost COP$8,000; the ride takes about 45 minutes. Private taxis from the airport cost around COP$50,000, and taxis from Santa Marta's Centro Histórico to Minca cost COP$40,000.

TOP EXPERIENCE

★ PARQUE NACIONAL NATURAL TAYRONA

An epic meeting of mountains and sea, **Parque Nacional Natural Tayrona** (PNN Tayrona, 34 km northeast of Santa Marta on the Troncal del Caribe highway, tel. 5/421-1732, www.aviaturecoturismo.com or www.parquesnacionales.gov.co, 8am-5pm daily, high season COP$63,500 non-Colombian visitors and COP$20,000 Colombian nationals, low season COP$53,500 non-Colombian visitors and COP$18,000 Colombian nationals) is the best-known national park in Colombia. It's home to gorgeous beaches, tropical rainforests, and archaeological sites.

The park covers 12,000 hectares (30,000 acres) from the edge of Taganga in the southwest to the Río Piedras in the east. The southern border of the park is the Troncal del Caribe highway and to the north is the Caribbean Sea. To the east and south of the PNN Tayrona is the PNN Sierra Nevada de Santa Marta, a much larger national park that encompasses the peaks of the highest coastal mountain range in the world.

The frequently tempestuous waters of the PNN Tayrona provide dramatic scenery, with palms growing atop massive island boulders and waves crashing against them. More than 30 golden-sand beaches in the park are set dramatically against a seemingly vertical wall of jungle. Although you can't see them from the park, the snow-covered peaks of the Sierra Nevada de Santa Marta are only 42 kilometers (26 mi) from the coast.

The park includes significant tracts of critically endangered dry tropical forests, mostly in its western section; these forests are much less dense than the humid tropical forests. At higher elevations you will see magnificent cloud forests. In addition to beaches, the coast is home to marine estuaries and mangroves. The park is laced with streams fed by chilly waters that flow from high in the sierra. In the western part of the park, many of these run dry during the dry season, while in the eastern sector they have water year-round.

The forest in PNN Tayrona is alive with plant and animal life. Some 1,300 plant, 396 bird, and 99 mammal species have been identified here. Four species of monkeys live in the park, and they can often be spotted. Five species of wild cats have been identified in the park: the margay, jaguar, ocelot, panther, and jaguarundi. Their numbers are few and these great cats are expert at hiding in the jungle—don't count on stumbling across them during your visit. Other mammals include sloths, anteaters, armadillos, deer, and 40 types of bats. Birds include migratory and resident species, such as the rare blue-billed curassow (locally called El Paují), a threatened bird that lives in the cloud forest, as well as toucans, macaws (*guacamayas*), and many hummingbirds.

PLANNING YOUR TIME

The best months to visit the park are February, March, September, and October. There are two rainy seasons: April-June and September-November, with the latter being more intense. During these times, trails can be extremely muddy.

If at all possible, avoid visiting PNN Tayrona during the high seasons of late December-mid-January, during Semana Santa (Holy Week), and, to a lesser extent, during summer school holidays mid-June-mid-July. During these times, the park is swarmed with visitors. Long holiday weekends (*puentes*) are also quite busy here; a weekday visit is by far the best.

Recently, the indigenous Kogi people, who still inhabit parts of the park, have begun closing the park to tourism for a month or so every year to protect the natural landscape from too much damage and to give wildlife a rest from human visitation; this often occurs right in January and February during the height of tourist season. Check the park website (www.parquesnacionales.gov.co) in advance for the most up-to-date information on closures.

While many people visit the park on day trips from Santa Marta or Taganga, spending one or two nights in the park is recommended, even though accommodations and food can be expensive.

Bring mosquito repellent (especially during rainy season), a flashlight or headlamp, hiking or athletic shoes if you will be hiking to El Pueblito, sunscreen, and cash. Darkness falls around 6pm year-round, and there is not much going on in the park, so bring playing cards and a book to read. Visitors are not permitted to bring alcohol into the park; your bags may be inspected upon entry. Passports are necessary for entry.

ORIENTATION

The majority of overnight visitors see just the extreme northeastern section of the park. This part of the park houses the main entrance, **El Zaino.** From El Zaino, visitors can access the **Cañaveral** area, which includes the Ecohab accommodations; campsites at **Castilletes;** and cabins and campsites at **Arrecifes.** Farther west along the coast are La Piscina and more campsites at **Cabo San Juan** (also called El Cabo). From Cabo San Juan, there is access to the archaeological site El Pueblito.

Closer to Santa Marta is the **Palangana** entrance, which provides access to Playa Neguanje and other remote beaches. No overnight stays are permitted in this part of the park.

For day-trippers, Playa Concha and Playa Cristal are accessible by boat from Taganga.

Recreation
BEACHES

The beaches in Parque Nacional Natural Tayrona are spectacular, but though the water may appear inviting, currents are deceptively strong, and, despite the warnings posted on the beach, many people have drowned here. Of the park's 34 beaches, there are only 6

where swimming is permitted. There are no lifeguards on duty in the park, and no specific hours for swimming.

The best swimming beaches include **Arenilla** and **La Piscina,** inviting coves of turquoise waters that are protected by natural rock barriers. It's a 20-minute walk northwest from Arrecifes to both of those beaches. A 15-minute walk to the west from the beach at La Piscina is Cabo San Juan; with a large campground nearby, it's a hub of activity in the park. Continuing west, farther along the coast, is a clothing-optional beach, **Playa Nudista.** Those up for an adventure can hike 2-3 hours west along the wilderness coastline from here to **Playa Brava,** a secluded beach that feels lost in time.

Some of the other beaches open to swimming are in the less-visited western part of the park. **Playa Neguanje** is accessed by car or taxi (COP$60,000 from Santa Marta) through the Palangana entrance (12 km/7.5 mi northeast of Santa Marta). **Playa del Muerto (Playa Cristal)** is another recommended beach in the same area. It's more than 20 kilometers (12.5 mi) from the park entrance to the beach.

It's possible to visit some of the beaches at the western end of the park all the way to Cabo San Juan by boat from Taganga, but park staff prefer that visitors enter the park by land. The waters can also be quite rough, especially December-February.

HIKING

The best-maintained and most beautiful hike in the park is the stretch between **Cañaveral and Arrecifes** (3 km/1.9 mi, 1 hour). Upon arrival, most visitors take this path to reach campsites or cabins at Arrecifes or Cabo San Juan. Wooden bridges meander through the jungle as you follow the sound of the crashing waves until you reach a beach strewn with massive boulders. To best enjoy this hike, consider sending your luggage onward

1: beach in Parque Nacional Natural Tayrona; **2:** Ecohab accommodations

to Arrecifes by horse (COP$25,000). Be on the lookout for capuchin monkeys, snakes, and birds.

A highlight of any visit to PNN Tayrona is the trek up to **El Pueblito** (also called Chairama, 3 km/1.9 mi, 1.5 hrs. one-way from Cabo San Juan), which consists of ruins of what was an important Tayrona settlement. The site contains well-preserved remnants of terraces, and a small Kogi community still lives nearby. The challenging path through the tropical jungle is steep and the stone steps can be slippery, but it's well worth it. Hikers can go up to El Pueblito without a guide, but inquire when you enter the park if you'd like to hire one. El Pueblito is usually accessed from within Tayrona by walking west along the beach from Arrecifes and following the signs from Cabo San Juan. A longer version of this hike can be started from the main highway, the Troncal del Caribe, at the Calabazo entrance to the park, around 24 kilometers (15 mi) northeast of Santa Marta. It's about a 2.5-hour trek from there. There's a good chance of spotting monkeys and birds on this longer hike.

Food and Accommodations

The park has two surprisingly upscale restaurants. One is in Cañaveral, close to the Ecohabs, and the other is in Arrecifes, near the *cabañas.* They are open daily 7am-9pm, and the specialty at each is fresh seafood. Expect to pay around COP$35,000 for a lunch or dinner entrée. Both restaurants accept credit cards. There are some snack bars in the park concentrated around the popular beach and campsites, serving fried fish, empanadas, and fresh fruit. The snack bars are usually open during daylight hours (9am-6pm daily).

There are numerous lodging options in PNN Tayrona for every budget: high-end Ecohabs, mid-level *cabañas,* and camping. The travel agency **Aviatur** (Bogotá office Av. 19 No. 4-62, tel. 1/587-5181 or 1/587-5182, www.aviaturecoturismo.com) manages most of the lodging facilities in the park. Neither the Ecohabs nor the *cabañas* could be considered a bargain, but the Ecohabs, where you can awake to beautiful views of the sea, are indeed special, and worth one or two nights. The *cabañas* are set back from the beach but are quite comfortable. Safety boxes are included in all rooms, and can be provided to campers as well. Some visitors prefer to leave a bag or valuables at a trusted hotel in Santa Marta.

The **Ecohabs** (COP$823,000-1,053,000 pp breakfast incl.), in the Cañaveral sector, consist of 14 private *bohíos* (thatched-roof cabins) that sleep 2-4 people. From a distance they look like giant nests amid the trees, but in reality they are modeled after the thatched-roof houses of the Tayrona people. There are two floors to the Ecohabs: the first comprises the bathroom and an open-air social area, and on the second is the bedroom. A flashlight is necessary if you need to go to the bathroom in the middle of the night, as you have to go outside and downstairs. This is inconvenient for some.

In nearby Arrecifes, there are six two-story *cabañas* (12 rooms, COP$462,000-628,000 pp breakfast incl.) with a capacity of four persons each. These are like jungle duplexes, with the two units divided by thin walls. There is also a **hammock area** (COP$38,000 pp) in Arrecifes with a capacity of 60 hammocks. Those choosing this option have access to lockers and the safety box at the lobby area.

There are **campgrounds** (COP$20,000 pp) in both Cañaveral and Arrecifes and also at Cabo San Juan, which is a 15-minute walk to the west from the beach at La Piscina. Cabo tends to get very crowded, bordering on unpleasant (thanks to not enough sanitary facilities), during long weekends and holidays. A better camping option is low-key Castilletes, which is just before the entrance to Cañaveral.

Transportation

From Santa Marta you can take any bus eastbound along the Troncal del Caribe to the park's main entrance (El Zaino). *Colectivo* buses can be caught at the intersection of Carrera 11 and Calle 11 (the market) in Santa Marta, and the trip takes about an hour and costs around COP$6,000. You can also take a cab for about COP$75,000.

Expect a thorough inspection of backpacks and bags upon entering the park. Visitors are not allowed to bring in plastic bags (to protect sea turtles), and no alcohol is permitted (although beer is served at restaurants and snack bars in the park). Be sure to bring bug repellent, a flashlight, and good hiking boots.

Visitors pay the entrance fee at the administrative offices. These fees are not included in the Aviatur package prices.

It's about 4 kilometers (2.5 mi) from the offices to Cañaveral, and vans travel this route on an ongoing basis (COP$3,000). From there it is 45 sweaty minutes on foot through the jungle to Arrecifes. Mules can be hired to carry your bags, or you can rent a horse for COP$20,000.

PNN Tayrona to Palomino

If you prefer less civilization and more tranquility, the coast between PNN Tayrona and Palomino has some interesting places to hang your *sombrero vueltiao* (Colombian hat) for a few days. Between these two very popular tourist destinations are some often overlooked beautiful coastal playgrounds, including both **Playa los Naranjos,** on the edge of the park and popular with surfers, and, just east, **Buritaca,** from which you can tube down a peaceful jungle-lined river; both beaches have some good accommodations options on them and are about 45 kilometers (28 mi) east of Santa Marta. Day trips to PNN Tayrona can be easily coordinated from this area.

ACCOMMODATIONS

Impossibly placed atop giant beach boulders, the guesthouse **Finca Barlovento** (Playa los Naranjos, 40 km east of Santa Marta, Bogotá tel. 1/325-6998, www.fincabarloventosantamarta.com, COP$480,000 d incl. 2 meals) is located between the sea and the Río Piedras. It's an amazing place to stay, and the food's good, too. There are just three rooms and one luxurious cabin here. Jungle excursions can be arranged by the hotel, but be sure to enjoy some beachside afternoons. You'll have the sand mostly to yourself.

The waves are the main draw at ★ **Costeño Beach Hostel** (Playa los Naranjos, 45 km east of Santa Marta, cell tel. 310/368-1191, www.costenobeach.com, COP$44,000 dorm, COP$143,000 d), but the property also gets exceptionally high marks from its guests for its laid-back atmosphere. Costeño Beach has dorms as well as a variety of private accommodations, including "cocohabs," on a former coconut farm. It's also solar-powered. The on-site surf school offers classes (COP$35,000) and board rentals (COP$40,000 per day).

La Brisa Tranquila (45 km east of Santa Marta, Buritaca, cell tel. 321/599-5966, www.labrisatranquila.com, COP$35,000 dorm, COP$160,000 d) is the tamer version of La Brisa Loca hostel in Santa Marta. This beachside hostel is only 5 kilometers (3.1 mi) from PNN Tayrona. It comprises six private rooms, beach huts, and dorms.

Playa Koralia (50 km east of Santa Marta, cell tel. 310/642-2574 or 317/510-2289, www.koralia.com, COP$280,000 d) is a beach-chic hotel on the water just east of PNN Tayrona. Accommodations are luxurious and comfortable, meals are healthy, and there's a spa and a bar. It's a popular place for weddings and celebrations for groups from Bogotá. Excursions to Tayrona and other sights can be arranged.

The recipe for pure relaxation, ★ **Gitana del Mar** (50 km east of Santa Marta, Buritaca, cell tel. 312/293-7053, www.gitanadelmar.com.co, COP$480,000 campsite, COP$720,000 d with all meals) has six "eco-chic" bungalows and several glamping tents, a stunning beachside location, and a spa and restaurant. There's no air-conditioning and the hotel strives to be as environmentally responsible as possible without sacrificing luxury. It also offers a calendar of wellness retreats and regular beachside yoga classes. Day passes are also available (COP$120,000 pp).

The environmentally conscious ★ **Bioreserve Quebrada del Plátano** (60 km east of Santa Marta, Buritaca, info@quebradadelplatano.com, cell tel. 312/338-4348, COP$80,000 campsite, COP$140,000 pp with meals) is a nature reserve and working farm with organic fruit, herbs, coffee, and vegetables. The water here comes from mountain springs, and all electricity is solar generated. Waterfalls and swimming holes are a short walk away. The reserve is located between the Río Buritaca and a smaller creek, about a two-hour hike from the town of Buritaca. Mules are available to help with your luggage. There is just one private room, one shared room, and an area for hammocks.

TOP EXPERIENCE

PALOMINO

Nestled under the towering, jungle-covered Sierra Nevada and fronting the open sea, Palomino is the Caribbean coast's ultimate backpacker mecca. Unfortunately, the beach has been steadily eroding for years and the surf is too rough for swimming. But the attraction here is much more than just sunbathing. Palomino is a crossroads of cultures, where hipsters from Bogotá, international travelers, and indigenous Kogi meet up to chew coca and discuss cosmic politics. Artisans from all over the world have set up shop and ply their wares in Palomino, renting informal stalls and kiosks from landowners along the main road. The bohemian vibe of the sprawling and verdant town traps travelers here for days, and recently Palomino has started to host large music festivals that showcase Colombia's top alternative music acts. Hiking and bird-watching in the mountains, tubing down the nearby Río Palomino, visiting Kogi communities, surfing, and just good old hammock lazing are all popular ways to pass the day here.

Palomino extends from either side of the main highway, **Troncal del Caribe.** There are no street names in Palomino; the main points of reference are the beach, the Trocal del Caribe highway, the **main road** that cuts north-south from the beach to the highway, and the gas stations Terpel and Mobil. Because of the encroaching sea, and the fact that much of the nightlife is located closer to the Troncal del Caribe, many hostels have set up shop about 500 meters (1,640 ft) from the beach along the main road. The closest thing Palomino has to a town center is on this main road on the northern side of the highway; many bars and restaurants are located on this stretch.

Recreation

Recreational activities in and around Palomino include an easy 20-minute walk west to mouth of the **Río Palomino** where it empties into the Caribbean; between the salt and fresh water is a bar of sand that's about as close to a nice beach as you'll find in the area, and where a variety of local seafood restaurants have set up shop. It's possible to tube down the river as well. **Tube rentals** (COP$40,000) are available all along the main road and include transport to a starting point along the river; floating the river usually takes about 2.5 hours and deposits you right at the mouth of the river on the beach, from where you can walk back to town and return your tubes.

There are hikes up to waterfalls like **Cascada los Coquitos** (1.5 hrs) and **Cascadas la Cristalina** (6 hrs). The fantastic jungle waterfalls at private nature reserve **Quebrada Valencia** (village of Buritaca, no phone, COP$3,000) are also worth checking out. There are also swimming holes and Kogi villages to discover, and bird-watching adventures into the mountains, all of which can be organized from your hostel or hotel.

Chajaka (office on the south side of the main coastal highway, cell tel. 313/583-3288, calixteheran@gmail.com) offers interesting day trips or multiday hiking trips (COP$120,000 pp per day) into the Sierra Nevada. Ask for Calixto Teheran, a longtime guide with Chajaka and a friendly expert who knows the Sierra well.

La Sirena Yoga (La Sirena hostel, cell tel. 312/861-4850, COP$25,000) offers 1.5-hour yoga sessions both morning and afternoon in a beachfront yoga studio in front of the hostel of the same name. Class frequency depends on the number of participants, so stop by in advance to inquire about times.

To rent a surfboard, visit **Chill and Surf** (The Dreamer hostel, cell tel. 315/610-9561, www.chillandsurfcolombia.com, 9am-4pm daily). It has a stand on the beach in front of The Dreamer, and also offers classes.

Entertainment and Events

Though it serves coffee and snacks all day, ★ **Maria Mulata** (main road, cell tel. 320/203-1537, 9:30am-2am daily, no cover) really gets kicking after the sun goes down, as live bands and guest DJs take over its small stage. An open-air garden setting, super-friendly staff, and Minca's Cerveceria Nevada beers on ice make dancing the night away with complete strangers—who become instant amigos—the order of the evening.

La Happycleta (main road, cell tel. 322/755-5740, 2pm-2am daily) is a small and friendly bar that opens onto the main road. With owners from Bogotá, it has a craft beer and bicycle theme and is frequently packed with other capital-city refugees discussing the daily news. Bike rentals are available here and a small guesthouse just around the corner offers a handful of private rooms (COP$60,000-80,000 d).

As the night winds up, crowds gather in front of **Nomada Bar** (main road, cell tel. 301/545-0907, 6pm-2am Mon.-Sat., no cover) to dance in the street to salsa and other Latin rhythms until the lights come on at 2am. But the party never really ends in Palomino, it just moves down to the beach until the sun comes up.

Started in 2014, **Festival Jaguar** (first weekend of Jan.) has become one of Colombia's biggest outdoor music fests. The beachfront festival features up-and-coming independent bands and DJs from across the country, as well as world-renowned Colombian headliners like

The Kogi People's Message to Their "Younger Brother"

a traditional Kogi village

Direct descendants of the Tayrona people who built Ciudad Perdida, the Kogi (which means "Jaguar") are one of only a handful of indigenous groups in Colombia—and the only advanced civilization on the continent—to fully survive the Spanish conquest, having escaped to the high peaks of the Sierra Nevada where they lived in isolation for hundreds of years.

In 1988, the Kogi permitted award-winning BBC journalist Alan Ereira to enter their lands so they could get a message out to the rest of the planet. The result was the documentary *From the Heart of the World: Elder Brother's Warning* (1990), in which the Kogi advise the modern world—their "younger brother": We must change or suffer environmental disaster. In 2012, Ereira was summoned back to the Sierra Nevada by the Kogi to produce *Aluna*, a renewed call to humanity to come to terms with the interconnectedness of the world. The film was screened at the United Nations Conference on Sustainable Development in Rio de Janeiro that same year. Aluna is the great mother to the Kogi, both the living earth and the creative force behind it. The Kogi people ritually consume coca leaf and practice meditation to tap into Aluna's insights.

All over Colombia, you'll see Kogi men and women, dressed in all white like the snowcapped peaks which they inhabit, selling their high-quality *mochilas* (shoulder bags) and other artisanal products. But Palomino, due to its proximity to many lower-lying Kogi communities, is where Kogi culture really meets the rest of the world.

DAY TRIPS AND TREKS TO KOGI COMMUNITIES

While most outsiders are restricted from entering the higher reaches of Kogi territory in the Sierra Nevada, visiting low-lying Kogi communities is fairly easy to do. In Palomino, **Tur Palomino** (main road, cell tel. 320/524-9992) offers day trips to Kogi communities, such as a 4x4 journey to Tungueka, home to around 180 traditional Kogi households, and a hiking trek to Sewiaka, which was recently built in partnership with the Colombian government and consists of about 50 traditional-style homes—built to house displaced Kogi people—circling a large ceremonial space and community library. Some hostels in Palomino, such as **Hostal Aluna,** also have strong relationships with some of the Kogi communities and can arrange visits.

Tours are also available from Santa Marta. **Kogui Tour** (Cl. 20 No. 4-60, cell tel. 312/833-0504) employs indigenous guides who lead multiday hiking treks to Kogi communities and mountain peaks such as Nevado Dumena (3,856 m/12,650 ft) and Nevado Debungie (3,200 m/10,500ft), the latter passing through several isolated Kogi villages on the way. It also offers tours to Ciudad Perdida.

Visitation options and prices vary at any given time, so contact the companies for itineraries and price details.

Bomba Estéreo and Systema Solar. Tickets to Festival Jaguar run around COP$100,000 for a single day, but you can get a small discount if you buy the full weekend pass. Hostels and hotels raise their prices and fill up during the festival; book accommodations in advance.

Food

Palomino has attracted both the best and the worst of the eternal nomad crowd from across Colombia and around the world. Food is either overpriced tourist fare or meticulously well-done budget gourmet eats that you won't find anywhere else in the country.

The ★ **cluster of seafood restaurants** at the mouth of the Río Palomino are run by a community association of local villagers who consistently serve high-quality plates of fresh local fish like *pargo rojo* (red snapper), *lebranche* (mullet), and the small but meaty *cojinoa* (yellow jack), beachside, for around COP$25,000.

You can smell the gooey goodness of ★ **Turcolandia** (main road, cell tel. 304/607-1341, 10am-11pm daily, COP$15,000) from blocks away. The pizzeria offers house-infused oils—like thyme, passion fruit, and coconut chile—to spice up your selection and make your pizza even more divine.

Fusion-style seafood specials make **Los 7 Mares** (main road near the beach, cell tel. 301/358-0807, noon-11pm daily, COP$32,000) a hip option. Its combination of local and Asian flavors, such as the pad thai with squid, get rave reviews. Both fish and veggie burgers are also available here, and the cocktails are just as creative as the food.

Always packed **Mykonos Bamboo** (main road, cell tel. 310/282-1218, 10am-9pm daily, COP$12,000) offers mains and sides that are priced individually, allowing you to create your own plate. A wide variety of fresh juices, as well as arepas and *patacones* (fried plantains) with a variety of toppings and stuffings, are also available.

Stop by **Panadería La Sierrita** (main road, cell tel. 316/451-2277, 7:30am-8:30pm daily, COP$5,000) for freshly baked artisan breads, locally produced coffee and chocolate, and some invigorating coca leaf kombucha.

Accommodations

Palomino dethroned Taganga as the country's top Caribbean backpacker resort several years ago thanks largely to one famous hostel: ★ **The Dreamer** (cell tel. 300/609-7229, www.thedreamerhostel.com, COP$45,000 dorm, COP$140,000 d). This is by far the most social option this side of Santa Marta. Dorm and private accommodations are in *malokas* (cabins) surrounding an always-happening pool area and outdoor bar and restaurant that opens onto the beach. The Dreamer is not just for partiers: You can always retreat to your cabin for some peace. If The Dreamer is booked, **The Tiki Hut** (cell tel. 314/794-2970, www.tikihutpalomino.co, COP$45,000 dorm, COP$160,000 d) is a suitable second choice, just next door. **La Sirena Eco Hotel** (cell tel. 310/718-4644, www.ecosirena.com, COP$250,000 d) provides a contrast to the nearby Dreamer. Here it's vegetarian food, yoga, reiki, massages, and quiet. The six beachside *cabañas* are simple and gorgeous, and the toilets are dry "eco" models. The restaurant serves delicious healthy breakfasts.

★ **El Matuy (Donde Tuchi)** (cell tel. 315/751-8456, www.elmatuy.com, COP$230,000 pp with meals) is a privately owned nature reserve with 12 cabins, each with a hammock out front, set amid palm trees and with no electricity (this means candlelit evenings and no credit card machine). The beachside spot is just east of La Sirena Eco Hotel. Staff can help organize horseback riding or other activities. Surprisingly, there's Wi-Fi available in the reception area (making it a popular place).

Stay in the heart of the action on the northern side of the Troncal del Caribe highway yet in peaceful surroundings at ★ **Hostal Aluna** (cell tel. 300/598-8057, COP$30,000 dorm, COP$80,000 d), a two-story eco-hostel made from all-natural materials. Aluna's small but lush garden has plenty of hammocks and a comfy outdoor lounge for relaxing. The

Bogotana owner has some great connections with local Kogi communities and can arrange visits. Just a block down the dirt road **Kanta Sana** (cell tel. 301/326-0301, www.kantasana. com, COP$35,000 dorm, COP$85,000 d) offers poolside cabanas, a spacious natural setting, and an on-site restaurant that specializes in ceviche. On weekends a DJ takes to the decks and the hotel throws a pool party that's open to the public.

On the southern side of the highway, in a hillside area called La Sierrita, there are a number of options for those who prefer mountains to beaches. **Casa Campestre Ameli** (La Sierrita, cell tel. 311/232-0034, www.hostalcasacampestreameli.mas57.co, COP$15,000 campsite, COP$25,000 dorm, COP$45,000 private room) is surrounded by beautiful gardens and offers budget-conscious accommodations. They are also in close contact with several Kogi communities and can arrange visits. **Mamatukua Hostel** (La Sierrita, cell tel. 320/354-8791, www.lasierrita. co, COP$155,000 d) is a sweet, relaxing hostel managed by a pair of Bogotanos. Set amid the trees of the sierra, the hostel has three rooms (with a shared bath) and a cabin. You'll wake to birdsong.

Transportation

There is regular bus transportation along the Troncal del Caribe between Santa Marta and Riohacha. From Santa Marta, at the market on Carrera 11 and Calle 11, take a bus bound for Palomino. It's about a two-hour trip and costs COP$15,000. On the highway where the bus drops you off, there are young men on motorbikes who will take you to your hotel for about COP$3,000.

PARQUE NACIONAL NATURAL SIERRA NEVADA DE SANTA MARTA

Colombia's second-oldest national park, **Parque Nacional Natural Sierra Nevada de Santa Marta** (www.parquesnacionales. gov.co) has an area of 383,000 hectares (945,000 acres), making it one of the country's largest parks—although much of the tropical alpine wonderland is off-limits to visitors.

The main attraction is the **Ciudad Perdida (Lost City)**, the most important archaeological site of the Tayrona, the pre-Columbian civilization that inhabited the Sierra Nevada. The Tayrona had a highly urbanized society, with towns that included temples and ceremonial plazas built on stone terraces. There are an estimated 200 Tayrona sites, but Ciudad Perdida is the largest and best known. Many of these towns, including Pueblito (in the Parque Nacional Natural Tayrona), were occupied at the time of the Spanish conquest. Today, an estimated 30,000 indigenous people who are descendants of the Tayronas—including the Kogi, Arhuaco, Kankuamo, and Wiwa peoples—live on the slopes and valleys of the Sierra Nevada de Santa Marta. They believe that the Sierra Nevada is the center of the universe and that the mountain's health controls the entire Earth's well-being. Many areas of the Sierra are sacred sites and barred to outsiders.

The Sierra Nevada de Santa Marta is best described as a giant pyramid, which is bordered on the north by the Caribbean and on the southeast and southwest by the plains of northern Colombia. Although some believe that the range is a distant extension of the Cordillera Oriental (Eastern Mountain Range) of the Andes, most geologists believe it is a completely independent mountain system.

The Sierra Nevada is the world's highest coastal mountain range, with the twin peaks of **Pico Cristóbal Colón** and **Pico Bolívar** (the two are called Chinundúa by indigenous groups in the area) reaching 5,776 meters (18,950 ft; Colón is said to be slightly higher than Bolívar, making it Colombia's highest mountain) but located only 42 kilometers (26 mi) from the sea. The range includes seven other snow-covered peaks that surpass 5,000 meters (16,400 ft): Simonds, La Reina, Ojeda, Los Nevaditos, El Guardián, Tulio Ospina, and Codazzi. Treks to these peaks used to be possible from the northern side of the mountains, starting at the Arhuaco indigenous village of Nabusímake (Cesar), but are no longer permitted by the indigenous communities.

The PNN Sierra Nevada de Santa Marta encompasses the entire mountain range above 600 meters (16,400 ft). In addition, a small segment of the park east of the PNN Tayrona, from the Río Don Diego to the Río Palomino, extends to sea level. This means that the park encompasses the entire range of tropical ecosystems in Colombia: low-lying tropical forests (sea level to 1,000 m), cloud forests (1,000-2,300 m), high mountain Andean forest (2,300-3,500 m), *páramo* (highland moor, 3,500-4,500 m), super *páramo* (4,500-5,000 m), and glaciers (above 5,000 m). However, because access to the upper reaches of the park is limited, what visitors will most be able to appreciate is low-lying tropical and cloud forest.

The isolation of the range has made it an island of biodiversity, and it hosts many plant and animal species that are found nowhere else. The Sierra Nevada de Santa Marta is home to 187 mammal species, including giant anteaters, spider monkeys, peccaries, tree rats, jaguars, and pumas. There are 46 species of amphibians and reptiles, including several that live above 3,000 meters (9,840 ft) that

are found nowhere else on the planet. There are an astonishing 628 bird species, including the Andean condor, blue-knobbed curassow, sapphire-bellied hummingbird, and black solitary eagle, as well as many endemic species. There are at least 71 species of migratory birds that travel between Colombia and North America.

TOP EXPERIENCE

★ Ciudad Perdida Trek

A highlight for many visitors to Colombia is the four- to six-day, 52-kilometer (32-mi) round-trip trek to the **Ciudad Perdida (Lost City)** in the Sierra Nevada. The Ciudad Perdida is within the confines of the Parque Nacional Natural Sierra Nevada de Santa Marta.

The Ciudad Perdida, called Teyuna by local indigenous tribes and Buritaca 200 by archaeologists, was a settlement of the Tayrona, forebears of the people who inhabit the Sierra Nevada today. It was probably built starting around AD 700, at least 600 years before Machu Picchu. There is some disagreement as to when it was abandoned, although there is evidence of human settlement until the 16th century. The discovery

the Lost City of the Tayrona civilization in the Sierra Nevada

Ciudad Perdida Tour Outfitters

The tour companies who lead Ciudad Perdida treks are all roughly the same, and can be booked in Santa Marta and at most hostels in Palomino and Tagana. Exceptional companies are Wiwa Tours (Cra. 3 No. 18-49, Santa Marta, tel. 5/420-3413, www.wiwatour.com) and Kogui Tour (Cl. 20 No. 4-60, Santa Marta, cell tel. 312/833-0504), which both employ indigenous guides. Other tour companies include:

- Baquianos Tour (Cl. 10C No. 1C-59, Santa Marta, tel. 5/431-9667, www.guiasybaquianos.com)

- Expotur (Cra. 3 No. 17-27, Santa Marta, tel. 5/420-7739; Cl. 18 No. 2A-07, Taganga, tel. 5/421-9577, www.expotur-eco.com)

- Magic Tour (Cl. 16 No. 4-41, Santa Marta, tel. 5/421-5820; Cl. 14 No. 1B-50, Taganga, tel. 5/421-9429, www.magictourcolombia.com)

- TurCol (Centro Comercial San Francisco Plaza, Cl. 13 No. 3-13, Local 115, Santa Marta; Cl. 19 No. 5-40, Taganga, tel. 5/421-2256, www.turcoltravel.com)

of the site in 1976 marked one of the most important archaeological events of recent years. From 1976 to 1982, archaeologists from the Colombian National Institute of History and Anthropology painstakingly restored the site.

Spread over some 35 hectares (86 acres), the settlement consists of 169 circular terraces atop a mountain in the middle of dense cloud forest. Archaeologists believe that this sophisticated terrace system was created in part to control the flow of water in this area, which receives torrential rainfall for much of the year.

Plazas, temples, and dwellings for tribal leaders were built on the terraces in addition to an estimated 1,000 *bohíos* (traditional thatched-roof huts), which housed between 1,400 and 3,000 people. Surrounding the Ciudad Perdida were farms of coca, tobacco, pumpkins, and fruit trees. The city was connected to other settlements via an intricate system of mostly stone paths.

PLANNING TIPS

The somewhat challenging hike to the Ciudad Perdida requires no special preparation. Booking your tour a few weeks in advance is necessary if you're planning to travel between mid-December and mid-January, during Semana Santa, or in June and July.

The trek is mostly uphill, starting at an elevation of around 150 meters (490 ft) and ascending to an elevation of 1,100 meters (3,600 ft). The out-and-back trek takes 4-6 days.

There is one set fee (COP$1,100,000) for the trek. This does not change, no matter if you're making the trek in four, five, or six days. Choose the four-day option only if you're shorter on time or in very good shape and prefer to go fast; this option requires six hours of hiking per day and rising early, with daily hiking distances varying from 7.5 kilometers (4.7 mi) to 15 kilometers (9.3 mi).

Thousands of people of all ages traverse the path each year and each group is usually 8-12 people. Numerous groups populate different parts of the trails at any one time, and campsites can get crowded at night.

Frequent rain showers mean the trail can be muddy, and the weather is extremely humid. There are numerous river crossings to be made, some more thrilling than others, but all manageable. To reach the spectacular terraces of Ciudad Perdida, you will climb about 1,200 often-slippery stone steps. In case of an emergency on the mountain, a burro or helicopter will be sent to retrieve hikers in distress for a fee.

Seasons and Climate

From mid-December through mid-January you'll have plenty of company on the way to the Ciudad Perdida: It's high tourist season. Other high seasons are during Semana Santa and when schools are on summer break (June-July).

The wettest times tend to be April-May and September-November. Expect a daily downpour and doable, but sometimes treacherous, river crossings. Rainy weather makes the trek more challenging. On the plus side, there are usually fewer crowds on the mountain at that time.

What to Pack

Bring a small to medium backpack, enough to carry a few days of clothes; good hiking boots with strong ankle support; sandals for stream crossings; long pants; mosquito repellent; sunscreen; a small towel; toilet paper; hand sanitizer; a flashlight (preferably a headlamp); sealable bags to keep things dry; a light rain jacket; and a water container.

Assume that everything in your backpack will get wet, but bring along extra plastic bags to minimize damage. If you have them, trekking poles are a nice addition, although it's easy to find a trusty walking stick along the way. There are beds with sheets and blankets provided, but a lightweight sleeping bag or sheet is a good idea, as the cleanliness of the provided bedding is questionable. Consider earplugs and sleeping pills—widely available at Colombian pharmacies. To limit carrying along wet clothes, consider wearing "disposable" T-shirts that can be left behind at the camps (they will be washed and used by locals).

Don't worry about bringing snacks—all meals are provided by your tour operator. Bring a small amount of cash, as some snack breaks at coffee or fruit stands run by local families are not included in the tour price.

To keep you occupied at night, a small paperback and a deck of cards are good to have handy.

Camping

The campsites along the way seem to turn into backpacker villages during high season, with upwards of 60 people there every night, but they are never rowdy. Upon arrival the routine is fairly standard. You'll be able to cool off in the pristine waters of nearby swimming holes, have dinner, and hit the hammocks. Sleeping in hammocks can be uncomfortable

for those not used to them, but bunk beds are also available.

THE TREK

On the first morning, you will rendezvous with your tour operator either in Santa Marta, Taganga, or Palomino, meet your fellow trekkers and guides, and take a minibus ride to the villages of Mamey and Machete, at the edge of the park, where a generous lunch at a small restaurant will be served before you set off.

The first day of hiking, about 3-4 hours, will take you through cleared farmland, not jungle, so be prepared for extensive sun exposure. You'll take a break along the way at a coffee and fruit stall. At your campsite, you will have the opportunity to plunge into a natural swimming hole of cool, crystalline waters.

The second day of the trek is the longest one, and most groups aim for an early start. Under the canopy of the Sierra Nevada, the trail hugs the Río Buritaca for much of the time. There are multiple river crossings, including a swinging bridge. Before arrival at camp, you'll pass by the thatched roofs of the Kogi indigenous settlement Mutanyí. (Your guide will instruct you on photography etiquette.) Kogi children may ask you for *dulces* (candy), but otherwise interaction with the people that live here is unlikely. Your group will arrive at camp after noon. The rest of the day includes lots of downtime.

On the third day, the various groups on the trail jockey to be the first to arrive at the Ciudad Perdida. A 5:30am start is worth it to experience a sense of discovery as you climb the steps to the ancient terraces. Mosquitoes may be out in full force, so apply insect repellent. Leave your pack at camp; just carry your camera, walking stick, and bottle of water. The sun can be quite potent at the ruins, so bring sunscreen as well. After a final water crossing, the famed 1,200 stone steps dramatically appear, a silent invitation to this sacred lost city.

Take your time going up the steps. At the

first series of grassy circular terraces, all that remains of the community's commercial center, your guide will give an introduction to the site. From there, climb the Queen's Path to the main site. Colombian soldiers guard the site and are always glad to chat up visitors. Take care when descending the steps on your way back, as they can become slippery.

La Guajira

A dazzling combination of desert and sea, the vast Guajira Peninsula has some of the most rugged, beautiful landscapes in Colombia. It is home to the matriarchal Wayúu indigenous people, who have maintained their independent way of life through centuries. They don colorful dresses that have caught on with the local population. Though many Wayúu people now live in cities and towns, their traditional *rancherías* (settlements) dot the desert. Open and outgoing compared to many more insular indigenous groups, the Wayúu are fully integrated into society in La Guajira.

The Colombian side of the peninsula (Venezuela claims the other part) can be divided into three sections. The Baja Guajira (Lower Guajira), near the Sierra Nevada de Santa Marta, is fertile agricultural and cattle-ranching land. The arid middle swath encompasses the pleasant beachfront departmental capital of Riohacha, the indigenous city of Uribia, and the border town of Maicao, home to the majority of the peninsula's population. The Alta Guajira (Upper Guajira), from Cabo de la Vela to Punta Gallinas, is sparsely populated and has some otherworldly landscapes that are the focus of most tourism to the area.

Lack of infrastructure makes visiting the Alta Guajira beyond Cabo de la Vela a challenge, so most people opt for organized tours. Many roads are unmarked tracks in the sand, meaning getting lost is inevitable. During the rainy months, September-November, it can be difficult to travel through the desert, which can become muddy to the point of impassability.

History
Spanish navigator Juan de la Cosa, who was a member of Columbus's first three voyages, disembarked in Cabo de la Vela in 1499, making the Guajira Peninsula one of the first places visited by Europeans in South America. It was not until 1535 that explorer Fernando de Enciso founded a settlement near Cabo de la Vela, which became a center of pearl extraction. This early settlement was relocated to Riohacha, which was founded in 1544. The traditional Wayúu inhabitants of the peninsula put up strong resistance to Spanish advances, even joining British and Dutch pirates to fight against them. During the 19th and 20th centuries, the peninsula was used primarily as a smuggling route.

For better or for worse, the fortunes of the Guajira changed in 1975 when the Colombian government entered into an agreement with oil giant Exxon to develop the Cerrejón open-pit coal mine 80 kilometers (50 mi) southeast of Riohacha. This project involved the construction of Puerto Bolívar, a coal port located in Bahía Portete, and of a railway to transport the coal. Production started in 1985. Coal has since become one of Colombia's main exports. The mine has generated more than US$2 billion in royalties for the Colombian government. But little of this wealth has trickled down to the people of La Guajira. The region is the fourth-poorest department in Colombia.

RIOHACHA
Called Süchiimma in the Wayúu language, meaning "city of the river," Riohacha (pop. 231,000), bordered on the east by the Río Ranchería, is La Guajira's slow-paced departmental capital. It is one of the oldest cities in Colombia, with a smattering of colonial

Riohacha

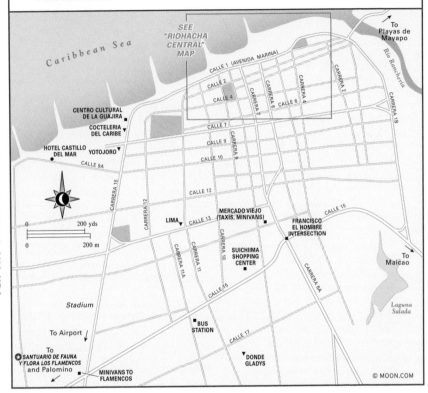

architecture at its center and a wide, beautiful city beach lined with a pleasant *malecón* (boardwalk) where families stroll at night and Wayúu women sell brightly colored *mochilas* (shoulder bags) and intricately patterned hats made from palm fronds.

While most people only visit Riohacha as a base from which to launch tours of Alta Guajira or visit the flamingos of the Santuario de Fauna y Flora Los Flamencos, the relaxed vibe, interesting mix of cultures (indigenous, African, and European), and relatively low prices of the city also make it a great place to simply recoup and enjoy life on an isolated stretch of Caribbean coast. Strong breezes and less humidity make the temperatures here less sweat-inducing than in many other coastal cities. Riohacha also plays host to one of the

largest and oldest Carnavals on the Caribbean coast outside of Barranquilla, with brightly costumed folkloric dancers parading through town and beauty pageants.

Sights

Parallel to Calle 1, also known as Avenida Marina, is the **Paseo de la Playa** *malecón* (0.8 km/0.5 mi long), where locals and tourists leisurely gather in the evenings. Along the *malecón* is the monument to *La Dama Wayúu* ("the Wayúu woman"), a tribute to the strength and beauty of the female leaders of this ancient matriarchal culture. The kilometer-long pier known as the **Muelle Turístico** that extends from the midpoint of the *malecón* is another favorite place for a walk, especially in the evening, with sea

Riohacha Central

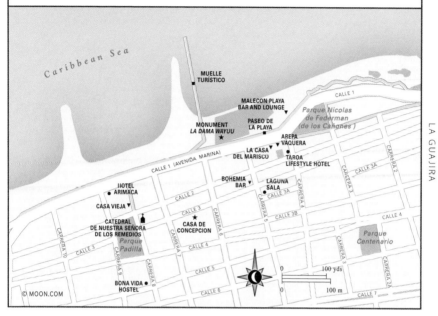

breezes providing relief from the heat of the day. From the pier there are especially good views of the rugged peaks of the Sierra Nevada in the distance.

With its striking murals depicting Wayúu culture, it's hard to miss the large **Centro Cultural de la Guajira** (Cra. 15 No. 1-40, tel. 5/727-0990, www.banrepcultural.org/riohacha, 8am-11:30am and 2pm-5:30pm Mon.-Fri., 9am-1pm Sat., free). Inside, the cultural center has a permanent exhibition space that tells the history of the area, from Spaniard pearl harvesters to modern times, when multinationals arrived to extract natural gas and coal. A good portion of the museum discusses Wayúu culture, and includes an exhibit on the area's traditions for Carnaval. The content of the exhibition is quite interesting and is a must-visit for anyone mildly interested in this unusual place. There are few English-language explanations of the exhibits. The center also houses a small public library.

Parque Padilla (Cl. 2 and Cra. 7), Riohacha's main plaza, is named after favorite son Admiral José Prudencio Padilla, who was the most prominent Afro-Colombian commander in the revolutionary wars. To one side of the plaza is the reconstructed **Catedral de Nuestra Señora de los Remedios** (Cl. 2 No. 7-13, tel. 5/727-2442, mass 6:30am and 7pm Mon.-Sat., 7am, 11am, and 7pm Sun.). This cathedral was erected in the 16th century, but completely rebuilt in the 1800s. The remains of Padilla repose here. The church is open to the public during mass, and occasionally at other times of the day. In the evening, the plaza buzzes with locals relaxing and catching up with friends and children playing.

At the eastern edge of the *malecón* is **Parque Nicolás de Federman** (Cl. 1 No. 4-1), also known as Los Canoñes because of the row of cannons here that were once used to defend the city from pirates. At night, bars open onto this plaza, and it fills with couples and groups of friends. Literature buffs will notice the park's *Monumento Mariposas Amarilla,* a sculpture depicting swarms of yellow butterflies; this is a tribute to Gabriel García Márquez, for whom yellow butterflies were an important symbol and which appeared prominently in his *One Hundred Years of Solitude.* The renowned writer was heavily influenced by Wayúu culture and inspired by the beauty of the Guajira region, where his ancestors were from. His parents' house, known as the **Casa de Concepcion** (Cl. 3 between Cras. 5 and 6, not open to the public) because the famous writer is believed to have been conceived there, is located a few blocks from the Catedral de Nuestra Señora de los Remedios in the city center.

Beaches

Riohacha boasts what is quite possibly the nicest **city beach** on the entire Caribbean coast outside of San Andrés. The wide and spacious beach runs alongside the *malecón* and has beachside umbrella chairs for rent and calm, baby-blue waters that beckon swimmers.

About 30 minutes northeast up the coast, a series of wide, white-sand playgrounds known as the **Playas de Mayapo** are even more impressive. The farthest east of these beaches, known as **Playa Jimatsu,** is home to several charming waterfront restaurants, including the Wayúu-run **Sutsha Wayúu** (Playa Jimatsu, cell tel. 311/431-9156, www.sutshawayuu.blogspot.com, 10am-8pm daily, COP$25,000), where fresh fish specials and comfy *chinchorros* (hammocks) await in the shade. The wide beaches give you lots of privacy for swimming and sunbathing. To get to the Playas de Mayapo take a *colectivo* taxi from downtown Riohacha's market plaza (Cl. 7 and Cra. 13) for COP$5,000 per person one-way, or hire a taxi for COP$50,000 round-trip.

Entertainment and Events

Occupying the balcony-ringed 2nd floor of a colonial house in the center of town, ★ **Bohemia Bar** (Cl. 3 No.5-10, cell tel. 300/837-1288, 6pm-2am Tues.-Sun.) is where the artsy/alternative crowd gets together to listen to vintage salsa and *son cubano* over ice-cold beers. With books on the walls and comfy sofas for relaxing, the bar-café is a great example of Colombian *tertulia,* where people gather to discuss and debate cultural-intellectual topics in a relaxed atmosphere.

Casa Vieja Cafe Bar (Callejón de las Brisas, tel. 5/729-1199, 2pm-10pm Sun.-Thurs., 2pm-3am Fri.-Sat.), which serves high-quality coffee and pastries daily, transforms into a popular dance club on weekend nights.

Fronting the boardwalk and right on the sand, **Malecon Playa Bar and Lounge** (Cl. 1 No. 32, cell tel. 301/475-3631, 6pm-2am daily) is an open-air bar-restaurant with an arrangement of sofas, tables, and tiki huts, as well as plenty of open space for dancing under the stars.

Riohacha's beachfront is also the stage for one of the biggest **Carnaval** celebrations on the coast outside of Barranquilla. Dating back to the 19th century, this is also one of the oldest continuously running Carnavals in Colombia, steeped in local traditions and heavily influenced by Wayúu culture. While the pre-Carnaval season in Riohacha lasts for weeks, the biggest celebration is on the weekend and weekdays leading up to the Tuesday before Ash Wednesday on the Catholic calendar, which usually falls near the end of February or early March. Riohacha's Carnaval features a massive parade of floats that starts at the stadium, located inland just southwest of downtown, and heads along the waterfront, concluding near the "I Love Riohacha" sign at the eastern end of the *malecón.* Like many others on the Caribbean, the town's Carnaval is centered on a beauty pageant that crowns a queen for the upcoming year. Recently, the city has added the crowning of an LGBT queen to the program. Besides the daily flour-throwing that is common in all Colombian Carnavals, Riohacha's version also includes a day when everyone covers themselves with mud and dances wildly in the streets.

Have You Been Drinking *Chirrinche,* or Are You Just Happy to See Me?

Asawaa *chirrinche*

Both *ron* (rum) and *aguardiente* (Colombia's national drink) are made from sugarcane and widely consumed all over Colombia, but in La Guajira, *chirrinche* reigns supreme. Also made from sugarcane, in this case the raw unprocessed *panela* (block sugar), which is cheap and plentiful here, *chirrinche* is a homemade affair, much like moonshine. The simple fermentation and distillation process has been perfected by the Wayúu people, who use *chirrinche* in ritual fiestas and make it in their *rancherías* (settlements) using makeshift yet highly effective equipment.

Semisweet and unfiltered, *chirrinche* is sold for dirt cheap at *tiendas* (stores) from Palomino to the Alta Guajira, and you'll no doubt see people downing it everywhere you go in the region; it's often packaged in used soda bottles. It tastes a bit rough around the edges, as it's unfiltered and often varies in alcohol content—although it's usually around 35 percent. While some say *chirrinche* is dangerous and can even cause blindness if consumed in excess, others tout its health benefits; it contains some hardy probiotics and the nutritional properties of raw sugar (including high iron and potassium content), unlike commercial sugarcane-based liquors that are more refined.

DISTILLERY TASTINGS AND TOURS

Learn more about *chirrinche* and try it for yourself at **Asawaa** (Cl. 3 No. 2-83, Riohacha, cell tel. 317/675-1971, www.asawaa.com, 10am-8pm Mon.-Fri., noon-8pm Sat., noon-6pm Sun.), located right in downtown Riohacha, just two blocks inland from Parque Nicolás de Federman. The Guajira's only high-end artisan producer of *chirrinche,* it also makes a wine-like apéritif made from *chirrinche* and the extract of *iguaraya* (a red cactus fruit) that's quite refreshing when chilled or enjoyed on ice. Tastes are given freely by the friendly staff and **tours of the processing facility** (COP$20,000 with advance notice) are also available. The **on-site shop and café** has a nice outdoor seating area, some hammocks, and variously sized bottles of product for sale.

Food

At the western end of the *malecón,* a cluster of ceviche shacks serve fresh shrimp, conch, octopus, and whatever else is fresh that day, cocktail-style, in a variety of different sizes and price points. Jaime Torres, known as "El Caribe," runs **Cocteleria Caribe** (10am-midnight daily), undoubtedly the best of the bunch. He makes his own aphrodisiacal ceviches, meant to fuel long days of work and long nights of loving, including the *rompe colchon* ("mattress breaker"), as well as fresh juices, accompanied by panoramic views of the sparkling Caribbean.

On the pedestrian-only Callejón de las Brisas, which connects Parque Padilla with the beachfront *malecón,* there are several inexpensive fresh juice joints with sidewalk seating as well as **Casa Vieja Cafe Bar** (Callejón de las Brisas, tel. 5/729-1199, 2pm-10pm daily), which serves high-quality coffee and pastries both inside and outside on its sidewalk patio.

The first thing to do at ★ **Yotojoro** (Cl. 7 No. 15-81, cell tel. 315/754-0176, 11am-10pm daily, COP$25,000), a well-known favorite among Riohacha's upper crust, is order a *limonada de coco* (coconut lemonade). Next, go for either the hearty *cazuela de mariscos* (seafood stew) or the signature dish, the *pargo monsenor* (grilled red snapper stuffed with shrimp in a tomato-coconut milk sauce). Seafood is the specialty here.

Gladys Beatriz Mendoza Guerra has been running the show at ★ **Donde Gladys** (Cl. 18 No. 9-2, no phone, 5pm-10pm daily, COP$20,000) since the 1980s, operating right out of her own house. This is the local go-to eatery for authentic creole cuisine, including the Guajira's signature *friche* (pan-fried goat innards). Armadillo, rabbit, and other regional specialties are also available.

There are several seafood restaurants along Avenida Marina/Calle 1 across from the *malecón.* A perennial favorite is **Casa del Marisco** (Cl. 1 No. 4-43, tel. 5/728-3445, 10am-10pm daily, COP$35,000), a restaurant that serves an array of fresh seafood dishes and pastas. Right next door, **Arepa Vaquera** (Cl. 1 No. 4-39, tel. 5/729-2838, 5pm-11pm daily, COP$12,000) serves gigantic arepas and stuffed *patacones* (fried plantains) that bring the locals out in droves.

Accommodations

Most visitors stay in Riohacha for only a night or two before heading onward. The options covered in this section are all centrally located, within walking distance of the city's attractions.

★ **Laguna Salá** (Cl. 3 No. 4-81, tel. 5/729-2462, COP$25,000 dorm, COP$87,000 d), just a block from the beach, offers a luxury experience on a backpacker's budget. Rooms are spotless, the 3rd-floor rooftop bar and pool features sweeping views over the city, a TV room has a cinema-sized flat-screen and beanbag chairs, and a full breakfast is included in the price.

The 46-room ★ **Taroa Lifestyle Hotel** (Cl. 1 No. 4-77, tel. 5/729-1122, www.taroahotel.com, COP$280,000 d) is the swankiest option in town, a good choice if you've been out in the desert and are ready to splurge. Go for a room with views of the boardwalk and sea, where you can swing in a hammock to your heart's content. Sip a cocktail on the top-floor terrace and enjoy the cooling breezes.

Situated in a colonial mansion, **Bona Vida Hostel** (Cl. 5 No. 8-20, cell tel. 314/637-0786, www.bonavidahostel.com, COP$32,000 dorm, COP$130,000 d) is just a block in from Parque Padilla and has a small pool on its central patio, a cozy terrace bar, and a cool, laid-back vibe. The friendly staff offer a ton of different tour options for exploring La Guajira.

The **Hotel Castillo del Mar** (Cra. 9A No. 16-150, cell tel. 315/792-4743, castillodelmarsuites@hotmail.com, COP$281,000 d, discount for multiple nights) sits right on the waterfront and offers a variety of beach bungalows and private rooms, as well as a shared terrace overlooking the Caribbean. The hotel is quiet and relaxed and yes, as the name implies, the building really does resemble a castle.

Information and Services

A smallish supermarket, **Cumana Express** (Cl 2. No. 7-46, no phone, 8am-9pm daily), is located a half block from Parque Padilla, which is ringed by **ATMs.** Discount supermarket **Metro** (tel. 5/728-9670, 8am-10pm Mon.-Sat., 8am-9pm Sun.), in modern shopping mall **Centro Comercial Suchiimma** (Cl. 15 No. 8-56, 10am-9pm daily), has all the provisions you need for an extended adventure in the desert.

Transportation

The **bus station** (Av. El Progreso and Cl. 11) has frequent service to Albania, Maicao, Santa Marta, and Barranquilla. There is also service to Valledupar, Cartagena, and Bogotá. Standard buses take longer, but are more comfortable. *Busetas* are faster minivans. Then there are shared taxis, which are more uncomfortable but much faster and take you directly to your hotel. Shared taxis to Uribia (where you can pick up trucks to Cabo de la Vela) leave from the market area (Cl. 15 and Cra. 1) in town and can be called to pick you up by your hostel or hotel. A cab to the bus station from downtown Riohacha costs only about COP$6,000; in fact, almost everywhere you want to go around town by taxi is COP$6,000.

The atmosphere at the bus station is rushed and harried; do your best to not let it stress you out. If you're westbound (to Palomino, Santa Marta, or beyond), the frantic bus station experience can be avoided by going to the **Francisco El Hombre traffic circle.** You'll see folks hanging out waiting for transportation here; just ask them which *buseta* is going your way.

Aeropuerto Almirante Padilla (RCH, Cl. 29B No. 15-217, tel. 5/727-3854) is five minutes north of town. There is one direct daily flight from Bogotá to Riohacha on both **Avianca** (www.avianca.com) and low-cost **Viva Air** (www.vivaair.com).

CROSSING INTO VENEZUELA

Canadians and most European citizens do not require a visa to enter Venezuela for stays of less than 90 days. The same used to be true for U.S. citizens, but since the economic crisis and growing tensions between the United States and Venezuela, U.S. citizens must now apply for a tourist visa three months ahead of time. You may be required to show proof of a hotel reservation and proof of an air ticket departing from Venezuela, and your passport must not expire within six months of entry into Venezuela. There is a Venezuelan consulate in Riohacha for further queries: **Consulado de Venezuela** (Cra. 7 No. 3-08, Edificio El Ejecutivo, Piso 2, tel. 5/727-4076, 8am-noon and 2pm-5pm Mon.-Thurs., 8am-1pm Fri.). There is an entry point to Venezuela at the town of Maicao, but the border is frequently closed. Be advised that this is considered one of the most dangerous border crossing into Venezuela.

★ SANTUARIO DE FAUNA Y FLORA LOS FLAMENCOS

Spotting flamingos is the order of the day at the **Santuario de Fauna y Flora Los Flamencos** (Camarones settlement, www.parquesnacionales.gov.co, 7am-5:30pm daily, free). This park, 25 kilometers (15.5 mi) southwest of Riohacha, includes the Laguna Navio Quebradado and the larger Laguna Grande, with the fishing settlement of Camarones on the park's eastern side and the Caribbean Sea just beyond the mangroves and tropical dry forests on the north.

The park is home to thousands of American flamingos and up to 180 other species of migratory and resident aquatic birds, such as ibis and storks. Sea turtles also arrive at the lonely beach here, where conservation efforts help keep the threatened animals safe. The 7,000-hectare sanctuary (17,300 acres), which is part of the national park system, encompasses a coastal estuary where the flamingos fish for tiny shrimp in the shallow waters (from whom the birds obtain their gorgeous rose-colored plumage).

The flamingos are migratory, and are most often observed during rainy seasons such as October-November, when their numbers reach into the thousands. During the rest of the year smaller flocks often reside in the park.

To see the flamingos up close, take an hour-long *chalupa* (wooden boat) excursion (COP$20,000 pp), captained by a local, onto one of the lagoons. The price of the excursion is negotiable, and the more people there are in a group, the lower the cost. To protect your skin from the powerful sun and glare off the water, visit the park early in the morning. Ample sun protection and drinking water are essential no matter the time of day.

GETTING THERE

The easiest way to get to the park is to arrange a taxi from Riohacha (COP$20,000 one-way). Either request for the driver to wait while you visit the park (additional COP$50,000), or, after finishing your tour of the park, take a *mototaxi* (COP$3,000) to the main road, where buses (COP$2,200) back to Riohacha regularly pass.

To take public transportation both ways, take a bus from Riohacha going toward Camarones for a trip of about 20 kilometers (12.4 mi) on the main road toward Santa Marta. From Camarones take a *mototaxi* (COP$3,000) to the entrance of the park, or walk the 3.5 kilometers (2.2 mi) to the park entrance.

To have someone else do the organizing and coordinating, contact **Expedición Guajira** (Cl. 2 No. 5-06, Riohacha, tel. 5/727-2336, cell tel. 311/439-4677 or 301/485-2837, franklin_penalver@yahoo.com), which will take you on an organized tour of the park for COP$95,000 per person. Insist on an early start.

TOP EXPERIENCE

ALTA GUAJIRA

The sparsely populated Alta Guajira (Upper Guajira) comprises the peninsula northeast of Riohacha. The area's three largest settlements, where most of the tourism infrastructure is located, are **Cabo de la Vela, Punta Gallinas** at the very northern tip, and **Nazareth,** in the northeast.

The terrain has a striking ochre color, with rocky and sandy patches. The vegetation is mostly shrubs and cacti. The Caribbean coast here is broken by three large bays with stunning turquoise and aquamarine waters: Bahía Portete, Bahía Honda, and Bahía Hondita. The last of these is easily accessible as a day trip from Punta Gallinas. There are a few low mountain ranges, including the Serranía de la Macuira (864 m/2,835 ft), located in the extreme northeast of the peninsula, but overall the terrain is low and slightly undulating.

The only major destination in the Alta Guajira that is accessible by public transportation is Cabo de la Vela. Most visitors choose to visit the region via organized tour, an easy option.

On the way to the Alta Guajira from Riohacha, you'll pass through **Uribia,** known as "The Indigenous Capital of Colombia." If you're making your own way to Cabo de la Vela, it's worth stopping here, if just for lunch. **Asadero Jlo** (Cl. 4A, cell tel. 323/351-0509, 10am-6pm daily) does an excellent *chivo en guiso de coco* (goat in coconut curry) for COP$10,000. The interesting octagonal main square is home to a crafts market and an ATM.

Tours

The typical Alta Guajira tour (COP$420,000 pp, including food and lodging) lasts three days, spending a day each in Cabo de la Vela (with a stop at the now-abandoned salt mines of the Salinas de Manaure) and Punta Gallinas. A longer option (COP$800,000-880,000 pp, including food and lodging) adds two nights in Nazareth to visit the Parque Nacional Natural Macuira. Tours operate out of Riohacha and include SUV transportation.

Inquire before booking how many people will be in your SUV, as tour operators often try to cram seven people into a vehicle, making for an uncomfortable ride. Drivers generally have a limited grasp of English. If you'd like some background information about the region and the Wayúu people before setting off, check out the Centro Cultural de la Guajira in Riohacha first.

The desert countryside seems endless and is beautiful in its own desolate way. You'll be amazed at how these drivers know which way to go, as there are no road signs, only cacti and the occasional goat. Every once in a while, you'll have to pay "tolls" to Wayúu children who have set up quasi roadblocks. To gain their permission to cross, drivers hand over crackers, cookies, or candy.

TOUR COMPANIES

Most tour companies are based in Riohacha, but it's also easy to book tours in Uribia and Cabe de la Vela. Many companies don't regularly accept credit cards for payment outside of Riohacha, though; to avoid carrying a lot of cash around, consider making a *consignación* (bank deposit), which can be done anywhere in Colombia. Get the tour company's bank account information and go in person to a branch of their bank, then make a cash deposit of the full trip amount. There are no ATMs in Cabo de la Vela or Punta Gallinas.

Mochileros People (Uribia, cell tel. 314/715-8132, maikerpinto1@gmail.com) employs Wayúu guides who know the desert like the backs of their hands. It runs all-inclusive tours aimed at backpackers that includes lodging in *chinchorros* (hammocks) and food at their beachfront lodges in Cabo de la Vela and Punto Gallinas. A three-day tour costs COP$440,000 per person, and a two-day tour of Cabo de la Vela costs COP$220,000. It's also possible to craft a custom private tour or roll with them on a day tour from Cabo de la Vela if you're already there.

Kai Eco Travel (Av. 1A No. 4-49, Riohacha, cell tel. 311/436-2830, www.kaiecotravel.com) has a range of tours for those who don't mind a group setting (maximum 6-8 people per group). A quick two-day jaunt to Cabo de la Vela costs around COP$220,000, with an extra night in Punta Gallinas bumping that up to COP$500,000. A full eight-day tour of the Alta Guajira that includes the Serranía de Macuira National Park runs COP$5,500,000 per person. If you're up for the real Guajira experience of sleeping in a *chinchorro*, the rates decrease slightly. Get details from Francisco at the Hotel Castillo del Mar in Riohacha.

Kaishi (Cl. 11B No. 16-125, Riohacha, cell

tel. 311/429-6315, www.kaishitravel.com, adelgadorozco@yahoo.com) is another agency with a very good reputation. It only offers private tours. The per-person price decreases as the passenger list expands, so it behooves you to go with a larger group of friends. A five-day private tour for two people that includes Cabo de la Vela and Punta Gallinas costs around COP$2,000,000 per person. The shorter three-day tour to Punta Gallinas with a brief stop in Cabo de la Vela costs around COP$1,300,000 per person.

★ Cabo de la Vela

Cabo de la Vela (known as Jepira in the Wayúu language), 180 kilometers (111 mi) north of Riohacha, is a small Wayúu fishing village spread along the Caribbean Sea. It comes as a pleasant shock to finally arrive at the waters of the Caribbean after several hours driving through the Guajira's arid landscape. Here the beaches are nice, the views otherworldly, and the atmosphere peaceful. Cabo de la Vela is a destination for windsurfers and kitesurfers, thanks to its smooth waters and ample winds that provide near-perfect conditions.

There are several excursions around Cabo; organized package tours should include all of them in the price. One is to **El Faro**, a lighthouse on a high promontory with nearly 360-degree views of the surrounding ocean. Another is to the **Ojo del Agua**, a small but pleasant beach near a freshwater spring. Farther afield is the **Pilón de Azúcar**, a high hill over the sea that affords incredible views to the surrounding region. Just below is **Playa del Pilón**, a beautiful ochre-colored beach where the waters are calm and bright blue. A short walk to the east is **Playa Arcoiris**, where waves crash against the rocky shore, and the sea spray forms a rainbow against the sunlight every 30 seconds or so—but you have to catch it before 10am or so. Farther east and visible in the distance is the **Jepirachi Wind Farm**, the first of its kind in Colombia; the turbines make for a somewhat surreal sight in the midst of this barren territory.

Travelers not on an organized tour can grab a *mototaxi* to any of these sites for around COP$5,000 per person. For COP$30,000 the *mototaxistas* will take you to them all on a full-day tour, including a lunch break in town; grab one out front of An'a Waya Restaurant before 8am or 9am, before it gets too hot and they're all snatched up by other tourists.

KITESURFING AND WINDSURFING

Cabo de la Vela is an excellent place to learn how to kitesurf or windsurf, as there's a good breeze here most of the year (the exception being September-November).

There are two excellent schools offering courses and equipment rental. **Eoletto** (10-min. walk from Ranchería Utta, cell tel. 321/468-0105 or 314/851-6216, www.windsurfingcolombia.com) is a windsurfing and kitesurfing school that also offers accommodations in hammocks (COP$20,000) in a quiet spot facing the water. An eight-hour windsurfing course costs COP$450,000; kitesurfing is COP$800,000. Rentals are available for COP$80,000 per hour.

Kite Addict Colombia (cell tel. 320/528-1665, www.kiteaddictcolombia.com) offers a 10-hour, three- to four-day basic course for COP$1,000,000, has *chinchorro* accommodations (COP$15,000 pp), and does kitesurfing excursions to Punta Gallinas. Kite Addict is located between the Mana shop and Posada Pujurú.

FOOD AND ACCOMMODATIONS

Family-run guesthouses are plentiful in Cabo de la Vela, and are quite rudimentary. Freshwater is scarce here in the desert, so long showers are not an option. Floors are usually sandy, and electricity is limited. The street in Cabo de la Vela along the sea is lined with guesthouses; most are basic but put your right on the edge of the Caribbean Sea. Being on the

beach at night, looking up at the stars, and listening to the sound of gentle waves breaking nearby is unforgettable. There are also a few lodgings outside of town toward El Faro.

The ★ **Ranchería Utta** (300 m northwest of town, Vía al Faro, cell tel. 312/687-8237 or 313/817-8076, www.rancheriautta.com, COP$20,000 hammock, COP$130,000 d) is a nice place to stay. It's just far enough from Cabo de la Vela that you can experience the magic of being far from civilization. Cabins are simple, with walls made from the hearts of *yotojoro* (cacti), a traditional form of construction in the desert. There are 11 *cabañas* with a total of 35 beds and plenty of inviting *chinchorros* (hammocks) for lazing about. A pleasant restaurant at the hotel serves breakfast (COP$7,000), lunch (COP$18,000), and dinner (COP$20,000). The fare is mostly seafood (lobster is a favorite but will cost extra), but vegetarians can be accommodated.

★ **Marparaíso** (cell tel. 300/279-5048, COP$15,000 hammock, COP$40,000 bed pp) is one of the nicer options on the row of lodgings that stretches up the bayfront. An on-site restaurant serves decently priced items (COP$15,000) over a stunning view of the sea.

Hospedaje Jarrinapi (cell tel. 312/600-2884, 321/831-7850, or 310/643-2786, www.hospedajejarrinapi.amawebs.com, COP$15,000 hammock, COP$35,000 bed pp) is another popular, beach-fronting, locally owned option. The large hotel offers 19 *yotojoro* (cactus) cabins for a total capacity of 60 people plus an extensive hammock area right on the sand. This hotel has electricity from the afternoon until dawn and has an orderly kitchen and restaurant.

TRANSPORTATION

Shared taxis (COP$25,000) ply the hour-long route from Riohacha to Uribia. Catch one in Riohacha at the intersection of Calle 15 and Carrera 5, or have your hostel or hotel call to have you picked up. They usually drop you off just outside of Uribia, where you can grab one of the **passenger trucks** (COP$30,000) from Uribia to Cabo de la Vela, which depart

1: Santuario de Fauna y Flora Los Flamencos; 2: *La Dama Wayúu* statue by Yino Márquez on the Riohacha waterfront; 3: hammock camping on the beach in Cabo de la Vela; 4: beach near Cabo de la Vela

from around 8am until 2pm every day. The uncomfortable ride, on a bench in the back of a truck, can take two or more hours, depending on how many stops are made, but this is a quintessential Guajira experience.

★ Punta Gallinas

Punta Gallinas is a settlement on a small peninsula jutting into the Caribbean at the very northernmost tip of the South American continent. It's home to about 100 Wayúu people, who claim this beautiful spot as their ancestral land. The landscape here is a symphony of oranges, ochres, and browns, dotted with cactus and shrubs. The peninsula is hemmed in to the south by Bahía Hondita, a large bay with bright aquamarine waters and thin clusters of mangroves, and to the north by the deep-blue Caribbean.

Sights in and around Punta Gallinas include the *faro* (lighthouse), which marks the northernmost tip of South America; **Bahía Hondita,** which is home to flamingos and mangroves; and the remote and unspoiled beaches at **Dunas de Taroa** (Taroa Dunes), where windswept and towering sand dunes drop abruptly some 30 meters (100 ft) into the sea, and at **Punta Aguja,** at the southwest tip of the peninsula of Punta Gallinas. These excursions are included in tour prices and are usually visited via 4x4 vehicles because the roads here nearly nonexistent. If you are on your own, hotels charge around COP$20,000 per person to see the dunes (five-person minimum), COP$150,000 for a group boat ride on the Bahía Hondita to spot flamingos, and COP$25,000 per person to go to Punta Aguja (five-person minimum).

FOOD AND ACCOMMODATIONS

There are two good lodging options in Punta Gallinas, both with splendid views of Bahía Hondita.

★ **Hospedaje Luzmila** (Punta Gallinas, cell tel. 311/678-4778 or 312/647-9881, luzmilita10@gmail.com, COP$20,000 hammock, COP$30,000 bed pp) has 10 *cabañas* with 20 beds spread alongside the bay.

Breakfast (COP$5,000), lunch (COP$15,000), and dinner (COP$15,000) are served in the restaurant. Lobster dishes cost extra.

★ **Donde Alexandra** (Punta Gallinas, cell tel. 315/538-2718 or 318/500-6942, alexandra@hotmail.com, COP$15,000 hammock, COP$30,000 bed pp) has 10 rooms and 25 beds. Meals are not included in the prices but are usually around COP$8,000 for breakfast, COP$15,000 for lunch, and COP$15,000 for dinner, unless you order lobster (COP$45,000). Donde Alexandra has sweeping vistas of the bay and beyond from the restaurant area.

TRANSPORTATION

Most travelers visit Punta Gallinas as part of an organized tour as it can only be accessed by 4x4 and roads are nearly non-existent.

Parque Nacional Natural Macuira

The remote **Parque Nacional Natural Macuira** (PNN Macuira, 260 km northeast of Riohacha, cell tel. 311/688-2362, macuira@ parquesnacionales.gov.co, 8am-6pm daily, free) covers an area of 25,000 hectares (61,780 acres) and encompasses the entire Serranía de la Macuira (Macuira mountain range), an isolated mountainous outcrop at the northeastern tip of the Guajira Peninsula. These mountains are a biological island in the middle of the surrounding desert. The Macuira range, which is 35 kilometers (22 mi) long and 864 meters (2,835 ft) in elevation at Cerro Palua, its highest point, captures moisture-laden winds from the sea that nourish a unique low-elevation tropical cloud forest teeming with ferns, orchids, bromeliads, and moss. At lower elevations, there are tropical dry forests.

The park includes 350 species of plants, 140 species of birds (17 endemic), and more than 20 species of mammals. The park is within the large Alta Guajira Wayúu Reservation. In the lower parts of the range, within the park, live many Wayúu families who raise goats and grow corn and other subsistence crops.

The gateway to the park is the Wayúu town of **Nazareth.** Visitors are required to register and participate in a brief presentation at the PNN Macuira park office, where they must also hire an authorized Wayúu guide. A few of the official independent guides are Ricardo Brito (cell tel. 312/654-5328), Pedro Quintero (cell tel. 313/648-8060), and María Eulalia Quintero (cell tel. 322/664-1319).

HIKING

There are multiple hikes varying 1.5-6 hours; the cost of a guided walk ranges COP$35,000-45,000 per eight-person group. Day hikes meander along riverbeds through tropical dry forest. One leads to the **Arewolü Sand Dunes** (2 hours, 1.5 km/1 mi, COP$45,000), which are, surprisingly, located in the midst of the forest. Another hike goes to **Cerro Tojoro** (2.5 hours, COP$25,000), which affords beautiful views of the coast and the mountain range. The most challenging hike, **Nazareth-Siapana** (7 hours, 12 km/7.5 mi, COP$120,000) traverses the entire length of the park. Plan to hike early in the morning to increase your chances of seeing birds and other wildlife. Hiking to the Macuira's unusual cloud forest is not permitted by the Wayúu.

FOOD AND ACCOMMODATIONS

There are only a few lodging options in Nazareth, the town closest to the park. One suitable choice is **Hospedaje Vía Manaure** (entrance to Nazareth, cell tel. 320/310-3783 or 314/552-5513, evelasiosuarez@msn.com, COP$20,000 hammock, COP$30,000 bed pp), which can accommodate 40 people and offers Wi-Fi. It has an on-site restaurant (breakfast COP$10,000, lunch COP$15,000, dinner COP$10,000) serving regional dishes. Make arrangements in advance for meals. Another choice is **Villa Inmaculada** (cell tel. 320/504-8519, COP$20,000 pp), offering the same services as Hospedaje Vía Manaure.

TRANSPORTATION

Getting to Nazareth and PNN Macuira requires patience, money, time, and determination. If you are touring the Alta Guajira, PNN Macuira can be added to your itinerary after Punta Gallinas, which usually adds several days and more than doubles the price. Otherwise, hire a car out of Riohacha for the day (about COP$500,000, negotiable). Another option is to take public transportation from Uribia to Nazareth (Sun. only, 5-6 hours, COP$60,000). Before visiting, contact the **PNN Macuira park office** (cell tel. 311/688-2362, macuira@parquesnacionales.gov.co) for more transportation options, road conditions, and updated park information.

Western Caribbean Coast

The portion of the Caribbean coast that stretches west from Cartagena—extending south to the dramatic Golfo de Urabá and jutting north through the Darién Gap and the border with Panama—is less visited and familiar than the coastline to the east, and may be just the ticket for those yearning to explore the undiscovered and escape the crowds.

The Golfo de Morrosquillo is home to the beach town of Tolú, the jumping-off point for visits to the Islas de San Bernardo, a group of small, idyllic Caribbean islands that are still relatively off the beaten path. Across the Golfo de Urabá, the tropical rainforests of the Darién provide an exuberant backdrop to the car-free seaside towns of Capurganá and Sapzurro, accessible only by boat and footpaths

Highlights

Look for ★ to find recommended sights, activities, dining, and lodging.

★ **Escape to Tropical Islands:** Day-trip or spend the night on the **Islas de San Bernardo,** a string of Caribbean islands just offshore (page 132).

★ **Spot Crocodiles and Turtles:** Learn about these reptiles on a boat tour through a lush mangrove reserve along the **Bahía de Cispatá** (page 134).

★ **Peace Out at Río Cedro:** This mostly undeveloped stretch of coastline, full of wildlife, offers a tranquil retreat (page 135).

★ **Relax Where the Wilderness Meets the Sea:** Hike around or play in the waters of Afro-Colombian villages **Capurganá and Sapzurro,** set on idyllic crescent-shaped bays backed by jungle (page 136).

Western Caribbean Coast

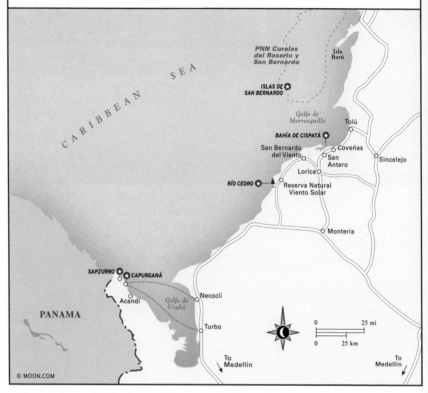

© MOON.COM

through the jungle. The diving off the coast here is superb.

What most visitors remember and cherish about a visit to this remote part of Colombia is being immersed in truly wild nature and authentic culture.

PLANNING YOUR TIME

Colombia's western Caribbean coast is made for slow travel. A dearth of flight possibilities and the necessity of traveling by boat to most of the major destinations, along with a largely undeveloped infrastructure, mean that patience will be not be just a virtue, but a necessity while traveling here. But for those

looking to drop out of the modern world and into a uniquely verdant and vibrant slice of raw Caribbean coastline, this region will be a delight. This stretch used to be almost completely off the radar for travelers, but this is quickly changing; however, you can still expect fewer crowds than elsewhere on the country's Caribbean coastline.

The two primary destinations are the Islas de San Bernardo, commonly visited from Tolú on the Golfo de Morrosquillo or Cartagena, and Capurganá and Sapzurro in the Darién region, accessible via the towns of Necoclí or Turbo on the Golfo de Urabá. Because of the huge expanse between these two sections,

Previous: view of Sapzurro Bay; swimming hole near El Cielo in Capurganá; coast near Tolú.

travelers typically choose one to focus on and incorporate into their itineraries. Although the Islas de San Bernardo can be visited on a day trip from Cartagena, you'll ideally give yourself 3-4 days to explore the Golfo de Morrosquillo. For Capurganá and Sapzurro you'll also want to budget 3-4 days. If you'd like to travel the entire western Caribbean coastline, plan on 7-10 days.

Safety

This region was greatly affected by violence during the worst years of the armed conflict between paramilitaries, guerrillas, and the military, with civilians often caught in the middle. This was especially so in the remote areas of the Darién, which was a major drug-trafficking route. Although drug smuggling in inland areas continues to this day, the places covered in this guide are safe. It's never a bad idea to ask locals about the security of an area, especially if you venture to parts not described in this guide.

Golfo de Morrosquillo

South of Cartagena, the Golfo de Morrosquillo is a broad, 50-kilometer-wide (31-mi-wide) inlet. Largely unknown to international visitors until recently, it's now becoming a common side trip from Cartagena due to the gorgeous Islas de San Bernado that lie just offshore. This chain of more than 40 Caribbean islands encompasses beautiful coral reefs, the world's most densely populated island—tiny Santa Cruz del Islote—and the picture-perfect Isla Múcura. The jumping-off point for the islands, the beach community of Tolú, is popular with vacationing Colombian families and is the largest town on this stretch of the coast.

On the southern edge of the gulf is the town of **San Antero,** which is home to a crocodile preserve on Bahía de Cispatá. Outside of San Antero is peaceful Río Cedro, a place to truly disconnect from the world. Inland from San Antero is the region's major city, **Montería,** the center of cattle country.

TOLÚ

Balmy beachside Tolú, 160 kilometers (100 mi) southwest of Cartagena, is best described as sleepy. Here, locals get around on foot or *bicitaxi* (bicycle cab), and it's hot and humid year-round. The beaches near town are pleasant, but many visitors come here in order to catch a boat to the Islas de San Bernardo.

In the evening, when the mercury has dropped a few degrees, locals congregate in the main plaza to exchange gossip and people-watch. On weekends, the town becomes livelier, with a steady influx of weekend warriors. Along the boardwalk that parallels the beach, vendors sell ceviche, bars blast music, and kids splash around in the warm water.

Tolú is home to a few decent beaches, perfect for lazing in the sun. Check out laid-back **Playa El Francés,** 5 kilometers (3 mi) north of Tolú. Another option is **Punta Bolívar,** nearly 30 kilometers (17 mi) southwest of Tolú.

Food and Accommodations

Half a dozen or so restaurants are clustered around the waterfront and blocks near the Chiringuito pier. Don't expect more than typical eats and fast food, but **Restaurante Donde Mamá** (Cra. 3 No. 15-11, tel. 313/546-8358, 6am-10pm daily, COP$16,000) serves up flavorful fish and meat plates. Service is a bit slow.

Hotel Casa Ines (Cl. 10 No. 2-96, Tolú, tel. 315/744-2538, COP$35,000 dorm, COP$70,000 s, COP$70,000-160,000 d) is located just two blocks from the beach and is run by a friendly local couple who can connect you with ecological and cultural projects in the area. Rooms are basic and clean, if a bit cramped, but the terrace bar overlooking the street is a great place to relax and socialize.

Catering mostly to Colombian families and groups, **Camino Verde** (Playa El Francés, Tolú, tel. 5/249-9464, www.vacacionescaminoverde.com, COP$290,000 d) is six kilometers (3.7 mi) east of Tolú, and a peaceful (but not fancy) beachfront spot to relax during the week. Rooms are generally set up family-style, with a double and a twin bed, and there's an outdoor pool and hot tub, as well as canopy beds set up on the sand. Most visitors drive here.

Transportation

There is frequent bus service from Tolú to Cartagena (3 hours, COP$40,000) and Montería (2.5 hours, COP$25,000). Buses to Cartagena and Montería are at Calle 15 where it intersects Carreteras 2A and 3A.

Satena (www.satena.gov.co) flies from Medellín to Tolú, making this a quick, easy, and often inexpensive beach destination.

To get around Tolú, take a *bici-taxi* (bicycle cab).

TOP EXPERIENCE

★ ISLAS DE SAN BERNARDO

The easiest and least expensive way to spend some time on the turquoise waters of the Golfo de Morrosquillo and relax on a tropical white-sand beach is to visit the **Islas de San Bernardo.** These islands, located about 16 kilometers (10 mi) offshore, are part of the Parque Nacional Natural Corales del Rosario y San Bernardo, although the islands have been privately developed.

If you don't have the time or budget to spend the night, a day tour is a good way to see the islands. Tours generally include a stop for a seafood lunch, snorkeling at **Isla Múcura,** and passing by a handful of the other islands, including **Santa Cruz del Islote,** the most densely populated island in the world, with one person for every 10 square meters. Book a tour of the islands with **Mundo Mar** (Av. 1 No. 14-40, Tolú, tel. 5/288-4431, www.clubnauticomundomartolu.com.co,

COP$85,000 pp), a reputable tour agency. Other tour agencies are located in the hotels that line Tolú's boardwalk. Most day tours depart at 8:30am and return to Tolú by about 4:30pm each day.

Day tours to the islands, particularly Isla Múcura, are increasingly popular from Cartagena as well. They leave from the docks just outside of the Torre del Reloj (clock tower) and the Old City walls at 4am, returning around 5pm, and run about COP$200,000, including lunch and the use of the facilities at one of the island resorts for the day. Agencies such as **Vive Cartagena** (cell tel. 300/894-4488, www.vivecartagena.com.co), which has booths set up all over the city, visit several different islands and offer various plans.

Food and Accommodations

To get to accommodations on the Islas de San Bernardo, you can hop on a boat from Tolú (8:30am daily, COP$50,000 pp one-way) via one of the many tour agencies on the waterfront; the ride takes about 1 hour. Some hotels offer their own transport services from Tolú or Cartagena, which takes about 2.5 hours.

For great Caribbean vibes on a floating piece of paradise, head to the ★ **Casa en el Agua** (Isla Tintipán, cell tel. 312/756-3439, www.casaenelagua.com, COP$70,000 hammock, COP$100,000 dorm, COP$300,000 d), a floating solar-powered hostel near Isla Tintipán. There is a restaurant here that serves all meals family-style. Activities include diving, island tours, and spearfishing. At night, it's possible to observe bioluminescent plankton. On nights where there's a full moon, Casa en el Agua hosts "reef raves." The quickest and easiest way to get here is from Tolú, but you can also get here via Casa en el Agua's boat service (1pm Mon., Wed., and Fri., COP$100,000); you must reserve a spot and confirm departure details in advance. Stop by the hotel's Cartagena office, located

---

1: boats, the main form of transportation to the Islas de San Bernardo; 2: relaxing on a pier; 3: a young crocodile at Bahía de Cispatá; 4: resort in the Islas de San Bernardo

right across from the Torre del Reloj on the Plaza de los Coches (La Matuna, Edificio Banco de Bogota, Av. Escallon Diagonal 35, office 505).

★ **Punta Norte** (Isla Tintipán, cell tel. 310/707-4005, www.hotelpuntanorte. com, COP$225,000 pp) is run by a friendly Uruguayan and is most often referred to as Donde El Uruguayo, or "The Uruguayan's Place." Bring plenty of insect repellent to this remote island paradise. Accommodations are not luxurious, but it's a relaxed place. The restaurant includes all meals, and fresh lobster is part of the deal! When you make your reservation, inquire about transportation timing and availability.

For white-sand beaches, warm aquamarine waters, and the occasional calorie-loaded cocktail, go to the resort of **Punta Faro** (Isla Múcura, cell tel. 317/435-9594, www.puntafaro.com, COP$1,040,000 d, two-night minimum). There are 45 simple rooms with no hot water in the showers and unreliable Wi-Fi. All meals (included) are served buffet-style. Spend your time here lounging on the beach, discovering nearby islands, participating in various water activities, riding bikes, and taking short hikes. It's a good place to bring kids. Private round-trip fast boat service from Cartagena costs an additional COP$175,000 per person.

Another option is **Hotel Isla Múcura** (Isla Múcura, cell tel. 300/7106033, http:// hotelislamucura.com, COP$350,000 d), which offers a variety of beach bungalows built for two and an on-site restaurant. It offers its own transport service from both Tolú (COP$50,000) and Cartagena (COP$100,000).

★ BAHÍA DE CISPATÁ

Perhaps the most interesting part of this region can be found along the coastline of **Bahía de Cispatá,** a serene bay lined with undisturbed mangrove forests, near the town of San Antero. Here, a project by **Asocaiman** (cell tel. 300/810-1161, www.asocaiman.org) helps in the protection and propagation of

American crocodiles and turtles. These creatures were once hunted for their meat and eggs, but today, locals are trained on the importance of protecting these species. A visit to the small bayside refuge, where many species of crocodiles and turtles reside before being released back into the wild, consists of a tour led by a former hunter. There is no set price for the tour, but guides can accept tips. Asocaiman also offers boat tours (COP$15,000-50,000 pp, depending on group size) of the mangroves, during which you'll have the chance to see animals in their natural habitat. Call Asocaiman in advance to coordinate your visit.

Food and Accommodations

Eat at ★ **Pesecar** (Bahía de Cispatá, cell tel. 312/651-2651, 7:30am-8:30pm daily). It's worth the trip to San Antero just for lunch here—very fresh seafood with an unbeatable bayside location.

San Antero borders the water and has some nice beaches at Playa Blanca. There is a long string of waterfront hotels popular with weekenders from Montería and Medellín. During the week, it's very quiet. The **Cispatá Marina Hotel** (tel. 4/811-0197 or 4/811-0887, www. cispata.com, COP$123,000 pp) has an enviable location overlooking Bahía de Cispatá and, on the other side, the beaches of Playa Blanca. The hotel comprises 16 cute red-roofed beachfront *cabañas* as well as smaller apartments. The hotel also has a large pool.

A locally run and quite friendly hotel with an on-site restaurant, the **Mangle Colora'o** (Vereda Amaya, tel. 4/811-0722, cell tel. 301/203-7071, COP$35,000 pp) is just across the street from Bahía de Cispatá.

Transportation

San Antero and Bahía de Cispatá are about 30 kilometers (18.6 mi) southwest of Tolú, on the Coveñas-Lorica highway. Regular public transportation is available for under COP$10,000 from the bus terminal along the main highway.

★ RÍO CEDRO

It's hard to find a place more tranquil than **Río Cedro**. This community of banana and plantain farmers on a mostly undeveloped coastline in Córdoba, near San Antero, is set amid an unusual tropical dry forest that is home to sloths, howler monkeys, iguanas, and many species of birds. The gray-sand beaches are strewn with driftwood, and pelicans glide in formation above the usually calm waters.

In peaceful Río Cedro, there are paths galore that wind through the forest and excellent swimming and kayaking opportunities. But perhaps the best activity of all is lazing in a hammock, enjoying the view. Take mosquito repellent.

The main destination here is the **Reserva Natural y EcoHotel Viento Solar** (cell tel. 317/377-6244, www.vientosolar.org, COP$145,000 pp, all meals included), a private beachfront nature reserve with a variety of private and shared rooms. It often hosts yoga, meditation, and traditional craft workshops, guided hiking and boating excursions,

and *yagé* (ayahuasca) retreats. Vegetarian meals are provided to guests. The owners have been working on reforesting the land here for more than 35 years, and the reserve is considered a model ecotourism project in Colombia. Visitors can explore the native forest, filled with fruit-bearing trees like mango and mamey, which are also used to provide nutrition to the Río Cedro community. Volunteer options are also available here, with a two-week minimum commitment.

Río Cedro is accessible from the town of Lorica, on the banks of the Río Sinú. To get to Lorica from San Antero, take one of the *busetas* (30 minutes, COP$10,000) that pass through town. From the Tolú-Montería highway in Lorica, take a shared taxi (one hour, COP$10,000) through San Bernardo del Viento to Moñitos—ask a local where to flag one down. From there, the lodge can arrange for a motorbike (45 minutes, COP$12,000) to collect you. Since it's a bit challenging to get here, plan on spending at least a night or two.

The Colombian Darién

Tropical rainforest-covered mountains frame the bright turquoise Caribbean Sea in the Darién region, a swath of land straddling the borders of Colombia and Panama and encompassing a dramatic meeting of land and water. The Colombian Darién is bookended by the delta of the Río Atrato, which flows into the Golfo de Urabá, on the east and the Serranía de Baudó mountain range on the west. Officially part of the Choco department of Colombia, this biodiverse region is completely different from the rest of the Colombian Caribbean coast. An Afro-Colombian community has made their home here for centuries, and the surrounding lush jungle is bursting with wildlife. Disconnected from the rest of civilization, there is a strong

island feeling to the coastal towns here, and wilderness beaches abound like nowhere else on the Caribbean.

Safety

The absence of roads, abundance of navigable rivers, and the cover provided by the jungle's canopy have made this region into a major corridor for the trafficking of illegal drugs, which has also meant that there has been a heavy presence of both guerrillas and paramilitaries. While the interior of the Darién region, particularly the Darién Gap—where Colombia borders Panama—is still considered one of the most dangerous places in the country, it is safe to visit the villages of Capurganá and Sapzurro.

★ CAPURGANÁ AND SAPZURRO

Perched on idyllic crescent-shaped bays are the twin car-free towns of Capurganá and Sapzurro. Capurganá is the larger of the two, and together they're the most popular destination in the Colombian Darién.

With a population of about 2,000, many residents in Capurganá still make their living by fishing, although tourism has increased in recent years, resulting in more guesthouses, hotels, and restaurants, many of which are run by Europeans. The town's *muelle* (port) bustles with activity during the day, with boats constantly bringing in passengers and supplies. In the evening, ramshackle bars, particularly around the town's soccer field, blast music for beer-drinking patrons. Nature is abundant here: Within minutes of leaving your hotel you'll be surrounded by the sounds of the jungle, accompanied only by the occasional green-and-black-speckled toad and maybe a band of howler monkeys.

Sapzurro, just north of Capurganá, is even more laid-back. This village is reachable only by foot or boat. Walking here on a jungle path over a mountain from Capurganá affords spectacular views of the coastline. From Sapzurro, you can also continue a short way north to cross the border into Panama, another incredible experience.

Prepare yourself for the weather here: Rain and humidity mean mud and mosquitoes, so you'll want durable shoes and layered clothing. Bring a flashlight or headlamp for walking at night.

Hiking

There are several jungle walks to make around Capurganá. These take you through dense jungle overflowing with tropical vegetation populated by howler monkeys, birds, colorful frogs, and snakes. While the walks are short and fairly straightforward, you may want to ask at your hotel or hostel for a guide, especially for the walk between Capurganá and Sapzurro. Guides cost about COP$15,000. Wear hiking boots (waterproof if possible) and a swimsuit underneath your clothes for dips in the water off of Sapzurro or in freshwater swimming holes, and set off in the morning hours to give yourself plenty of time to get back.

An easy walk to make, without the need of a guide, is to **La Coquerita** (20-minute walk north from town, cell tel. 311/824-8022, COP$3,000), a delightfully ramshackle waterside hangout where you can have a refreshing coco-lemonade or maybe some guacamole and *patacones* (fried plantains) and take a dip in the refreshing freshwater or saltwater pools. There are also some handicrafts on sale here. To get there, walk along the Playa Caleta just north of the port, passing in front of the Hotel Almar. Continue along the jungle path that hugs the coastline. La Coquerita is less than 1 kilometer (0.5 mi) from town, and the path is well marked. Look out for the black and fluorescent green frogs along the way, but don't touch them; they're poisonous.

El Cielo waterfall is a 50-minute walk (about 3 km/1.8 mi) through the jungle from Capurganá. The path is flat and easy, although you'll have to make about a dozen crossings of shallow streams. Bring a bathing suit to cool off in the swimming holes you'll encounter. To get to heavenly El Cielo, set out on the road that runs parallel to the airstrip and then ask locals for directions. On the way to El Cielo, look for **El Trébol Piscina,** a pool where you can take a dip in cool waters and have lunch.

Find the white sands and calm swimming pool-like waters of **Playa Aguacate** (Avocado Beach), tucked into the lush Aguacate Bay. A trail to the bay begins at the southern end of Capurganá's town beach. The 3-kilometer (1.9-mile) walk takes about 45 minutes and hugs the coast the entire way, so scrambling over a couple of headlands is necessary. Don't do this walk during the rainy season, however; the trail can get eroded and slippery. Playa Aguacate can also be reached via a 20-minute boat ride (COP$10,000 pp one-way) from the town dock. Just south of the bay that Playa Aguacate is nestled in lies a long stretch of sand aptly named **Playa Soledad,** which offers privacy most of the week and shallow turquoise-green waters for wading.

The **path to Sapzurro** leads you through the exuberant rainforest to a lookout point and then down directly to the beach. The hike takes two hours. Start at the soccer field, on the southern end of Capurganá, and ask the way. Midway up the uphill path is a shack that is the home of a man who claims to protect the jungle. Once you find him, you know you're on the right track. He expects those who pass through to pay him about COP$2,000. At the top of the mountain is a nice overlook with views of Capurganá and the coastline. The hike is not difficult, but the path can get muddy and slippery in places. Wear hiking boots and pick up a walking stick along the way to help you manage the steep parts.

Once in Sapzurro, you're a short hike (15 minutes) from the border with **Panama** and the village of **La Miel.** This easy walk begins on the same street as Cabañas Uvali. The border crossing is at the top of a steep hill embedded with steps. You'll need to show a passport to cross over to Panama. The village of La Miel is tiny but has a pleasant beach where you can swim, backed by jungle-covered mountains. There's also a decent waterfront eatery, **Restaurante-Lounge Chiriqui** (La Miel, cell tel. 310/627-5430, 8am-5pm daily, COP$25,000) that serves fresh fish and has awesome views, making it a good place to have lunch before heading back to the Colombian side of the coast.

Diving and Snorkeling

The warm, turquoise waters off the coast of Capurganá, all the way up to San Blas in Panama, make for fantastic diving, and there are over 30 diving sites to choose from. The best time for underwater exploration is May-November. During those months, visibility is exceptional, with hardly any waves. There are coral walls, reef rocks, and caves to explore. **Dive and Green Diving Center** (facing the Capurganá port, cell tel. 311/578-4021 or 316/781-6255, www.diveandgreen.com, 8am-7pm daily) is the best place to organize a diving trip (certified diver excursion COP$190,000) or to take a five-day PADI certification course (COP$820,000) with a bilingual instructor. For these packages it's best to pay in cash, as credit card transactions have an additional fee. For those interested in snorkeling, Dive and Green can make arrangements for you, though they don't themselves lead snorkeling trips. Dive and Green offers all the equipment you need. If you're on the fence about whether diving is for you, the company offers a Discover Scuba Diving day (COP$150,000). Dive and Green also has accommodations (COP$25,000 pp), comprising four rooms in a house adjacent to its offices. The house faces the water, guaranteeing a pleasant evening breeze.

Food

Most hotels in Capurganá have on-site restaurants, but you can also dine on freshly caught seafood at informal residences-turned-eateries around town, especially at lunchtime; look for tables set up out front and makeshift signs listing daily specials.

In Capurganá ★ **Donde Josefina** (Playa Caleta, cell tel. 316/779-7760, noon-9pm Tues.-Sun., COP$35,000) is the top restaurant for a delicious gourmet seafood dinner, right on the beach in the heart of town. Dining on lobster in a coconut-and-garlic sauce under the swaying branches of a palm tree is an iconic way to enjoy the evening. **Hernan Patacón** (no phone, hours vary, COP$20,000) is a food stand serving fresh fish and shrimp. It's located in front of Capurganá's clinic. A decent **bakery** overlooking the soccer field in the center of town serves breakfast, and is open daily.

In Sapzurro, the best places for a meal are **Doña Triny** (Hostal Doña Triny, cell tel. 312/751-8626 or 313/725-8362, noon-10pm daily, COP$20,000), a two-story brick house facing the water, and the **Gata Negra** (cell tel. 314/725-0325, www.lagatanegra.net, open

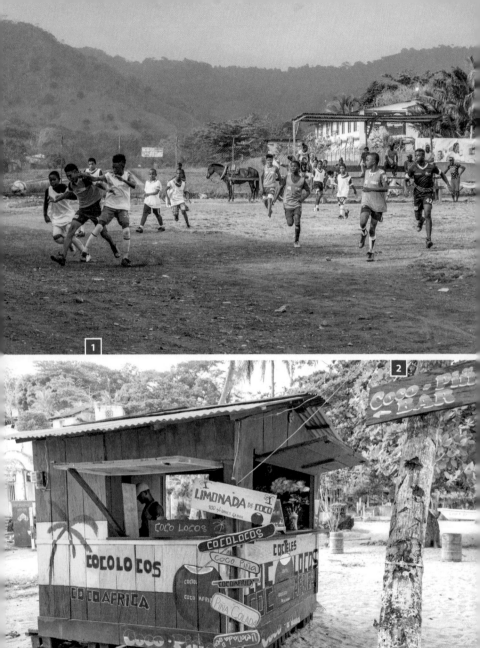

daily) for authentic home-style Italian dishes. Call in advance to let either restaurant know you're coming.

Accommodations

There are a surprising number of excellent and inexpensive accommodations options in both Capurganá and Sapzurro, as well as in nearby beach areas. While there are a few large, all-inclusive hotels offering welcome drinks and the works, the most interesting and comfortable options are the smaller guesthouses and hostels. Many larger hotels are owned and operated by out-of-towners but it is also easy to rent informal rooms from locals (look for signs that say "habitaciones").

One of the best "urban" lodging options in Capurganá is **Posada del Gecko** (in town, cell tel. 314/525-6037, www.posadadelgecko. com, posadadelgecko@hotmail.com, COP$25,000 dorm, COP$80,000 d), which is run by an Italian-Colombian couple and offers both dorms and private rooms spread over two houses, with a capacity of 28 people. In between the buildings is a spacious garden ideal for lounging in a hammock or the hot tub. Enjoy a good Italian dinner by candlelight at the restaurant (7:30pm-11pm daily); it's open to nonguests as well, but it's best to stop by in advance and make a reservation. The hotel can arrange three-day excursions to the San Blas Islands (Panama), in which you visit a Kuna indigenous community, frolic on pristine white-sand beaches, and snorkel.

Several excellent guesthouses reside amid the trees in the Playa Roca area, about a 15-minute walk south or horse ride from Capurganá. This is more pleasant than staying in the Centro: At night you'll need no air-conditioner, and in the morning you may awake to birdsong. ★ **Cabaña Darius** (Playa Roca, cell tel. 314/622-5638, www. cdarius.blogspot.com, capurga05@gmail. com, COP$90,000 pp incl. 2 meals) is a lovely guesthouse among the trees that includes seafood-based dinners plus breakfast

in the rates. Rooms are spacious and clean, and it's cool enough at night that you won't miss air-conditioning. Balconies and hammocks provide lounging spaces, but the top selling points are the warm hospitality and good food.

A low-key place to stay in the Capurganá area is on Playa Aguacate, south of town. The German owner of the ★ **Bahía Lodge** (Playa Aguacate, cell tel. 314/812-2727, www.bahialodge.com, COP$270,000 pp incl. 2 meals) has carved a little paradise out of the jungle—once there you won't want to leave. Its simple and comfortable cabins, each with a sea view, are popular with honeymooners and those celebrating special occasions.

In Sapzurro, there are quite a few inexpensive lodging options, but fewer restaurants than in Capurganá. Most hotels offer meals, though, and are usually the best bet, as they tend to be open more frequently. The ★ **Hostel El Chileno** (cell tel. 313/685-9862, COP$30,000 dorm, COP$50,000 pp d) has basic beachfront cabins and is named after the Chilean owner. It can organize oversea transportation directly to Cartagena. A wide front patio offers seating, including tables and chairs, plus hammocks for simply taking in spectacular views of the bay. Free avocadoes and mangoes are a nice perk. The hostel is located at the entrance to Sapzurro near the path to Capurganá.

Just steps from the beach in Sapzurro, ★ **Gata Negra** (cell tel. 314/725-0325, www.lagatanegra.net, COP$50,000 pp d, COP$70,000 pp cabana) is a cozy guesthouse surrounded by a tropical garden full of fruit trees and birds. There is no formal restaurant here but the owners serve Italian dishes based on local seafood if you place a dinner order ahead of time. Note there's no Wi-Fi here.

Cabañas Uvali (in town, cell tel. 314/624-1325, COP$40,000 pp) is a friendly, clean, and straightforward little place. It's about a five-minute walk from the beach. **La Posada Hostal & Camping** (cell tel. 312/662-7599 or 310/410-2245, www.sapzurrolaposada.com, COP$15,000 pp camping, COP$95,000pp d),

---

1: kids playing soccer; 2: Capurganá beachfront bar

close to the path to Capurganá, has one luxury cabaña with a view, two private rooms, and a large space for camping under a big mango tree. It also has a little tiki bar over the water, which can be set up for a romantic dinner under the stars.

Information and Services

Bring extra cash to Capurganá and Sapzurro: There are no ATMs, and credit cards are not accepted in most establishments. The nearest bank, **Banco Agrario** (Cl. Las Flores with Cl. Consistorial, tel. 4/682-8229, 8am-11:30am and 2pm-4:30pm Mon.-Fri.), is in Acandí, a half-hour boat ride south from Capurganá.

Transportation

Capurganá and Sapzurro are currently accessible only by boat. To get to the towns, you must take a *lancha* (boat) to Capurganá from the coastal town of **Necoclí** or the rough port city of **Turbo,** both on the Golfo de Urabá.

All boats arrive at the *muelle* (dock) in Capurganá, in the middle of town. Most hotels are within walking distance, although those on Playa Roca are a 15-minute walk south. If you have heavy luggage, ask for a horse (about COP$10,000) when you disembark. Hotels in Playa Aguacate and Sapzurro are reachable only by taking another *lancha* from the docks in Capurganá, about a 20-minute ride. Those hotels will arrange your transportation from Capurganá in advance.

Buses run to Necoclí from Montería (2.5 hours, COP$33,500) and Cartagena (9 hours, COP$85,000). From Necoclí, there's direct **fast boat** service (tel. 4/821-4164 or cell tel. 315/687-4284). It takes 1.5 hours and leaves at 11am (COP$85,000 one-way,

COP$170,000 round-trip). If you need a place to spend the night in town, **Casa Neco** (Cra. 49 No. 46-150, Necoclí, cell tel. 313/599-8441, COP$35,000 dorm, COP$75,000 d) is just a block from the beach and offers clean rooms that open onto a garden patio. There is a shared kitchen and bike tours are available.

Buses also run from Montería (4 hours, COP$28,000), Medellín (8 hours, COP$54,000), and cities across the Caribbean coast to Turbo on the Golfo de Urabá. From Turbo, it's possible to take a 2.5- to 3-hour **boat ride** to Capurganá. These usually depart daily 7am-8am, costing about COP$60,000. The early-morning departure means that you will probably have to spend the previous night in Turbo. **Residencias La Florida** (Cra. 13 No. 99A-56, Turbo, tel. 4/827-3531, COP$35,000 d) is an acceptable lodging option. It's close to the port and its bustling market, and the hotel staff is quite helpful in arranging your onward transportation. Be advised that December-March the boat ride from Turbo to Capurganá can be awful due to high winds and unrelenting waves.

To return to the mainland from Capurganá, it's best to reserve a day in advance for *lanchas* bound for Necoclí or Turbo, especially during peak tourist times. Your hotel should be able to do this for you by calling ahead to the *muelle,* where the contact is Ariel Palacios (cell tel. 312/264-5924).

To travel onward to Panama past the border town of La Miel, you must go to the Colombian **Ministerio de Relaciones Exteriores** (Cl. del Comercio, Capurganá cell tel. 311/746-6234, 8am-5pm Mon.-Fri., 9am-4pm Sat.) to get an exit stamp before leaving Capurganá.

San Andrés and Providencia

Situated in turquoise waters, these idyllic
Caribbean islands feel a lot more like Jamaica or Belize than Colombia.
As a stand-alone Caribbean getaway or an extra stop on any Colombian
adventure, the San Andrés islands will not disappoint: The beaches
here are legendary, the food is good, and the reggae-infused nightlife
is markedly different from what you'll find in the rest of the country.
Sunbathing, snorkeling, diving, kitesurfing, and just plain chilling
are the order of the day. Seafood, particularly fresh crab and *caracol*
(conch), is always on the menu, best accompanied by cold beer. And
the locals are as friendly and laid-back as it gets.

The San Andrés Archipelago is made up of seven atolls and three
major islands: San Andrés, Providencia, and Santa Catalina. San

Highlights

Look for ★ to find recommended sights, activities, dining, and lodging.

★ **Wander the Jardín Botánico:** At this lush reserve you'll learn about the archipelago's native, medicinal, and edible plants (page 148).

★ **Snorkel and Dive in the Seaflower Biosphere Reserve:** The San Andrés Archipelago is part of a UNESCO-designated marine reserve (pages 150 and 162).

★ **Hop on a Boat Tour:** Head out on a *lancha* to **Johnny Cay,** renowned for its white-sand beaches, and **Rose Cay,** known as The Aquarium for its abundant marinelife (page 152).

★ **Chill Out at Beachfront Reggae Bars:** Relaxing to the rhythms with a cold beer on the beach in **San Luis** is a perfect way to end the day (page 153).

★ **Explore Different Ecosystems:** Kayak through mangroves and walk a trail through tropical dry forest at **Parque Nacional Natural Old Providence McBean Lagoon** (page 160).

★ **Hike to the Highest Point on Providencia: The Peak** offers excellent views over the mountainous landscape and aquamarine Caribbean Sea (page 162).

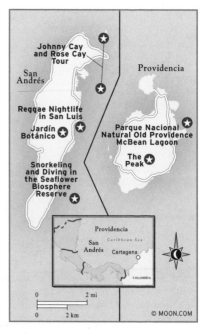

Andrés is 775 kilometers (492 mi) northeast of the Colombian mainland and only 191 kilometers (119 mi) east of Nicaragua. The islands are small: San Andrés, the largest island, has an area of 26 square kilometers (10 square mi), Providencia just 17 square kilometers (6.5 square mi), and Santa Catalina, attached to Providencia by a photogenic pedestrian bridge, is 1 square kilometer (247 acres) in size.

The island of San Andrés is a popular vacation destination for middle- and upper-class Colombians and well as international visitors, meaning lots of low-priced domestic flights from major cities, but higher prices on restaurants and accommodations. Providencia and its tiny tagalong neighbor of Santa Catalina are more expensive than San Andrés but offer a sense of how the Caribbean used to be. Here you'll enjoy small bungalow-style hotels, home-cooked creole food, and picturesque palm-lined beaches.

English and a creole patois are spoken on the islands, although Spanish is rapidly taking over in San Andrés and the tourism sector.

HISTORY

Little is known of the early history of San Andrés, Providencia, and Santa Catalina. In pre-Columbian times, the Miskito people of Central America visited the islands but didn't settle there until after European colonization.

In 1631, 100 Puritans from England arrived via the *Seaflower* and founded a colony on Providence Island (the English name for Providencia). The colonists imported slaves and established a plantation-based economy. Spaniards attacked the islands in 1641 and put an end to the Puritan experiment. Over the next 50 years, the island was fought over by Spain and England.

In 1821, the archipelago became part of the newly independent Republic of Gran Colombia. During the 19th century, an influx of immigrants from the British Caribbean included many former slaves, known as Raizals, who formed the beginnings of the islander community.

Colombia exerted what many considered abusive power over the islands in the early 20th century, even forbidding English from being taught in schools at one point, giving rise to several separatist and self-determination movements. In 1953, dictator Gustavo Rojas Pinilla declared San Andrés a free port. This led to a massive influx of outsiders, and the English-speaking native islanders became a minority, losing control of much of their land. Providencia, which was not declared a free-trade zone, was spared this onslaught.

The 1991 Colombian constitution gave the islands some autonomy and put an end to immigration from the mainland. Providencia enacted strict zoning and land-ownership regulations that have preserved the islander identity and community. The archipelago's Raizal community signed a Declaration of Self-Determination in 2002 that was submitted to both the Colombian government and the United Nations (UN) and sought recognition of their autonomy and qualification for receiving domestic and international aid. But the Colombian government still classifies them as "Afro-Colombian" rather than "indigenous," which would give afford the islanders more autonomous rights.

In recent decades, Nicaragua has contested Colombian jurisdiction over the islands. In 2012, the UN's International Court of Justice decided that 70,000 square kilometers (43,500 square mi) of sea surrounding San Andrés that had previously been considered Colombian were in fact Nicaraguan. For islanders this meant losing traditional fishing areas. The court's decision is being appealed, but Nicaragua is also pushing for more territory. After the ruling, the Colombian government began giving small subsidies to fishers and is investing in measures to try to save the

SAN ANDRÉS AND PROVIDENCIA

Previous: colorful house in San Luis; *coco loco* vendor; iguana on Johnny Cay.

San Andrés and Providencia

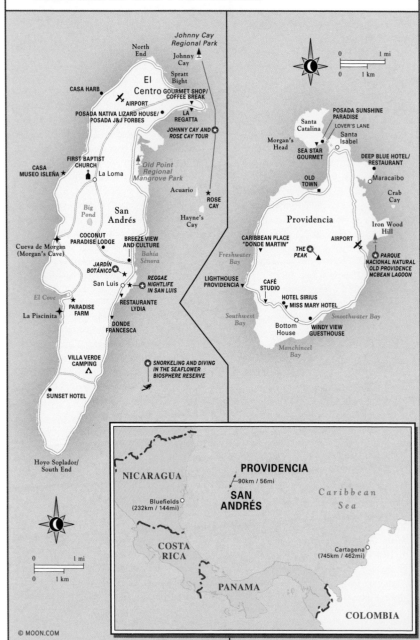

North End

Johnny Cay Regional Park

Johnny Cay

Spratt Bight

El Centro

CASA HARB

AIRPORT

GOURMET SHOP/ COFFEE BREAK

POSADA NATIVA LIZARD HOUSE/ POSADA J&J FORBES

LA REGATTA

JOHNNY CAY AND ROSE CAY TOUR

FIRST BAPTIST CHURCH

CASA MUSEO ISLEÑA

La Loma

Old Point Regional Mangrove Park

Acuario

ROSE CAY

Big Pond

San Andrés

Hayne's Cay

COCONUT PARADISE LODGE

BREEZE VIEW AND CULTURE

Cueva de Morgan (Morgan's Cave)

Bahía Sénora

JARDÍN BOTÁNICO

San Luis

REGGAE NIGHTLIFE IN SAN LUIS

El Cove

PARADISE FARM

RESTAURANTE LYDIA

La Piscinita

DONDE FRANCESCA

VILLA VERDE CAMPING

SNORKELING AND DIVING IN THE SEAFLOWER BIOSPHERE RESERVE

SUNSET HOTEL

Hoyo Soplador/ South End

0 1 mi
0 1 km

Santa Catalina

POSADA SUNSHINE PARADISE

LOVER'S LANE

Santa Isabel

Morgan's Head

SEA STAR GOURMET

DEEP BLUE HOTEL/ RESTAURANT

OLD TOWN

Maracaibo

Crab Cay

Providencia

Iron Wood Hill

CARIBBEAN PLACE "DONDE MARTIN"

THE PEAK

AIRPORT

PARQUE NACIONAL NATURAL OLD PROVIDENCE MCBEAN LAGOON

Freshwater Bay

LIGHTHOUSE PROVIDENCIA

CAFÉ STUDIO

HOTEL SIRIUS

MISS MARY HOTEL

Southwest Bay

Bottom House

WINDY VIEW GUESTHOUSE

Smoothwater Bay

Manchineel Bay

NICARAGUA

Bluefields (232km / 144mi)

PROVIDENCIA

90km / 56mi

SAN ANDRÉS

Caribbean Sea

COSTA RICA

Cartagena (745km / 462mi)

PANAMA

COLOMBIA

0 1 mi
0 1 km

© MOON.COM

island's fishing industry, including building a new fishing terminal on San Andrés.

THE LANDSCAPE

The archipelago covers 280,000 square kilometers (174,000 square mi) of marine area. It includes three major islands, seven atolls, and some well-preserved coral reefs, particularly the barrier reef surrounding Providencia and Santa Catalina, home to more than 80 species of coral and 200 species of fish. The three islands and much of the surrounding Caribbean Sea were designated the Seaflower Biosphere Reserve by UNESCO in 2000 in recognition of the region's status as a biodiversity hot spot.

The islands were once covered by forest. Though much has been cleared, especially in San Andrés, significant tracts remain, with cedars, cotton trees, stinkingtoes, birch gums, and other indigenous species. The abundance of fruit-bearing trees and plants includes breadfruit, tamarind, mango, coconut, and guava. There are several large, well-preserved mangrove lagoons, notably the McBean Lagoon in Providencia and Old Point Mangrove Regional Park in San Andrés.

The islands support a wide range of reptiles, including snakes, iguanas, geckos, and lizards. Other land animals include crabs, especially the black and shankey crabs, which migrate to and from the sea to spawn, protected by army personnel who block traffic on Providencia's roads during the migration. Four species of protected sea turtles nest here. Approximately 100 bird species have been identified on the islands, but only 18 are resident. The island's only nonhuman land mammals are bats. Dolphins and whales are sighted occasionally.

Despite environmental degradation, especially in San Andrés, the archipelago remains one of the best-preserved corners of the Caribbean.

PLANNING YOUR TIME

San Andrés is a possible long-weekend getaway from mainland Colombia; visiting the islands can be accomplished in five nights, although a full week allows for a more relaxed pace, especially if you want to do some serious diving. Wait 24 hours after diving to get in an airplane, due to pressurization concerns.

A visit to Providencia from San Andrés can be a budget buster, but is well worth the expense if you're interested in getting away from it all. Getting to Providencia and Santa Catalina involves an extra flight or catamaran ride, and hotels and restaurants are generally more expensive than in San Andrés (which itself is more expensive than the mainland).

High tourist seasons on the islands are during Christmas and New Year's. It may be hard to find a hotel from mid-December until mid-January, when throngs of Colombian families and a growing number of Brazilians and Argentinians take over San Andrés. Also popular are Semana Santa (Holy Week) and school vacations, which fall between mid-June and August. May and September are quiet. Because it's more difficult to reach, Providencia rarely feels crowded.

The average daily temperature is 27°C (81°F). During the dry season (Jan.-Apr.), water rationing can be necessary, especially in Providencia, where it rains as little as five days per month. The rainy season extends June-November, when it can rain 20-24 days per month. October is the rainiest month and is also when hurricanes occasionally churn up the warm Caribbean waters. March and April are the best months for snorkeling and diving because the waters are calm. December and January are windy, making snorkeling and diving challenging. Strong winds can prompt airlines to cancel flights into and out of Providencia.

San Andrés

Surrounded by a large barrier reef, San Andrés is a Caribbean island playground for a growing number of domestic and international tourists. Here the waters are seven shades of blue, the sandy beaches are white, and a *coco loco* (the official island cocktail) is always available. Days here are spent sun-worshipping, island-hopping, snorkeling and diving, partying on the beach, and enjoying fresh seafood. For many Colombians, the deals at the many duty-free stores are too good to pass up—and one reason why they visit the island in the first place.

San Andrés has a population of about 75,000, about two-thirds of whom are of mainland Colombian origin. The rest are English- and creole-speaking native islanders, known as Raizals or *nativos,* whose ancestors were enslaved and brought to the islands; they're related to the inhabitants of the nearby Corn Islands of Nicaragua and the Miskito coast region of Central America. There is also a community of "Turcos" or "Arabes," whose roots can be traced to mostly Lebanon and Syria. Their presence on the island is not an insignificant one, as demonstrated by a brilliantly white modern mosque that stands prominently in the commercial center.

Orientation

The island of San Andrés resembles a seahorse floating gently eastward in the western Caribbean Sea. It's only about 13 kilometers (8 mi) long from top to bottom and 3 kilometers (2 mi) wide, and has a total area of 26 square kilometers (10 square mi). The *Circunvalar* ring road more or less circles the entire island.

The "town" of San Andrés is usually called **El Centro.** It's in the snout of the seahorse, in the northeast. This is the center of activity and where the majority of the island's restaurants, hotels, and shops (nearly all of which are owned and operated by mainland Colombians) are found. The center of

action here is the *paseo peatonal,* or *malecón,* along Avenida Colombia, known in English as the Spratt Bight Pathway. This delightful 1.6-kilometer (1-mi) pedestrian promenade along Spratt Bight Beach is lined with hotels and restaurants and stays bustling late into the night.

The town of **San Luis** extends along the southeastern edge of the island. It has a much more local feel and is more laid-back than El Centro. This area has some hotels, restaurants, and waterfront reggae bars, mostly situated along a series of beaches, including **San Luis Beach** and **Rocky Cay Beach,** which is named after a small offshore island just east.

The west side of the island is quieter, with a handful of points of interest, hotels, and restaurants. The coastline on the west side is all coral; there are no beaches.

At the southernmost point of the island is the **Hoyo Soplador** blowhole.

The middle part of the island, called **La Loma** (The Hill), is the highest point on the island. The main point of reference here is the stately white First Baptist Church. This area is home to the largest community of native Raizal islanders and is an interesting place to immerse yourself in local life.

SIGHTS

Spratt Bight Pathway and Beach

Always packed, **Spratt Bight Pathway and Beach** is the center of action in El Centro. The pedestrian walkway is lined with restaurants, hotels, and souvenir shops on one side and the beach on the other. Spratt Bight Beach is wide and pleasant, and boasts the clearest waters and whitest sands on the entire island. Offshore coral reefs break the tide and create a swimming pool effect, making the waters

1: Spratt Bight Beach; **2:** San Luis Beach; **3:** beachfront dessert; **4:** First Baptist Church in La Loma

safe for swimming for all ages. Because the duty-free shops sell *cerveza* and bottled liquor for absurdly cheap prices (the only things that are inexpensive in San Andrés), the walkway and beach are also party central until late into the night. Expect *champeta* dance shows and impromptu salsa parties.

Old Point Mangrove Regional Park

See the largest remaining mangrove forests left on the island at **Old Point Mangrove Regional Park** (Via San Luis, Km. 26, tel. 8/513-1130 or 8/512-6853, www.oldpoint. tours, 9am-5pm daily, COP$14,000). An extensive network of platform walkways allows visitors to explore the environs without disturbing the ecosystem. The park is also home to several unique species of animals, including Jamaican fruit-eating bats and green-breasted mangos, a type of hummingbird.

Supported by environmental agencies, **Ecofiwi Turismo Ecológico** (Vía San Luis, Mango Tree sector, cell tel. 316/567-4988 or 316/624-3396, ecofiwi@gmail.com, 9am-4pm daily, COP$80,000 pp) offers two-hour **kayak tours** of the mangroves at Old Point, led by local guides. The kayaks are completely transparent—allowing you close-ups of sealife such as upside-down jellyfish and sea cucumbers. You may also see seagrass beds and birds including pelicans and herons. Snorkeling is also part of the tour (equipment included).

★ Jardín Botánico

Extending over 8 hectares (20 acres) of wilderness, the **Jardín Botánico** (Vía Harmony Hill in front of Hotel Sol Caribe Campo, tel. 8/513-3390, 9am-5pm Mon.-Sat., 10am-5pm Sun., COP$10,000) is easily the most peaceful place on San Andrés. In this lovely botanical garden run by the Universidad Nacional, you can stroll along several paths and view trees and plants that grow in San Andrés. Of particular interest are the many fruit trees, like the ever-present and abundant breadfruit, as well as mango, mamey, *tamarindo*, and more.

There is also an impressive section on medicinal plants used by the locals including the *yarumo* (used for asthma) and herbs like oregano and achiote, which are used in cooking but also have medicinal properties. Several species of native animals live in the garden including blue lizards, iguanas, and the chincherry, a bright yellow bird that darts among the foliage.

From a five-story lookout tower, you can take in impressive views of the eastern coast of the island and its barrier reefs. Guided tours, included in the price of admission, are available (but not required), and take about an hour.

Casa Museo Isleña

Casa Museo Isleña (Km. 5 Av. Circunvalar, tel. 8/512-3419, 9am-5pm Mon.-Sat., 9am-6pm Sun., COP$10,000) is a reconstruction of a typical San Andrés-style wooden house that provides a glimpse into island life in the 19th century. After a required guided tour (15 minutes), your cheerful guide will tell you "now let's dance!" Reggae dancing is a rather strange component of the museum experience, but then again, it's hard to say no. Those smiling guides are a persuasive lot.

Cueva de Morgan (Morgan's Cave)

It would seem that all caves hidden along the coasts of San Andrés and Providencia are reputed to hold hidden treasures stashed away by notorious pirates. On the western side of San Andrés is the immensely popular **Cueva de Morgan** (Morgan's Cave, tel. 8/513-2946, 9am-6pm daily, COP$18,000), a sort of theme park where Welsh privateer/pirate Captain Henry Morgan allegedly stored some of his loot (but there's no evidence to prove this). There isn't much to see at the cave itself. That's why the park owners added on some reconstructions of traditional wooden island cabins that serve as mini-museums on island culture and ways of life. You visit these on a guided tour that is included in the cost. One is an art gallery where local dancers often perform to calypso beats. Also on the premises is the Coconut Museum, which is a house made out of coconuts. All in all, it's a tourist trap.

Paradise Farm

Job Saas, a native islander, operates **Paradise Farm** (Cove Seaside, Km. 11 Polly Higgs Rd., tel. 8/513-0798 or cell tel. 315/770-3904, donations accepted). Saas decided to transform the former standard family farm into one with a focus on environmental conservation and the preservation of local Raizal culture. Here you can see animals, such as iguanas and turtles, and plants that are threatened due to over-development on San Andrés. Saas uses the same farming techniques that his family has applied for decades and also runs a fresh produce stand in San Luis. Saas hosts local musical groups and, if you're lucky, you can hear his band play.

La Piscinita

Located in a cove on the rocky coastline is **La Piscinita** (Hwy. 1 near Via Tom Hooker), "the swimming pool," one of the west side's major attractions. You can snorkel right offshore in this natural pool, which is a good spot for children; they'll be able to spot a variety of brightly colored fish in the clear waters. Bread to feed the fish is included in the price of admission (COP$8,000) but consider abstaining; feeding bread to fish is harmful to them and the environment, and you can still swim with the fish, which are abundant here. Bring your own snorkel equipment unless you want to pay COP$10,000 per hour to rent the (very used) gear available here. An on-site restaurant serves overpriced island specialties, but the quality is decent.

Hoyo Soplador

At **Hoyo Soplador** on the island's southern tip, the attraction is a blowhole in the coral where, when the tide and winds are right, water sprays up, reaching heights of more than 10 meters (33 ft) and drenching those who stand beneath it. Expect lots of families and a cluster of overpriced restaurants. There is no fee to see the hole, but vendors will strongly encourage visitors to purchase something.

First Baptist Church

The white clapboard **First Baptist Church** (La Loma, no phone, services 7:30pm Thurs. and 10:30am Sun., COP$5,000 donation requested) was built in 1844 and rebuilt before the turn of the 20th century using wood imported from Alabama. It was the first Baptist church established on the island. A guide will tell you the history of the church and allow you to climb up to the bell tower for a commanding view of the island. The Sunday worship service can last several hours. Church members dress up for services, and you'll often see a smattering of tourists in the balcony on Sundays. This is an excellent place to hear gospel music.

Big Pond

Managed by a Rastafarian community, the **Big Pond** (La Loma, no phone, 9am-5pm daily, COP$5,000) is on the backside of La Loma, and home to a few domesticated caiman. They're usually lazing about in the sun near the edge of the pond and don't mind posing for photos. The caiman live in harmony with turtles, and herons watch the action from a tree nearby. You can order a beer at the bar, where reggae music blares from speakers. Entrance to Big Pond includes an escort/tour guide down to the waterfront and an explanation of local village life.

RECREATION
Beaches

You'll find San Andrés's best beaches just offshore on **Johnny Cay,** which boasts postcard-quality white sands and gleaming sapphire waters, as well as restaurants and bars overlooking the Caribbean. The only downside is that it's absolutely packed every day of the week.

Spratt Bight Beach, along El Centro's pedestrian walkway, is also popular and crowded, for good reason: It's quite spectacular as far as urban beaches go, with calm, crystalline waters and a wide swath of sand for sunbathing. People-watching here is also prime, and after sunset there tends to be a beach-party atmosphere.

South of El Centro, along the eastern coast of the island, are the beaches of San Luis. From **Rocky Cay Beach,** you can wade through the shallow waters to tiny Rocky Cay, just offshore. Just south of Rocky Cay Beach is **San Luis Beach,** a long stretch of golden sand adjacent to the town of San Luis. Both beaches are dotted with local-style restaurants and some of the island's top eateries, as well as reggae bars; relaxing in the Caribbean breeze backed by tropical tunes here makes you feel like you've found heaven on earth. San Luis beaches are much more laid-back than Spratt Bight or Johnny Cay, though the water quality isn't quite as crystalline, and there is stronger surf.

TOP EXPERIENCE

★ Snorkeling and Diving

Part of UNESCO's **Seaflower Biosphere Reserve,** San Andrés is surrounded by a well-preserved coral reef teeming with marinelife that makes it a diver's and snorkeler's paradise. On the eastern edge is the windward barrier, 15 kilometers (9.3 mi) long and 60-80 meters (200-260 ft) wide, with significant live coral communities. Beyond the reef, the shelf ends abruptly with a vertical wall that drops hundreds of meters. To the west, the windward barrier protects a large marine lagoon that has seagrass cover. The reef on the western, leeward side is a bit less well preserved due to tourism and boat traffic, but it also has beautiful patches of coral and significant marinelife. In all, the waters surrounding San Andrés include more than 40 species of corals and 131 species of fish. It'd common to see large schools of brightly colored jacks, tangs, grunts, and snapper, as well as barracudas, groupers, and parrot fish. Other marine creatures include turtles, stingrays, moray eels, octopus, squid, and lobster.

A unique feature of San Andrés is that the dives are very close to shore, which means a 10- to 30-minute boat ride maximum. The water is warm and has excellent visibility year-round. The best conditions for diving are January-May, with stronger winds in June and July. Popular dive sites are **The Pyramids,** a shallow 4-meter (13-foot) dive with striking anemones and fish; **Nirvana,** a reef at about 15 meters (50 ft) that teems with marinelife; **Trampa Tortuga,** a reef at about 15 meters (50 ft) with great visibility; and **Blue Wall,** on the eastern edge of the windward barrier, which starts at 6 meters (20 ft) and drops to 60 meters (200 ft). It contains magnificent corals and large tube sponges.

Most dive operators also offer short (three-hour) introductory courses for beginners, costing around COP$155,000 per person, which allow you to do an easy dive without being certified. There are also many opportunities to do full introductory and advanced courses with certification. A three-day open-water certification course typically costs around COP$800,000.

Highly recommended diving operators on San Andrés include **Banda** (Hotel Lord Pierre, tel. 8/513-1080, www.bandadiveshop.com, beginner's dive COP$185,000, open-water course COP$1,200,000), where friendly owner Gloria will help with everything, and German-run **Karibik** (Av. Newball 1-248, Edificio Galeón, tel. 8/512-0101 or cell tel. 318/863-9352, www.karibikdiver.com, two dives COP$190,000, night dive COP$160,000), which prides itself on its dive safety.

Snorkeling is particularly spectacular off of **Rose Cay,** aptly known as **The Aquarium (El Acuario)**—it has great visibility—which is usually visited on a tour along with Johnny Cay. Another popular snorkeling spot is **La Piscina,** on the western side of the island; a rocky cove creates a natural "swimming pool" effect. Snorkeling gear is available for rent at both locations for around COP$10,000, but bringing your own gear is a better idea.

1: turtle in the Seaflower Biosphere Reserve; **2:** kayaks for rent

Tours
★ JOHNNY CAY AND ROSE CAY TOUR

Located just a mile off the northern tip of the island and visible from the sands of Spratt Bight Beach, **Johnny Cay Regional Park** (COP$8,000 park admission fee) is a picture-perfect palm-fringed island surrounded by shimmering turquoise water. The 4-hectare (10-acre) nature reserve is easy to reach via a 15-minute *lancha* ride (COP$35,000 round-trip) from Sunrise Park, just next to the ferry terminal on Avenida Colombia in El Centro. These are organized as group tours and leave at 9am daily, returning around 4pm. It's best to book the tour a day ahead—your hotel may be able to do this for you—but you can also just show up ahead of time on the day of. You usually get a couple of hours on the beach before lunch (additional cost) is served by local restaurants in the shade of the palms; the freshly caught fried fish is good, if overpriced. Besides glorious beaches—the water here is shallow and calm for wading and swimming, and the sands good for sunbathing—Johnny Cay is also home to a significant iguana population that likes to hang out near the northern side of the island.

Most tours also include stops to view manta rays and old shipwrecks as well as an hour-long, post-lunch stop at **Rose Cay,** also known as **The Aquarium (El Acuario)**, located south of Johnny Cay off the eastern side of San Andrés. The waters surrounding the tiny island are calm and clear, and brightly colored tropical fish as well as a wide variety of crustaceans and echinoderms (think sea urchins and starfish) are plentiful in the offshore coral reef, making this the island's most popular snorkeling spot. Lockers are available and a restaurant-bar serves seafood specials and cold beer—but since there's no competition, be prepared for high prices. From The Aquarium, you can also walk through the shallow waters over to **Haynes Cay,** where there's a more developed eatery. Bring your own snorkeling gear and water socks for navigating the coral.

You can also negotiate with private boat owners from Sunrise Park if you want to head to the islands on your own time. This can be expensive for Johnny Cay for a day's charter (upward of COP$200,000) and so might be best for a group of friends. Once you have a private boat charter, however, you may be able to visit other sites as well.

OTHER TOURS

Another option to get out on the water is to take a glass-bottom boat tour with **San Andrés Unlimited** (Tom Hooker Rd. No. 8-75, South End, tel. 8/513-0035 or 8/513-0129, cell tel. 316/889-8701 or 310/625-2938, www.sanandresultd.com). During this tour, the boat makes several stops at coral reefs, sunken ships, and exotic islands. You'll be able to get in the water and snorkel several times to observe sealife. The nearly two-hour tour costs around COP$50,000 per person but is free for guests of their *posada* (inn) on the west side of the island (COP$150,000 d).

Kitesurfing

Balmy but strong breezes around San Andrés mean there are ample opportunities to kitesurf here. Located in El Centro and running a tent right on Spratt Bight Beach, **Club Kitesurf San Andres** (Cl. 1 No. 1B-24, cell tel. 312/280-6283, www.kitesurfsanandresschool.com) offers everything from basic skill classes (COP$1,500,000 pp, 3 hours) to rentals and sales for experienced kitesurfers. Down in San Luis, **Kitesurf Rocky Cay** (Cocoplum Hotel, cell tel. 317/462-6763, www.kiterockycay.com, 9am-5pm Mon.-Fri.) offers personalized one-on-one classes with local instructor Eliu Silvera (COP$150,000 per hour), plus sales and rentals.

ENTERTAINMENT
Nightlife

The *Coco loco* (a coconut filled with rum) is the island's cocktail of choice, and the mix of coconut water and liquor is quite delicious. You'll find them sold everywhere, so be sure to try one (an especially good one is offered at Donde Franz in San Luis).

EL CENTRO

The nightlife scene in El Centro mostly caters to visiting Colombians and international visitors, so venues here feel tourist-oriented rather than authentic. Clubs are generally open Thursday-Saturday during off-season and every night during high season. Cover charges range from free to COP$20,000 at most clubs, depending on season and night of the week. Things get cranking around 10pm.

The perennial top discos are **Coco Loco** (Av. Colombia, tel. 8/513-1047), **Discotek Extasis** (Hotel Sol Caribe, Av. Colón No. 2-77, tel. 8/512-3043), **Blue Deep** (Sunrise Hotel), and **Discoteca Coco's** (Hotel Tiuna). Over at **Bocca de Oro** (Cra. 1 No. 2252, cell tel. 316/426-2690), top local bands perform live on the weekends.

If you're not into the club scene, a good place to go is the **Beer Station** (Av. Colombia No. 55A1, cell tel. 316/471-7872, http://beerstation.com.co, noon-1am daily). With a sports bar theme indoors and a terrace overlooking Spratt Bight Beach outdoors, it's a popular option for a cold craft beer, cocktail, or light meal.

Another fun alternative is to join the impromptu street parties that take place along the Spratt Bight Pathway, fueled by cheap alcohol from the duty-free shops. The area around **Hotel Tiuna** (Av. Colombia No. 4-31, tel. 8/513-1351, www.tiuna.com) is especially rambunctious as revelers flow in and out of the hotel's top-floor Discoteca Coco's. An outdoor stage on Carrera 2, about three blocks in from Spratt Bight Beach, hosts live calypso and reggae bands most evenings around 8pm that are free and put on by the local government.

★ SAN LUIS

In San Luis, nightlife moves at a completely different pace than in El Centro. Sipping on a cold beer as reggae music pumps out of a loudspeaker accompanied by the sounds of the Caribbean as it laps the shore is the perfect way to end a day on the island. Several locally owned beachfront bars have turned this style of bar into an art form. At **Arnold's Place** (San Luis Beach, no phone, hours vary), family and friends come together for fresh fish barbecues on the weekends and stay for the after-party, which consists of enjoying rum drinks on the sand at sunset as reggae plays in the background. It's as friendly and local as it

Madguana Beach bar in San Luis

gets. Up on the north end of San Luis Beach is another great place for sunset, **Donde Franz** (San Luis Beach, no phone, hours vary). It serves cocktails—including a tasty *coco loco*—and fresh seafood appetizers both beachfront and upstairs on its rooftop dining room.

Madguana Beach (Rocky Cay Beach, no phone, hours vary, no cover) is a beachfront bar that makes a great spot for a night swim to the soothing sounds of reggae. It has a small stage for local and visiting musicians to perform on should the mood strike and keeps the party going until about midnight on weekends; otherwise, it typically closes about an hour or so after the sun sets.

Festivals and Events

San Andrés is host to several lively cultural fairs and festivals throughout the year, some well worth planning a trip around. These events are free and open to the public.

Around the first weekend in September, the **Green Moon Festival** is an explosion of reggae music and cultural activities that bring visiting musicians and artists from other Caribbean countries. During the last weekend in September, the **Ethnic Roots International Theatre Festival,** which aims to preserve the *nativo* cultures of Colombia through theater, comes to the island. Besides performances by local Raizal theater groups exploring their unique history, the festival also hosts groups from the Colombian mainland and showcases, for example, Afro-Colombian performances from the Pacific coast and indigenous presentations from the Guajira.

The entire month of November fills the island with parades and concerts for the **Fiestas Patronales de San Andrés,** which celebrates the island's patron saint, Saint Andrew. This colorful festival concludes with a coconut carnival and the crowing of a coconut queen.

SHOPPING

Ask any Colombian about San Andrés and they will tell you that one of the top things to

do here is to go shopping for cheap and duty-free goods. There are numerous duty-free shops in El Centro, where deals can be had on booze, perfume, watches, luggage, and the like. **La Riviera** is the best known of these. It has multiple locations close to the Spratt Bight walkway.

Casa BazArte (San Luis, cell tel. 317/375-4779, 9am-6pm daily) has local handicrafts like papier-mâché (a typical island handicraft), paintings, and wallets made of coconut fiber, among more common Colombian wares. Luly, the owner, can hook you up with local artisans if you're interested. The shop is located in a protected heritage house that's over 90 years old; its cheerful turquoise-blue paint job makes it hard to miss.

FOOD

Seafood is on every menu in every restaurant in San Andrés. Fish, *langosta* (lobster), *cangrejo* (crab), and *caracol* (conch) are likely to come from the waters off of San Andrés and Providencia. A Caribbean specialty you'll likely find only on San Andrés, Providencia, and Jamaica is *rondón* (rundown). This filling stew has fish or conch, pig's tail, dumplings, yuca, and other ingredients slow-cooked in coconut milk.

All restaurants are beach casual, and most of the larger ones accept credit cards. Service is often laid-back. Inexpensive local dishes such as *caracol* stew, lobster and crab empanadas, banana bread, and coconut and lime pies are sold by local women in the afternoon and night along **Spratt Bight Pathway** and also at the **entrance to the beach in San Luis** at the intersection of Sound Bay Road.

Seafood

Ask anyone in town to recommend the best seafood place on the island and a solid majority will mention ★ **La Regatta** (next to the Club Náutico, tel. 8/512-0437, www.restaurantelaregatta.com, noon-11pm daily, COP$50,000), an open-air restaurant that juts onto the water. For a sampling of the finest of San Andrés seafood, try their Fiesta Náutica,

Sustainable Seafood

which includes lobster tails, prawns, and crab, or go for the *tesoros del mar,* a filling seafood stew. The restaurant is festively decorated. Reservations are a good idea.

Near the north end of Spratt Bight Beach, the blue-collar **Fisherman's Place** (Cra. 9 No. 1-10 Spratt Bight, tel. 8/512-2774, 11:30am-4pm daily, COP$25,000) is a restaurant run by a cooperative of local fishers. Overlooking the water, it's also close to the airport runway. Try the *rondón* or the lobster.

Although the namesake for **Miss Celia** (Av. Newball and Av. Raizal, tel. 8/512-6495, restaurantemisscelia@gmail.com, noon-10pm daily, COP$30,000) passed away, the restaurant continues in this colorful spot. Located in front of the Club Náutico, Miss Celia is surrounded by flower gardens, and the sounds of local music add to the atmosphere. Lobster is the house specialty and there are also various rice dishes, some with shrimp, some vegetarian. For dessert there's homemade ice cream.

The Grog (Rocky Cay Beach, Cocoplum Hotel, tel. 8/513-3244 or cell tel. 311/232-3247, 11am-6pm Wed.-Mon., COP$40,000) is everything you'd expect in a Caribbean seafood restaurant. In an idyllic location on the beach and steps from the water, it's famous for its *cazuela de mariscos* (seafood stew). This is also a great spot for a grilled fish lunch on a lazy afternoon.

Tables right on the sand and hip tropical decor make ★ **Donde Francesca** (El Pirata Beach, San Luis, tel. 8/513-0163, cell tel. 318/616-8547, restaurantedondefrancesca@gmail.com, 11am-6pm daily, COP$50,000) an atmospheric spot to try out some of the island's gourmet fare. The acclaimed and varied menu includes *langosta tempura* (tempura lobster) and *pulpo reducción al balsámico* (balsamic octopus). The drinks, such as the gin cocktails and margaritas, are good too, and are made from non-bottled ingredients. It's easy to understand why folks arrive for lunch at 11am and don't leave until sundown.

In-the-know locals make a weekly visit to ★ **Restaurante Lydia** (Ground Rd. No. 64-65, San Luis, tel. 8/513-2192, COP$38,000) a ritual. It's open only for lunch (11am-5pm) Sundays and holiday Mondays. It gets great reviews from foodies and is considered one of the top places to try an authentic *rondón;* expect to be full for the rest of the day. Lydia's crab empanadas are also recommended.

Right on the beach is **El Paraiso** (Sound Bay No. 69-87, San Luis, tel. 8/513-3881, 9am-5pm daily, COP$35,000), a no-nonsense seafood restaurant where thick filets of freshly caught *pargo* are served with sides of breadfruit and coconut rice for decent prices. A variety of chairs and lounges are available to guests for after-lunch lounging on the sand and cocktailing the afternoon away.

The **Restaurante Punta Sur** (Km. 15.8, South End, tel. 8/513-0003, cell tel. 312/449-0301, 10am-6pm daily, COP$35,000) is close to the Hoyo Soplador. Sitting on the terrace when the waves come crashing in, it feels like you might be taken out to sea. Bring a bathing suit and chill out in their small pool overlooking the sea. *Arroz con camarones* (rice with shrimp) and grilled lobster are the most popular menu items at this well-liked spot on the southern tip of the island.

International

★ **Gourmet Shop** (Av. Newball in front of Parque de la Barracuda, tel. 8/512-9843, cell tel. 315/770-0140, noon-11pm Mon.-Sat., 6pm-11pm Sun., COP$35,000) is an excellent choice for a break from seafood (although it also makes an excellent grilled octopus). The salads, pasta, and other dishes are good, and on every table is a big bottle of imported spicy chili sauce. A wide variety of wine is for sale along the walls, and thousands of empty wine bottles decorate the ceiling.

Mr. Panino (Edificio Bread Fruit Local 106-7, tel. 8/512-3481 or 8/512-0549, 10:30am-10pm Mon.-Sat., 11am-4pm Sun., COP$40,000) is a reliable, somewhat up-scale Italian restaurant, popular at both lunch and dinner, but more pleasant in the evening. There is typically a set lunch menu of Colombian fare. It's nice to sit at the high wooden tables in the back. Try the *risotto con langostinos*, a prawn risotto that's a generous plate to share. Service can be chilly.

Margherita e Carbonara (Av. Colombia No. 1-93, tel. 8/512-1050, 11am-11pm daily, COP$35,000) gets packed at night during high season thanks to its prized location near the big hotels and nightclubs. Stick with the pasta and pizza at this boisterous family-style place.

It's a rarity to find vegetarian options in San Andrés, but **New Dawn Paradise** (Vía Tom Hooker No. 1-107, tel. 8/513-0015, cell tel. 314/444-9418, 11am-3pm Sun.-Fri., COP$15,000) delivers. This simple restaurant is in the modest home of super-friendly Enaida Veloza, who serves vegetarian hamburgers, salads, and the like, as well as baked goods. Many of the vegetables come from her prosperous organic garden.

Bakeries and Cafés

From the outside, ★ **Coffee Break** (Av. Colombia No. 3-59, in front of Parque de la Barracuda, tel. 8/512-1275, 7am-11pm daily) often appears empty or even closed. But when you go inside, it's almost always packed with visitors and locals alike sipping on Vietnamese coffee, munching on nachos, or smearing cream cheese on toasted bagels. Customers here take their time (likely because of the air-conditioning).

Part of the Casablanca Hotel, the groovy turquoise **Sea Watch Caffé** (Av. Colombia, tel. 8/512-4115, 7am-11pm daily, COP$25,000) is as close as it comes in Colombia to a New York-style coffee shop. Here you can have a leisurely breakfast as you watch the tourists file by on the walkway out front. Also on offer are pizza, hamburgers, ceviche, pasta, and desserts.

A bakery-café popular with both locals and visitors is **Bread Fruit Bakery** (Av. Francisco Newball No. 4-169, outside the Sunrise Hotel, tel. 8/512-6044, 7:30am-8:30pm Mon.-Sat.), named after the breadfruit tree, which is typical to the area. This solid breakfast spot offers outdoor seating and table service as well as freshly baked pastries to go.

ACCOMMODATIONS

On this island where tourism is king, lodging options are plentiful, except during high season (mid-December to mid-January, Holy Week, and, to a lesser extent, during school vacations June-July). Mid- to upper-range all-inclusive hotels are popular with Colombian families and couples but there is also an extensive network of *posadas nativas* (native guesthouses), owned and operated by locals, many of whom have deep roots on the island. Staying at a *posada nativa* is the best way to get to know the local culture.

Most visitors stay in El Centro, where beaches, restaurants, nightlife, and services are all in walking distance, but quiet San Luis or the village of La Loma are also pleasant options. This may require mastering public transportation or taking cabs if you want to go downtown, but renting a motor scooter, golf cart, or bicycle is also relatively easy.

The western side of the island has coral coastline instead of beaches, and the few hotels there cater mostly to divers, so this side feels more isolated.

El Centro

Boutique hotel ★ **Casa Harb** (Cl. 11 No. 10-83, tel. 8/512-6348, www.casaharb.com, COP$860,000 d) is by far the most luxurious place to stay in San Andrés. The six suites, lobby, dining area, and spa are thoughtfully decorated with fantastic art and furniture from Morocco to Malaysia, personally chosen by owner Jak Harb. The fabulous on-site restaurant is open to the public (but call first).

Just outside of El Centro in a more residential area, ★ **Posada Nativa Lizard House** (Av. 20 de Julio No. 189, tel. 8/512-5400, COP$40,000 dorm, COP$100,000 d) offers cozy rooms around a small but lush tropical patio. Ernesto, the owner, offers a wealth of information on the history of the islands and will direct you to authentic eateries in town. Right next door, ★ **Posada J&J Forbes**(Av. 20 de Julio, cell tel. 317/575-4379, COP$100,000 d) is a *posada nativa* run by a friendly young local couple. Their furnished apartment suites come with full kitchens and access to a rooftop terrace. The supermarket on the corner is handy, too.

On an unassuming street in a quiet neighborhood two blocks from the beach, **Hostal Mar y Mar** (Av. Colombia No. 1-32, Sarie Bay, cell tel. 317/783-6420, www.hostalmarymar.com, COP$140,000 d) offers 12 clean and comfortable rooms. Noise from airplanes may be a nuisance in the mornings.

The party-hearty set will enjoy **Hotel Tiuna** (Ave. Colombia No. 4-31, tel. 8/513-1351, www.tiuna.com, COP$383,000 d including breakfast and dinner). Located right on Spratt Bight Pathway across from the beach, this 158-room hotel has a classic Miami Beach vibe. The top-floor Discoteca Coco's draws crowds most nights of the week, and the two on-site restaurants, swimming pool, café, and movie theater make this more of a resort than a hotel. In addition to a basic plan that includes breakfast and dinner, there's also a Super Tiuna Plan that includes all meals and drinks (11am-11pm), plus entry to the disco and a trip to Johnny Cay, but this option requires a minimum four-night stay; inquire for price details.

The Colombian all-inclusive chain Decameron has several properties on the island. Arguably the best of them is the **Decameron Aquarium** (Av. Colombia No. 1-19, tel. 8/513-0707, www.decameron.co, COP$800,000 d), with a fantastic location just blocks from Spratt Bight Pathway and Beach and accommodations hovering over the water. During high season it gets crowded here, but in the off-season you may have the facilities—including open-air dining and a pool overlooking the Caribbean—practically to yourself. Guests can dine at other Decameron locations on the island, but may have to make reservations in advance, which can be a hassle. Wi-Fi is available at an additional cost.

Blindingly white **Hotel Casablanca** (Av. Colombia No. 3-59, tel. 8/512-4115, www.hotelcasablancasanandres.com, COP$780,000 d with breakfast) faces the Spratt Bight Pathway and overlooks the sea. Of its 91 rooms, 10 are *cabañas*. There is a small pool and, more importantly, a pool bar, Coco's. The hotel has three on-site restaurants. Casablanca gets mixed reviews, but is one of the better options along Spratt Bight.

The small hotels in the busy downtown are far more reasonably priced than those with a view to the sea and are just a few blocks away. The most popular choice for backpackers is the five-floor **El Viajero** (Av. 20 de Julio No. 3A-122, tel. 8/512-7497, www.elviajerohostels.com, COP$60,000 dorm, COP$250,000 d), which is part of an Uruguayan chain. It has several air-conditioned gender-separated dorms, as well as private rooms. The top-floor bar serves cold beer and assorted rum drinks, and there are several common areas with wireless Internet and computers. A small breakfast is included, and a kitchen is provided for guest use.

San Luis

★ **Breeze View and Culture** (Av. Loma Barrack, San Luis, cell. tel. 315/518-3258, COP$50,000 dorm, COP$100,000 d) is a comfortable *posada nativa* located right across the street from the sea and just down the hill from the Jardín Botánico. The five rooms here, including one with water views, are sparsely but comfortably decorated by Greg, who inherited the house from his mother. His front porch eatery, Greg's Place, has some of the best-priced fresh-fish lunch specials (COP$15,000) on the entire island.

Tucked away on a quiet lane is ★ **Villa Verde Camping** (Vía Tom Hooker 1A-24, cell tel. 315/770-0785, temporadasanandres@yahoo.es, COP$70,000 campsite, COP$110,000 d), a charming guesthouse that offers rooms in the owner's home, an inviting pool surrounded by trees, hammocks under the trees, and camping on the lush grass.

Brightly colored **Cocoplum Hotel** (Vía San Luis No. 43-49, tel. 8/513-2121, www.cocoplumhotel.com, COP$388,000 d) in the San Luis area has the most important feature for a beach hotel: It's actually on the beach, with rooms that are steps from the water. The rooms are colorful but basic, many have balconies, and the included breakfast is decent.

About five minutes from the beach, **Posada Buganvilla** (Vía Tom Hooker No. 3-41, cell tel. 315/303-5474 or 317/804-1952, posadabuganvilla@gmail.com, COP$180,000 d) is a cheerfully colored house in a quiet location, with four air-conditioned rooms, tile floors, and shared bathrooms. The guesthouse offers bikes for rent.

La Loma

This neighborhood, home to the island's highest point—hence the name La Loma (The Hill)—is situated in the interior of the island and is almost completely inhabited by English-speaking native islanders, some of whom run *posadas nativas*. A fine option is ★ **Coconut Paradise Lodge** (Vía La Loma, Claymount No. 50-05, tel. 8/513-2926 or cell tel. 301/543-2344, oldm26@hotmail.com, COP$90,000 d with breakfast), a beautiful turn-of-the-20th-century wooden home with just four rooms. It's close to the botanical gardens and the San Luis beaches. Try for

the top-floor room, which has great views and a refreshing breeze. Across the street is **Caribbean Refuge** (Vía La Loma, tel. 8/523-2878 or cell tel. 313/823-3587, COP$65,000 pp dorm, COP$140,000 d), run by Clemencia Livingston. It's a spotless, modern house (though lacking in charm), and Clemencia is a very gracious host.

West

For those interested in diving, ★ **Sunset Hotel** (Km. 13 Circunvalar, cell tel. 318/523-2286, www.sunsethotelspa.com, COP$255,000 d) is a great option on the quiet west side of the island. It has 16 bright and basic rooms that surround a small pool. While there is no beach, the hotel's dive shop, Sharky's, offers diving lessons and organizes diving excursions. You can go snorkeling in the waters across the street. Weeklong diving packages are a good option. Great sunsets are included at no extra cost. You can also rent bikes here.

INFORMATION AND SERVICES

A **tourist office** (Av. Newball, tel. 8/513-0801, 8am-noon and 2pm-6pm daily) is located downtown across from Club Náutico. Tourism bureau staff are also on hand at a **tourist information kiosk** (intersection of Av. Colombia and Av. 20 de Julio, 8am-7pm daily) on Spratt Bight Beach.

There is a small branch of **Universidad Nacional** (National University, San Luis, tel. 8/513-3310 or 8/513-3311, 8am-noon and 2pm-6pm Mon.-Fri.), and the library is open to the public. Anyone is welcome to work or read there.

TRANSPORTATION

San Andrés's **Aeropuerto Gustavo Rojas Pinillas** (ADZ) is about 2 kilometers (1.25 mi) northwest of El Centro, and very close to many hotels. Cabs to and from the airport cost COP$15,000. San Andrés is served by all the major Colombian airlines, with most options from Bogotá and Medellín. There are nonstop flights from Cartagena on **VivaColombia** (www.vivacolombia.co) and **Copa Airlines** (www.copaair.com); Copa also offers nonstop flights from Barranquilla and Panama City, with connections to and from several major Latin American cities including Lima, São Paulo, Santiago, and Mexico City.

Public buses serve the entire island; rides cost about COP$2,000 each way. To get to San Luis, flag down a bus from the Parque de la Barracuda just south of El Centro.

Renting a car is possible, but parking is scarce, distances are not far, and, more importantly, there are more fun options than driving a car. Most visitors rent moto scooters or heavy-duty, gas-powered golf carts referred to as **mulas** (literally, mules).

Millennium Rent A Car (Av. Newball, Parque de la Barracuda, tel. 8/512-3114, 10am-6pm daily) rents standard golf carts (COP$90,000 day) and *mulas* (COP$200,000 day). **Rent A Car Esmeralda** (Av. Colombia,

in front of Buxo del Caribe, tel. 8/513-1170 or cell tel. 315/303-7037, 10am-6pm daily) offers similar prices. Although you can rent both golf carts and *mulas* for multiple days, their use is prohibited after 6pm.

At **Renta de Motos T.T. 9** (Av. Boyacá, Calle las Proveedoras, tel. 315/749-8325), you can rent a motor scooter starting at COP$60,000 for the day.

Rent a bike at the **Bicycle Rental Shop** (Cra. 1B, Sector Punta Hansa, in front of Edificio Hansa Reef, cell tel. 318/328-1790 or 321/242-9328, 8am-6pm daily, COP$45,000/day).

Both taxis and *mototaxis* ply the main thoroughfares of El Centro as well as the Circunvalar between San Luis and El Centro. Within El Centro, you shouldn't pay more than COP$8,000 for a taxi or COP$4,000 for a *mototaxi*. Expect to pay around COP$20,000 for a taxi between El Centro and San Luis, or around COP$6,000 for a *mototaxi*.

Providencia and Santa Catalina

Of volcanic origin, Providencia and Santa Catalina are older islands than San Andrés, and more mountainous. But they are much smaller in area and population than it, having a total area of about 18 square kilometers (7 square mi) and a population of only 5,000. Only 300 people live on minuscule Santa Catalina, an island known as the "Island of Treasures" and which was once home to an English fort. Located about 90 kilometers (56 mi) north of San Andrés, these islands are the easygoing cousins of hyperactive San Andrés. Secluded palm-lined beaches, gorgeous turquoise Caribbean waters, mellow locals, fresh seafood, and rum drinks make it easy to become smitten with Providencia. Tiny Santa Catalina is home to historic Fort Warwick and a beautiful waterfront promenade.

Orientation

The two islands of Providencia and Santa

Catalina combined are about 7 kilometers long and 4 kilometers wide (4 mi by 2.5 mi). A ring road encircles the entire island of Providencia. The harbor/downtown area of Providencia is called **Santa Isabel** and is the center of island activity. Connected to the northwest corner of Providencia by a 200-meter (600-ft) pedestrian bridge is **Santa Catalina,** a tiny island without any motorized vehicles.

Other settlements on Providencia are usually referred to by the names of their beaches or bays. The main ones are on the western side of the island: **Manchineel Bay (Bahía Manzanillo),** on the southern end, which has some excellent beaches; **Southwest Bay (Bahía Suroeste);** and **Freshwater Bay (Bahía Aguadulce),** home to most of the island's hotels and restaurants. **Smoothwater Bay (Bahía Aguamansa),** on the southeastern edge of the island, is more remote.

Smoothwater is adjacent to **Bottom House (Casa Baja),** which is more residential. **Maracaibo** is on the northeast part of the island, between Santa Isabel and the airport. In the middle of the island is its highest point, **The Peak.**

★ PARQUE NACIONAL NATURAL OLD PROVIDENCE MCBEAN LAGOON

The **Parque Nacional Natural Old Providence McBean Lagoon** (office Jones Point, east of airport, tel. 8/514-8885 or 8/514-9003, www.parquesnacionales. gov.co, oldprovidence@parquesnacionales. gov.co, 9am-5pm daily, COP$18,000 non-Colombians, COP$11,000 Colombians, COP$5000 students) is a small national park on the northeast coast of the island. It occupies about 1,485 hectares/3,670 acres (1,390 hectares/3,435 acres of that is sea). Here you can observe five different ecosystems: coral reefs, seagrass beds, mangroves, dry tropical forests, and volcanic keys.

Just offshore, **Crab Cay** (Cayo Cangrejo) is one of the main attractions of the park, and it's a convenient spot for some splashing about in the incredibly clear, warm waters. This is a great place for some easy snorkeling; in addition to tropical fish, you may see manta rays or sea turtles. A short five-minute nature path takes you to the top of the island. A snack bar on Crab Cay sells water and snacks such as ceviche. It is open every day until around 1pm.

Boat tours, organized by all hotels and dive shops, motor around the coast of Providencia, stopping at beaches and at Crab Cay for snorkeling or swimming. These tours depart the hotels at around 9am each morning and cost about COP$40,000 per person. Once you disembark at Crab Cay you pay the park entry fee of COP$18,000. Following the stop at Crab Cay the boats go to Southwest Bay for a seafood lunch (not included in the price of the tour). Otherwise you can hire a boat yourself at around COP$350,000 total. Upon arrival at the island, you'll be required to pay the park entry fee. All hotels can arrange this more exclusive option.

The park's **Iron Wood Hill Trail** is a 3-kilometer (1.8-mi) round-trip nature trail along which you can explore the tropical dry forest landscape and see different types of lizards, birds, and flora. There are nice views from here of the coastline. This path is less popular than the hike to The Peak, but many find it more beautiful. Tourists are encouraged to go with a local guide arranged by the **park office** (Jones Point, east of airport, tel. 8/514-8885, 8/514-9003, www. parquesnacionales.gov.co, 8am-12:30pm and 2pm-6pm daily, COP$25,000 pp plus park entry fee), but the trail is straightforward, and most visitors simply head off on their own. Be sure to pay the park entry fee before leaving.

An additional activity is to hire a **kayak** and paddle to Crab Cay or through the park's McBean Lagoon mangroves. Passing through the mangroves you'll enter the **Oyster's Creek Lagoon,** where you'll see several species of birds, including blue and white herons and pelicans, as well as crabs, fish, and some unusual jellyfish. This is an interesting trip. Try to go early in the morning or late in the afternoon, as the sun can be brutal. Kayaks can be rented at the **Posada Coco Bay** (Maracaibo sector on the northeastern side of the island, tel. 8/514-8226, cell tel. 311/804-0373, www.posadacocobay.com, COP$60,000). A kayak with a guide costs COP$90,000, and for snorkeling equipment tack on another COP$10,000.

LIGHTHOUSE PROVIDENCIA

Lighthouse Providencia (Hoy's Hill, cell tel. 313/380-5866 or 318/758-1804, www. lighthouseprovidencia.com, 5pm-9pm Mon.-Sat.) is a cultural center/café that's worth a stop. It hosts a range of cultural activities,

1: aerial view of Providencia; **2:** kayaking through the mangroves at Parque Nacional Natural Old Providence McBean Lagoon; **3:** sailboat race at Manchineel Bay; **4:** horses cooling off at Southwest Bay

including art exhibitions and film showings, all with an environmental bent, including a film on the famous black crab migration that brings the island to a virtual standstill. Try to come for sunset, as the café terrace has spectacular views over the Caribbean Sea.

RECREATION
Beaches
The best beaches on Providencia can generally be found on the western side of the island. From Manchineel Bay (Bahía Manzanillo) on the southern end to Allan or Almond Bay in the northwest, they are each worth exploring if you have the time: the waters are calm, the sand golden, and there's always a refreshing breeze.

Manchineel Bay (Bahía Manzanillo), home to Roland Roots Bar, is an exotic beach where you can relax under the shade of a palm tree. (Be careful of falling coconuts.) In **Southwest Bay (Bahía Suroeste)**, there are a couple of hotels and restaurants nearby, and you can sometimes see horses cooling off in the water or people riding them along the shoreline. The beaches of **Freshwater Bay** are very convenient to several hotels and restaurants.

The beach at **Allan Bay (or Almond Bay)** is more remote. It's notable for its large octopus sculpture on the side of the road (you can't miss it) and nicely done walkway down to the beach from the ring road. The beach area is a public park, and there is a snack bar and stand where you can purchase handicrafts. You'll have to either drive to this beach or take a taxi.

A couple of coves on Santa Catalina have some secluded beaches on the path to Morgan's Head, and they offer snorkeling opportunities as well.

TOP EXPERIENCE

★ Snorkeling and Diving
Providencia, part of the **Seaflower Biosphere Reserve** and surrounded by a 32-kilometer-long (20-mi-long) barrier reef, is a fantastic place to dive or learn to dive. The water is always warm, and visibility is usually 25-35 meters (82-115 ft). The best time of year to dive is June-October. In January the water can be particularly rough.

Popular diving sites are **Felipe's Place,** comprising several ledges with significant coral and marinelife; **Turtle Rock,** a large rock at 20 meters (66 ft) covered with black coral; **Tete's Place,** teeming with fish; **Confusion,** with corals and sponges at 20-40 meters (66-131 ft); and **Nick's Place,** a deep crack in the island's shelf that starts at 18 meters (60 ft) and drops to 40 meters (131 ft). Good snorkeling can be done near **Cayo Cangrejo,** at the small islands of **Basalt** and **Palm Cays,** and around **Morgan's Head** in Santa Catalina, among other places.

The **Hotel Sirius** (Southwest Bay, tel. 8/514-8213, www.siriushotel.net) is serious about diving and offers a PADI certification (COP$950,000) that includes four open-water immersions over five days. It also offers a mini-course (COP$220,000) that includes a double-immersion excursion. Hotel Sirius's diving courses have an excellent reputation.

Felipe Diving (Freshwater Bay, cell tel. 316/628-6664 or 317/805-8684, www.felipediving.com) is also highly recommended. Its options include an open-water course (COP$890,000), and it also rents diving and snorkeling gear.

Snorkeling is a popular activity frequently offered on tours of Providencia and Santa Catalina, but it can also be done independently near **Morgan's Head** in Santa Catalina and **Freshwater Bay.** Bring your own gear or rent from Felipe Diving.

Kayaking
For kayak rentals and mangrove tours, contact guide **Israel Livingston Archbold** (cell tel. 318/587-7898). A two-hour tour for two people costs COP$130,000. Israel's tours depart from Posada Coco Bay in Maracaibo.

Hiking
★ THE PEAK
The Peak (El Pico) is the highest point (360 meters/1,181 ft) on Providencia, and the

360-degree views from this mountaintop are impressive. This hike takes about 1.5 hours to the top and less than an hour down. The path to The Peak begins in the middle of the island and meanders along relatively well-marked trails through tropical rainforest and tropical dry forest. You'll likely come across lizards, cotton trees, and maybe a friendly dog who will follow you up to the top and back.

From the top you'll be able to see the barrier reef that extends for 32 kilometers (20 mi) off of the east coast of the island. This reef is the second longest in the Caribbean and is part of the Parque Nacional Natural Old Providence McBean Lagoon.

To get to the trailhead, go to the Bottom House (Casa Baja) neighborhood in the southeastern corner of the island just to the east of Manchineel Bay. Although you may come across a sign pointing toward The Peak, roads are not well marked. Ask at your hotel for directions to the starting point.

At the beginning of the walk, follow a path straight ahead, veering to the right. Five minutes later, go right, before a two-story house. You'll then go left (not to the right of the concrete well). From here, you will pass a small garden, then follow a rocky creek, fording it several times. You'll go through a gate and eventually veer left as you begin climbing the hill. After you cross over a wooden bridge, the path becomes steep; hold onto the wooden handrails. Occasional signs identify some of the trees or fauna you might see along the way.

During rainy seasons, the path can become muddy and slippery. Make sure to bring a bottle of water with you. Guides are not necessary for this walk, but it's not impossible to get lost. All hotels can contract a guide for you, and this usually costs around COP$50,000.

Be careful of thorny cockspur trees along the route, which also harbor ferocious ants.

SANTA CATALINA

English colonists and privateers once ruled from atop Santa Catalina, keeping their eyes peeled for potential enemies—usually the Spanish Armada or competing Dutch pirates.

Today you can see remains from 17th-century English rule at **Fort Warwick,** adjacent to a big rock known as **Morgan's Head.** If you squint hard enough, it resembles the head of Henry Morgan, the notorious Welsh pirate and admiral of the Royal Navy who marauded the Spanish New World colonies during the mid-17th century; Morgan captured Santa Catalina from the Spaniards in 1670. Morgan's Head is next to **Morgan's Cave,** where the pirate supposedly hid his loot. You can go snorkeling inside the cave, where you may encounter the occasional (harmless) shark. Start this hike at the colorful pedestrian bridge that connects Providencia with Santa Catalina in the Santa Isabel area. When crossing the bridge, particularly in the evening, you may be able to spot graceful manta rays in the water. Once on Santa Catalina, take a left and follow the path.

Tours

Paradise Tours (Freshwater Bay, tel. 8/514-8283, cell tel. 311/605-0750, paradisetourscontact@gmail.com) is your one-stop shop, offering tours around the island and snorkeling, diving, and fishing excursions. One of its popular options is the Reefs and Snorkeling Tour (3-4 hours, 4-person min., COP$85,000), during which you boat to coral reefs around the island, exploring the underwater cities that exist just below the surface. Snorkeling equipment costs extra. A full-day trip to idyllic **El Faro Island** and reef, nine kilometers (5.6 mi) off of Providencia, costs COP$110,000. It's an excellent place for snorkeling in warm, crystalline waters.

On land, Paradise Tours offers several hiking options, such as to The Peak, where you can see coral reefs in the distance; to Manchineel Hill, where you might see wild orchids on your way; and to Iron Wood Hill in the Parque Nacional Natural Old Providence McBean Lagoon. These cost COP$85,000.

A popular excursion is to take a **boat tour** around the island. The tours, departing at around 9am and returning at 3pm, make several stops, including Crab Cay and Santa Catalina. Any hotel can assist you in arranging a tour; boats make the rounds to pick up tourists at various hotels. These tours cost around COP$50,000 per person and usually leave from Freshwater Bay. If you prefer, you can rent a boat for just yourself and your crew; that will cost up to COP$350,000.

Discover Old Providence (Bottom House, cell tel. 318/587-7898 or 316/761-5770, enjoyprovidence.pespo@gmail.com) offers fishing, hiking, and kayak tours in and around Providencia.

A recommended guide who can assist with transportation on the island is **Bernardo "Big Boy" Henry** (cell tel. 313/811-0121 or 311/853-5166, bbernardhenry@gmail.com). It generally costs about COP$25,000 to get from one part of the island to the other.

ENTERTAINMENT
Nightlife

Bob Marley never seems to fall out of fashion at **Roland Roots Bar** (Manchineel Bay, tel. 8/514-8417, hours vary). This spot beneath the coconut palms is the perfect place to spend a lazy, sunny day in Providencia. Or go at night, when you can order your rum drink to go and walk to the beach and stargaze, or hang out by a bonfire. On Sunday afternoons it's a popular spot for locals. Roland's competition is **Richard's Place** on the beach in Southwest Bay. You can broaden your Caribbean music horizons here with reggae roots, rocksteady, ska calypso, ragamuffin, and soca dub—but more often than not, it's Marley on the sound system. Both bars serve fried fish during the day.

Festivals and Events

In early January of each year (usually a Saturday), the Parque Nacional Natural Old Providence McBean Lagoon organizes the colorful **Festival del Chub** (tel. 8/514-8885 or 8/514-9003, Jan.). Chub is a plentiful but not very popular fish (it can have a strong aroma). The purpose of the festival is to encourage fishers and consumers to choose

chub instead of other fish such as red snapper, the stocks of which have been depleted throughout the Caribbean. The festival is held at Rocky Point (Punta Rocosa), where chub is widely eaten. In addition to the food component, which features dishes like chub burgers and chub ceviche, there is also a sailing race from Southwest Bay to Manzanillo. It's fun to hang out at **Roland Roots Bar** (Manchineel Bay, tel. 8/514-8417) in the morning to watch the sailors ready their boats for the race.

Between April and August each year the **black crab migration** takes place. This species of crab lives in the mountainous interior of the island for most of the year, but when the rainy season begins (usually April or May) thousands of the female crabs, carrying up to 120,000 eggs each, make an arduous journey to the sea to deposit their eggs. The migration peaks during nighttime hours, so watch your step. More crabs can be seen on the western side of the island. A second migration occurs a few weeks later, when the young crabs make their trip from the sea up to the mountain. During both migrations, the main road on the island may be closed—enforced by military personnel—as a means of protecting the crabs from vehicles.

SHOPPING

Kalaloo Point Café-Boutique (near Halley View lookout, eastern side of the island, tel. 8/514-8592 or cell tel. 317/387-6448, 10am-8pm Mon.-Sat.) is a cute shop and café in a wooden house that sells tropical dresses by a Colombian designer and various knickknacks. There's also a small library.

FOOD

Providencia is synonymous with fresh Caribbean seafood. Many restaurants in Providencia do not accept credit cards. Hotel restaurants are open every day, while others often close on Sundays.

Freshwater Bay (Bahía Aguadulce)

★ **Caribbean Place** (tel. 8/514-8698, noon-3pm and 6pm-10pm Mon.-Sat., COP$30,000), also known as "Donde Martin," is one of the best seafood spots in Providencia. Try the fish in ginger-butter sauce or the coconut shrimp, and, for dessert, the coconut pie. Cheerfully decorated, it's a great choice for both lunch and dinner.

For a pizza night, try **Blue Coral** (tel. 8/514-8718, 11am-3pm and 6pm-9pm Mon.-Sat., COP$20,000). Though not out of this world, the pizzas and pastas here can taste exotic after several days of seafood. Service is lackluster.

Morgan's Market (8am-noon and 3pm-8pm Mon.-Fri., 9am-noon and 4pm-8pm Sat.-Sun.) is one of the main grocery stores on the island. It's hard to miss this hub of activity. There's a sandwich and juice stand inside as well.

Southwest Bay (Bahía Suroeste)

★ **Café Studio** (on ring road, tel. 8/514-9076, 11am-10pm Mon.-Sat., COP$30,000), on the side of the road near Southwest Bay, is a favorite among visitors—and not just because of its trademark cappuccino pie. Everything is good here, it's open for both lunch and dinner, and it's the island's best spot for afternoon coffee and dessert. Café Studio has a varied

menu with pastas, interesting seafood dishes, and salads. An awesome blues soundtrack plays in the background. It's run by a local and his Canadian wife.

★ **Miss Mary Hotel** (tel. 8/514-8454, noon-3pm and 6pm-9pm daily, COP$30,000) offers an exotic menu different from most of the other restaurants on the island, with hummus and other vegetarian options galore. The open-air restaurant overlooks the beach. On the beach nearby is **Restaurante Arturo** (cell tel. 317/620-0814, 11am-5pm daily, COP$25,000), where the specialty is *rondón*. It's also open-air and has a relaxed atmosphere.

Maracaibo

The ★ **Deep Blue Hotel Restaurant** (Maracaibo Bay, tel. 8/514-8423 or cell tell. 315/324-8443, www.hoteldeepblue.com, noon-3pm and 6pm-10pm daily, COP$45,000) is the most elegant and pricey restaurant on the island, and open to the general public. Menu items, often Caribbean seafood, are innovative and beautifully presented, and the service is excellent. An impossibly beautiful setting in a swanky dining room overlooking the sea makes this the perfect place for a special dinner.

view from Miss Mary Hotel

SAN ANDRÉS AND PROVIDENCIA
PROVIDENCIA AND SANTA CATALINA

Santa Isabel and Santa Catalina

Old Providence Taste (Old Town Bay, to the west of Santa Isabel, tel. 8/514-9028 or cell tel. 311/264-6789, 11:30am-3pm Mon.-Sat., COP$25,000), on the beach to the west of Santa Isabel, is run by a local sustainable seafood and farming co-op. Each day they offer a different menu depending on what fishers and farmers bring in. It's the best deal on the island. They can also organize visits to farms and excursions with local fishers.

For an evening out in Santa Catalina, try ★ **Sea Star Gourmet** (Santa Catalina, cell tel. 316/824-0451, noon-4pm and 6:30pm-9pm Mon.-Fri., noon-4pm Sun., COP$35,000), an open-air restaurant with fine service where you can feast on fish fillets, lobster bathed in a coconut-ginger sauce, or *arroz con cangrejo* (crab stir-fry).

A quirky option is **Don Olivo** (Santa Catalina, cell tel. 310/230-5260), which is made up of a few small tables in front of a wooden house. Monsieur Olivier and his Colombian wife, Amparo, serve Caribbean dishes with a French flair. You have to ring the bell for service, and it's best to call first. Expect to be regaled with stories.

ACCOMMODATIONS

Providencia and Santa Catalina offer an array of interesting and comfortable accommodations. Most options are in Freshwater Bay, but each area on this enchanting island has its charms. Note that Internet service is unreliable, and it's best to communicate with hotels via phone call or text message (rather than email) for reservations and inquiries.

Freshwater Bay (Bahía Aguadulce)

Three affiliated locations of the all-inclusive Decameron chain are in Freshwater Bay, but they're locally operated. The least expensive option is **Relax** (Freshwater Bay, tel. 8/514-8087, COP$250,000 d). It has a small pool, hot water, and eight rooms, and is near a couple of restaurants and stores. It's across the road from the beach. **Miss Elma** (Freshwater Bay, tel. 8/514-8229 or 8/514-8854 or cell tel. 310/566-3773, COP$290,000 d) has just six rooms, all of which overlook the sea, and a restaurant on the beach. **Hotel Posada del Mar** (Freshwater Bay, tel. 8/514-8052, www.posadadelmarprovidencia.com, COP$300,000 d) is a 24-room hotel with air-conditioning and a pool. Instead of a beach, a grassy lawn overlooks the water.

Somewhat far from everything is the **Posada Refugio de la Luna** (Bluff, tel. 8/514-8460, providenciarefugiodelaluna@gmail.com, COP$260,000 d), a guesthouse with just one comfortable and spacious room. Carmeni, the owner, is a papier-mâché artist; her studio is upstairs.

Southwest Bay (Bahía Suroeste)

★ **Hotel Sirius** (tel. 8/514-8213 or cell tel. 318/743-5367, www.siriushotel.net, COP$350,000 d) is a beachside hotel that specializes in diving and snorkeling excursions and offers guests free rides in a glass-bottomed boat. It has some huge rooms, and the friendly manager will make every effort to ensure you have a pleasant stay in Providencia.

Cabañas Miss Mary (tel. 8/514-8454, hotelmissmary@yahoo.com, COP$250,000 d) is just steps from the beach in the southwest part of the island. It has eight rooms, five of which have beach views.

Smoothwater Bay (Bahía Aguamansa)

English writer Sam Cuming (author of *A Short History of Providence and San Andrés*) owns ★ **Windy View Guesthouse** (Bottom House, tel. 8/514-8750 or cell tel. 310/589-4888, www.windyviewprovidence.blogspot.com or www.providencewindyview.com, COP$250,000 d). This gorgeous spot with two rooms and a nautical feel is brimming with books.

Casa Posada Angels (Smoothwater Bay, cell tel. 321/414-5241, anniprovi@gmail.com, COP$80,000 pp) is a guesthouse managed by

Anni, an expat journalist from New Zealand who has lived in the islands for many years. There is one small cabin and a room in the main house. Across the street is a rickety pier and water access that nobody else seems to know about.

For cute accommodations in an A-frame house next to a big mango tree, hang your hat at **Posada Miss Rossy** (Almond Bay, tel. 8/514-8327 or cell tel. 316/315-2350, COP$85,000 pp). There is one room with a double bed and a room with two twins, perfect for a small group.

Maracaibo

By far the most luxurious option on Providencia is ★ **Deep Blue** (Maracaibo Bay, tel. 8/514-8423, www.hoteldeepblue. com, COP$675,000 d). It has 13 rooms of various types, each with a view, and some with Jacuzzis. A deck with a small pool provides spectacular views of the water. The friendly and professional staff can organize interesting day trips to nearby islands. Note there's no beach, and unless you plan on dining exclusively at Deep Blue's elegant restaurant, you'll need to find transportation to other eateries on the island.

Located directly over the lapping waters on the eastern side of Providencia, **Posada Coco Bay** (Maracaibo, tel. 8/514-8903 or 8/514-8226, posadacocobay@gmail.com, www.posadacocobay.com, COP$180,000 d) is a small guesthouse with five comfortable rooms, three of which are on the water side. The other two (more spacious) options are across the street. You can go snorkeling just outside the hotel, and you can rent kayaks here, but there is no beach. You must rent a golf cart or *mula* to get to island restaurants and beaches.

Santa Isabel and Santa Catalina

The **Hotel Old Providence** (Santa Isabel, tel. 8/514-8691 or 8/514-8094, COP$155,000 d) is the only option in the "town" area of Providencia. It's close to Santa Catalina

and offers basic, comfortable rooms with air-conditioning.

★ **Posada Sunshine Paradise** (Santa Catalina, tel. 8/514-8208 or cell tel. 311/227-0333, COP$180,000 d) is a charming guesthouse surrounded by flower gardens, and has four clean rooms. A major selling point is the warm hospitality of the owner, Francisca.

Posada Santa Catalina (Santa Catalina, tel. 8/514-8392 or cell tel. 310/842-3278, www.posadasantacatalina.blogspot.com, COP$350,000 pp) uses solar panels for electricity, a rarity in the islands. This guesthouse offers five large rooms, with good beds, set amid fruit trees. The friendly owners grow the medicinal noni fruit here, as well as unusual herbs for teas; you might be able to try some.

INFORMATION AND SERVICES

There is a **tourist office** (Santa Isabel, tel. 8/514-8054, ext. 12, www.providencia.gov.co, 8am-noon and 2pm-6pm Mon.-Fri.) in the town area near the port. It may be able to assist with accommodations, including *posadas nativas* (guesthouses owned and operated by locals) and give you some maps. The town has a bank, an ATM, and an Internet café.

In case of an emergency the police can be reached at 112 or 8/514-8000. For medical emergencies, call 125.

Many hotels on the island sell *A Short History of Providence and San Andrés* (COP$30,000), by resident author Sam Cuming. It's a good read for those interested in the mostly forgotten history of these tiny islands.

TRANSPORTATION

There are two ways to travel to Providencia: by plane or by fast catamaran boat service from San Andrés.

Satena (Centro Comercial New Point, Local 206, San Andrés, tel. 8/512-1403 or 8/514-9257, www.satena.com) offers two daily flights—one early-morning flight and one in the late afternoon—to Providencia's **Aeropuerto El Embrujo** (PVA), which is near the Parque Nacional Natural Old Providencia McBean Lagoon. Charter flights are usually organized by **Decameron** (Colombian toll-free tel. 01/800-051-0765, www.decameron.co) from San Andrés to Providencia. All flights are on small propeller planes, and there are strict weight limitations. Passengers are only allowed 10 kilograms (22 pounds) in their checked baggage, and each passenger is required to be weighed upon check-in along with their carry-on bag, which makes for an amusing photo op. The average weight per passenger cannot exceed 80 kilograms (176 pounds), including luggage. The flight takes about 35 minutes.

The **Catamaran Sensation** (tel. 8/512-3675 or cell tel. 318/347-2336, www.catamaransanandresyprovidencia.com, COP$200,000 one-way, COP$380,000 round-trip) provides **fast boat service** between San Andrés and Providencia. The trip takes approximately four hours from San Andrés to Providencia (and three hours in the other direction). It provides service Sunday-Monday and Wednesday-Friday during low season. There is greater frequency during high season. Boats leave San Andrés at 8am from the Muelle Toninos and depart Providencia from the docks in Santa Isabel at 2:30pm. The catamaran service, while cheaper than air travel, often gets ghastly reviews due to the rough seas and resulting seasickness among the passengers. When the winds are strong and the waters are choppy between the two islands, especially June-July and again December-January, the ride can be extremely rough, requiring boat attendants to constantly circulate among the passengers to distribute seasickness bags. This is especially true on the San Andrés-to-Providencia leg. Waters are normally calmer traveling the other direction.

Taxis are expensive in Providencia, costing around COP$20,000 no matter where you go. *Mototaxis* (motorcycle taxis) are much cheaper and you can find them almost anywhere. You can also flag down passing vehicles and hitchhike (expect to pay a small fee). You can rent *mulas* (gasoline-powered golf carts, COP$150,000 per day) and motorbikes (COP$100,000 per day) in Providencia. All hotels can arrange this. Reputable rental agencies include **Renta Car y Motos Old Providence** (Santa Isabel, tel. 8/514-8369 or cell tel. 313/450-4833, 9am-6pm Mon.-Sat.) and **B&Q Providence Center Hans Bush Felipe** (cell tel. 311/561-1537, hours vary).

Background

The Landscape

Colombia covers a land area of 1.14 million square kilometers (440,000 sq mi), roughly the size of Texas and California combined, making it the fourth-largest South American country in area after Brazil, Argentina, and Peru. It is located in the northwest corner of South America, with seacoast on both the Pacific and the Atlantic, and it borders Venezuela, Brazil, Peru, Ecuador, and Panama. The Amazonian departments of Putumayo, Caquetá, Amazonas, and Vaupés in the south of the country straddle the equator.

For a country of its size, Colombia has an astonishing variety of

landscapes, including the dense rainforests of the Amazon and the Pacific coast, the vast grassland plains of the Llanos, the lofty Andes Mountains, and the Caribbean islands of San Andrés and Providencia. Colombia's mountainous regions themselves hold a succession of vertically layered landscapes: tropical rainforests at their base, followed by cloud forests at higher elevations, topped by the unique tropical high mountain *páramo* (highland moor) above 3,500 meters (11,480 ft). The country boasts several peaks higher than 5,000 meters (16,400 ft), including Nevado del Ruiz (5,325 meters/17,470 ft) and Pico Cristóbal Colón (5,776 meters/18,950 ft).

GEOGRAPHY

Colombia's Caribbean coast runs 1,760 kilometers (1,100 mi) from the border of Panama to Venezuela, just longer than the California coast. However, the term "Caribe" or "Región Caribe" refers to much more than the narrow strip of coast; it encompasses basically all of Colombia north of the Andes, including a vast area of plains. This region covers 15 percent of the surface of Colombia and is home to 20 percent of the population.

The terrain is mostly low-lying and undulating. Near the border with Panama, the land is covered by dense tropical forests, similar to those on the Pacific coast. Farther east is the Golfo de Urabá, a large, shallow bay. Between the Golfo de Urabá and Cartagena is the Golfo de Morrosquillo, a broad inlet that is 50 kilometers (31 mi) wide. Off the shore of the Golfo de Morrosquillo are two small archipelagos, the Islas de San Bernardo and the Islas del Rosario, with beautiful coral reefs. Inland to the south is a large area of savannas in the departments of Córdoba and Sucre largely devoted to cattle ranching. This area was once covered by dry tropical forests, which have been largely felled.

Bahía de Cartagena, farther east, is a magnificent deep bay that caught the attention of the early Spanish explorers. To the southeast of Cartagena is the lower valley of the Magdalena and Cauca Rivers, a vast expanse of low-lying lagoons and lands prone to seasonal flooding. The Río Magdalena flows into the Caribbean east of Cartagena at the port city of Barranquilla. Farther to the east along the coast is a major mountain range, the Sierra Nevada de Santa Marta. It was formed by the collision of the South American plate and the Caribbean plate to the north and is entirely independent of the Andes. This range is home to Colombia's two highest peaks, Pico Cristóbal Colón and Pico Bolívar (5,776 meters/18,950 ft), and is considered the highest coastal mountain range in the world. The Sierra Nevada de Santa Marta contains the same range of vertically layered landscapes as the Andes, from low-lying tropical forest through cloud forest, Andean forests, *páramo*, and glaciers. There are eight peaks with elevations greater than 5,000 meters (16,400 ft).

Northeast of the Sierra Nevada de Santa Marta is La Guajira, an arid peninsula jutting into the Caribbean. Punta Gallinas, at the tip of La Guajira, is the northernmost point in South America. There are a few low-lying mountain ranges in La Guajira, such as the Serranía de la Macuira (864 meters/2,835 ft), which is covered with rainforest. The Sierra Nevada de Santa Marta and Serranía de la Macuira are biological islands, and their upper reaches are home to numerous endemic species that evolved in isolation.

CLIMATE

Colombia has a typically tropical climate, with no change of seasons. Climate is related primarily to elevation, and there are defined annual precipitation patterns.

Cartagena, which is at sea level, has an average temperature of 27.5°C (81.5°F); Medellín, which is at 1,600 meters (5,250 ft), has an average temperature of 22°C (71.5°F); and the capital city of Bogotá, which is built

---

Colombia's National Parks

Parque Nacional Natural Tayrona

From undisturbed coral reefs to the Amazonian jungle to snow-covered mountain ranges, Colombia's national park system is a treasure, and making the effort to visit the parks is worthwhile for any visitor. The country's system of natural parks and protected areas covers more than 14 million hectares (34.6 million acres), around 13.4 percent of the country. It includes 43 Parques Nacionales Naturales (National Natural Parks), which are areas of major ecological interest that have remained largely untouched by human intervention, and 12 Santuarios de Flora y Fauna (Flora and Fauna Sanctuaries), areas that are devoted to the preservation of specific ecosystems. Of the 43 parks, 24 are open for tourism. The rest are officially off-limits, due to lack of infrastructure, security concerns, or in order to respect the territory of indigenous communities.

In 1960, PNN Cueva de los Guácharos, in the southwest, was the first park to be established. The number of parks steadily increased, especially from 1986 to 1990 when President Virgilio Barco doubled the park holdings from roughly 5 million hectares to 10 million hectares (12 million to 24 million acres). In 2013 President Juan Manuel Santos doubled the size of the PNN Serranía de Chiribiquete to its present 2.8 million hectares (7 million acres), or three times the size of Yellowstone National Park.

Charged with the considerable task of administering this huge system are a mere 430 rangers—roughly one person for every 33,000 hectares (82,000 acres). Rangers face a great challenge in protecting the parks against threats related to human encroachment, particularly cattle ranching and the planting of illicit crops. There are other threats as well, such as illegal mining and logging. Paradoxically, what has preserved many of the parks until now has been the lack of security due to Colombia's internal conflict. As security conditions improve, there will be increasing pressure on these natural habitats. The Parks Service is actively engaging with the communities that live near the parks and is transferring the operation of much of the ecotourism infrastructure to community-based organizations as part of an effort to enlist local communities in the preservation of the land.

Entry permits and entry fees are only required in a handful of highly visited parks, such as Parque Nacional Natural Tayrona. At these, you will automatically be charged if you book lodging in advance, or if not, upon arrival. If you want to be meticulous, you can obtain the entry permit and pay entry fees in advance by contacting the **Parques Nacionales** (tel. 1/353-2400, www.parquesnacionales.gov.co) in Bogotá.

at 2,625 meters (8,612 ft), has an average temperature of 13.5°C (56°F).

In the mountainous areas, temperature decreases approximately six degrees Celsius per every 1,000 meters (3,280 ft) of elevation (or three degrees Fahrenheit per every 1,000 ft). The common designations for the altitudinal zones are as follows: *tierra caliente* (hot lands) is anywhere below 1,000 meters of elevation; *tierra templada* (temperate lands) is anywhere between 1,000 and 2,000 meters; and *tierra fría* (cold land) is anywhere above 2,000 meters (6,562 ft). Roughly 80 percent of the country is *tierra caliente,* 10 percent is *tierra templada,* and 7 percent is *tierra fría.*

Precipitation patterns vary throughout the country. On the Caribbean coast, the dry period is December-April and the rainy season is May-November. In the Pacific it rains almost the entire year, but there is a slight dry spell December-March. In the Andean region, there are generally two periods of *verano* (dry season, literally "summer"), December-March and June-September, and two periods of *invierno* (rainy season, literally "winter"), in April-May and October-November. In the Llanos, there are two very marked seasons: a very dry *verano* November-March and a very wet *invierno* April-October. In the Amazon, it rains almost the entire year, but there is a slight dry spell August-October.

Extreme weather in Colombia is rare, but the country is susceptible to weather phenomena such as El Niño or La Niña, when temperatures in the Pacific Ocean rise or fall, respectively.

San Andrés and Providencia are occasionally, and the Caribbean mainland of Colombia rarely, in the path of Atlantic hurricanes August-October.

Plants and Animals

When it comes to biodiversity, Colombia is a place of superlatives. Though representing only 0.2 percent of the earth's surface, it is home to about 10 percent of all the species in the world. The country has an estimated 55,000 plant species, including 3,500 species of orchids. Only Brazil, with seven times the land surface, has as many plant species. Colombia is the country with the greatest number of bird species in the world—about 1,800. It's also home to about 3,200 fish, 750 amphibian species, 500 reptile species, and 450 mammal species. No wonder Colombia was designated as one of 17 so-called megadiverse countries, a select club of countries that are home to an outsized proportion of the world's biodiversity. Other megadiverse countries include Australia, Brazil, China, Democratic Republic of Congo, Indonesia, Madagascar, Mexico, the United States, and South Africa.

This enormous biodiversity is the result of Colombia's location in the tropics, where year-round sunlight and high precipitation are conducive to plant growth, plus the country's mountainous topography with numerous climatic zones and microclimates that have created biological islands where species have evolved in relative isolation. Furthermore, the recent ice ages were not as severe in this part of the world, and as a result many ancient species were preserved. Finally, Colombia's location at the crossroads of Central and South America has further enriched the country's biodiversity.

RAINFOREST

Rainforests are among the most complex ecosystems on Earth. They have a layered structure with towering trees that soar 30-40 meters high (100-130 ft) to form the forest's canopy. Some of the most common rainforest trees are the ceiba, mahogany, myrtle, laurel, acacia, and rubber trees. Occasionally, particularly high trees known as *emergentes* pierce the canopy, reaching as high up as 60 meters

Colombian Fruits

Colombia is a land bursting with exotic fruit. Sold from the back of pickup trucks by farmers on the roadside, overflowing at stalls in colorful markets in every town and village, lined up in neat rows in the produce section at fancy grocery stores and at juice stands—just about anywhere you go, delicious fruit is in reach.

You know pineapples, papayas, mangoes, and bananas, but be sure to try these tropical delights that you may not have encountered outside of Colombia.

- *Chirimoya* (cherimoya): This green fruit that resembles a smooth artichoke is covered with a smooth, silky skin and filled with delectable, sweet pulp.

- *Granadilla:* Crack open this orange-yellow fruit and slurp down the slimy gray contents, seeds and all. It's delicious.

- *Guanábana* (soursop): By far the strangest-looking fruit, soursops resemble prehistoric dinosaur eggs. Inside the large green spiky fruit is a milky and slimy flesh. *Guanábana* is great in juices and desserts.

- *Higo* (prickly pear): This green fruit comes from cactus plants and has sweet, if tough, orange-colored meat.

- *Mamoncillo:* Tough-skinned grapes (don't eat the skin), *mamoncillos* are usually sold only at street markets.

- *Mangostino* (mangosteen): Crack open a deep-purple mangosteen and enjoy the sweet segments inside. They're full of antioxidants.

- *Níspero* (sapodilla): A fruit with a deep brown color that tastes like a prepared sweet.

- *Pitahaya* (dragon fruit): Looking like a yellow grenade, *pitahayas* have a sweet white meat inside.

- *Uchuva* (Cape gooseberry): Known in English as Cape gooseberries, these tart yellow berries are a cousin of the tomato and are tasty on their own or in salads, but are often used in jams and sweets.

(200 ft). Below the canopy is the *sotobosque*, a middle layer of smaller trees and palms that vie for the sunlight filtering in through the canopy. In the canopy and *sotobosque* there are many epiphytes (plants such as orchids and bromeliads) that have adapted to live on top of trees so as to be nearer to the sunlight. Near the ground live plants that require little sunlight, including ferns, grasses, and many types of fungi. The two main rainforests in Colombia, the Amazon and the Chocó, have the same layered structure, though they have some differences in their flora and fauna.

The Amazon rainforest is home to an impressive array of vertebrates. Over millennia, a large number of canopy-dwelling species evolved. Monkeys, such as the large and extremely agile spider monkey, the woolly monkey, and the howler monkey, evolved prehensile tails that allowed them to move easily from branch to branch. Anteaters, such as the tamandua and the *oso mielero* (giant anteater) and the incredibly cute *kinkajú* (kinkajou), also developed prehensile tails. Other inhabitants of the canopy include sloths, such as the adorable three-toed sloth, whose strategy is not agility but passivity: It eats tree vegetation and is covered with algae that gradually turns the animal green to allow for good camouflage. The canopy is also home to myriad bats and many birds, including exotic eagles, curassows, toucans, woodpeckers, cotingas, and macaws.

Notable is the majestic harpy eagle, with

powerful claws and the ability to fly unencumbered through the canopy. It preys on monkeys and sloths, which it kills with the force of its claws. The *tigrillo* (tiger cat) is a small and extremely endangered species. It has a long tail that helps with its balance as it moves from tree to tree.

On the ground, large vertebrates include the extremely endangered tapir, an ancient mammal species that can grow two meters long (over six ft) and weigh 300 kilograms (660 pounds). It is equally at ease on land as in the water. Other land mammals include the giant armadillo, giant anteater, deer, and boars, such as the *saíno* and *pecarí*. Smaller mammals include the *guatín* and *borugo,* both rodents. These animals are often prey to the puma and jaguar, both of which inhabit the Amazon but are difficult to observe in the wild.

The rivers of the Amazon are home to more than 1,500 species of fish, including endangered pirarucu, one of the largest freshwater fishes on Earth. There are also dolphins, both pink and gray. The former evolved separately from the oceangoing dolphins when the Amazon was an inland sea. The Amazonian gray dolphins are sea dolphins that adapted to living in freshwater. Other aquatic mammals include the highly endangered manatee and otters.

The Chocó rainforest is particularly rich in palms, of which 120 species have been identified. In fact, it is sometimes referred to as the "Land of the Palms." The forest also abounds in cycads, ancient plants that have a stout trunk and crowns of hard, stiff leaves. Chocó is also notable for more than 40 species of brightly colored poisonous frogs, known locally as *ranas kokois.* These small frogs are covered with a deadly poison and have evolved stunning coloration, from bright orange to red, gold, and blue. They are active in the day and therefore relatively easy to spot. Of Colombia's 1,800 species of birds, more than 1,000 have been identified in the Chocó, including a large number of hummingbirds.

Offshore, the Pacific Ocean welcomes the annual migration of Antarctic humpback whales. The beaches of the Pacific coast are popular nesting areas for sea turtles, in particular the *tortuga golfina* (olive ridley) and *tortuga carey* (hawksbill) sea turtles.

CLOUD FOREST

Rainforests that grow at higher altitudes on the flanks of the Andes are known as montane rainforests or cloud forests because they are often enveloped in mist that results from the condensation of warm air against chillier mountain currents. Unlike the lowland rainforest, cloud forests only have two layers, the canopy and ground layer. Generally, the vegetation is less dense than that in the lowland rainforest. However, it is home to many palms, ferns, and epiphytes, particularly orchids.

The type of cloud forest vegetation is dictated by altitude. *Selva subandina* (sub-Andean forest) vegetation grows between the altitudes of 1,000 and 2,300 meters (3,300-7,500 ft), where temperature varies 16-23°C (61-73°F). Plant species include the distinctive Seussian white *yarumo* with its oversized leaves, as well as cedar, oak, and mahogany trees. Many palms grow here, including the svelte wax palm and *tagua*, which produces a nut that resembles ivory. Ferns include the striking *palma boba* or tree fern. Colombia's premier crop, coffee, is grown at this elevation.

At elevations between 2,300 and 3,600 meters (7,500-12,000 ft), the vegetation is described as *selva Andina* (Andean forest). This vegetation is even less dense and at higher elevations the trees are smaller. *Selva Andina* includes many oak, *encenillo, sietecuero* (glory bush), and pine trees.

Mammals include the spectacled or Andean bear, the only species of bear in South America, the mountain (or woolly) tapir, anteaters, armadillos, sloths, boars, foxes, and *olingos,* small arboreal carnivores of the raccoon family. In 2013, the *olinguito* (small *olingo*), an incredibly cute animal, was declared a new species. Other unusual animals include the slow-moving *guagua loba* and *guatín,* both of which are rodents. In addition, numerous species of monkeys inhabit the cloud forest, including noisy troops of howler monkeys. Birds include many types of *barranqueros* (motmots), including the spectacular blue-crowned motmot. Other common birds include *tángaras* (tanagers), woodpeckers, warblers, parrots, owls, and ducks, including the beautiful white-and-black torrent duck.

TROPICAL DRY FORESTS

Tropical dry forests exist in areas where there is a prolonged dry season. The vegetation includes deciduous trees that lose their leaves during the dry season, allowing them to conserve water. Trees on moister sites and those with access to groundwater tend to be evergreen. Before Columbus, this ecosystem covered much of the Colombian Caribbean coast. However, much of it has since been cut down for cattle ranching. Pockets still exist east of the Golfo de Morrosquillo and at the base of the Sierra Nevada de Santa Marta. Tropical dry forests are the most endangered tropical ecosystem in the world.

Though less biologically diverse than rainforests, tropical dry forests are home to a wide variety of wildlife. They were once the stomping ground of the now highly endangered *marimonda*, or white-fronted spider monkey.

TROPICAL GRASSLANDS

Los Llanos (The Plains) of Colombia are covered with lush tropical grasslands. Vegetation includes long-stemmed and carpet grasses in the drier areas and swamp grasses in low-lying humid areas. There are also thick patches of forest throughout the plains and along the rivers (known as gallery forests). These plains are teeming with wildlife, including deer, anteaters, armadillos, tapirs, otters, jaguars, pumas, and *chigüiros* (also known as capybaras), the world's largest rodent. The Llanos are also home to the giant anaconda and to one of the most endangered species on Earth, the Orinoco crocodile, which reaches up to seven meters (23 ft) long.

History

BEFORE COLUMBUS

Located at the juncture of Central and South America, what is now Colombia was a necessary transit point for the migration of people who settled South America. However, because these peoples left few physical traces of their passage, little is known of them. The oldest human objects found in Colombia, utensils discovered near Bogotá, are dated from 14,000 BC. With the expansion of agriculture and sedentary life throughout the territory of present-day Colombia around 1000 BC, various indigenous cultures started producing stunning ceramic and gold work, as well as some monumental remains. These remains provide rich material evidence of their development. Nonetheless, there are significant gaps in the understanding of the history of these early peoples.

From around 700 BC, the area of San Agustín, near the origin of the Río Magdalena in southern Colombia, was settled by people who practiced agriculture and produced pottery. Starting in the 1st century AD, the people of San Agustín created hundreds of monumental stone statues set on large platforms, which comprise the largest pre-Columbian archaeological site extant between Mesoamerica and Peru. By AD 800, this society had disappeared.

In the northwestern plains of Colombia, south of present-day Cartagena, starting in the 1st century AD, the Sinú people constructed a large complex of mounds in the shape of fish bones. These mounds regulated flooding, allowing cultivation in both rainy and dry seasons. During rainy seasons, the water flooded the lower cavities, allowing for cultivation on the mounds; during dry season, cultivation took place in the cavities that had been enriched by the floodwaters. These monumental formations are still visible from overhead. By the time of the Spanish conquest, these people no longer inhabited the area.

From AD 500 to 900, the area of Tierradentro, west of San Agustín, was settled by an agricultural society that dug magnificent decorated underground tombs, produced large stone statues, and built oval-shaped buildings on artificial terraces. As with the San Agustín and the Sinú people, it is not known what happened to these people.

At the time of the conquest, present-day Colombia was populated by a large number of distinct agricultural societies that often maintained peaceful trading relations among themselves. The two largest groups were the Muisca people, who lived in the altiplano (highlands) of the Cordillera Oriental, and the Tayrona, who lived on the slopes of the Sierra Nevada de Santa Marta. Other groups included the Quimbaya, who settled the area of the present-day Coffee Region; the Calima, in present-day Valle del Cauca; and the Nariños, in the mountainous areas of southwest Colombia.

These indigenous societies were mostly organized at the village level with loose association with other villages. Only the Muisca and the Tayrona had a more developed political organization. Though these were all agricultural societies, they also engaged in hunting, fishing, and mining and produced sophisticated ceramics and goldwork. Each group specialized in what their environment had to offer and engaged in overland trade. For example, the Muiscas produced textiles and salt, which they traded for gold, cotton, tobacco, and shells from other groups.

The Muiscas, a Chibcha-speaking people, were the largest group, with an estimated 600,000 inhabitants at the time of the Spanish conquest. They settled the Cordillera Oriental in AD 300 and occupied a large territory that comprises most of the highland areas of the present-day departments of Cundinamarca and Boyacá. At the time of the conquest, they were organized into two large confederations: one in the south headed by the Zipa, whose capital was Bacatá near present-day Bogotá, and another headed by the Zaque, whose capital was at Hunza, the location of present-day Tunja. The Muiscas had a highly homogeneous culture, skilled in weaving, ceramics, and goldwork. Their cosmography placed significant importance on high Andean lakes, several of which were sacred, including Guatavita, Siecha, and Iguaque.

The Tayrona, who settled the slopes of the Sierra Nevada de Santa Marta, were also a Chibcha-speaking people. They had a more urban society, with towns that included temples and ceremonial plazas built on stone terraces, and practiced farming on terraces carved out of the mountains. There are an estimated 200 Tayrona sites, of which Ciudad Perdida (Lost City), built at 1,100 meters (3,600 ft) in the Sierra Nevada de Santa Marta, is the largest and best known. Many of these towns, including El Pueblito in the Parque Nacional Natural Tayrona, were occupied at the time of the Spanish conquest. The Kogis, Arhuacos, Kankuamos, and Wiwas, current inhabitants of the sierra, are their descendants and consider many places in the sierra sacred.

THE SPANISH CONQUEST (1499-1550)

As elsewhere in the New World, the arrival of Europeans was an unmitigated disaster for the Native American societies. Though there were pockets of resistance, on the whole the indigenous people were unable to push back the small number of armed Spanish conquistadores. Harsh conditions after the conquest and the spread of European diseases, such as measles and smallpox, to which the indigenous people had no immunity, killed off millions of natives. The Spanish conquest of present-day Colombia took about 50 years and was largely completed by the 1550s.

In 1499, the first European set foot in present-day Colombia in the northern Guajira Peninsula. In 1510, a first, unsuccessful colony was established in the Golfo de Urabá near the current border with Panama. In 1526, the Spanish established Santa Marta, their first permanent foothold, from where they tried, unsuccessfully, to subdue the Tayronas. In 1533, they established Cartagena, which was to become a major colonial port.

In 1536, Gonzalo Jiménez de Quesada set off south from Santa Marta to conquer the fabled lands of El Dorado in the Andean heartland. After a year of grueling travel up the swampy Río Magdalena valley, 200 surviving members of Jiménez de Quesada's 800 original troops arrived in the Muisca lands near present-day Bogotá. After a short interlude of courteous relations, the Spaniards' greed led them to obliterate the Muisca towns and temples. They found significant amounts of gold, especially in the town of Hunza, but they were, by and large, disappointed. In 1538, Jiménez de Quesada founded Santa Fe de Bogotá as the capital of this new territory, which he called Nueva Granada—New Granada—after his birthplace.

Sebastián de Belalcázar, a lieutenant of Francisco Pizarro, led a second major expedition that arrived in the Muisca lands from the south. Having conquered the Inca city of Quito, Belalcázar and his army traveled north, conquering a vast swath of land from present-day Ecuador to the *sábana* (high plateau) of Bogotá. Along the way, he founded several cities, including Popayán and Cali in 1536. He arrived shortly after Quesada had founded Bogotá. Incredibly, a third conquistador, the German Nikolaus Federmann, arrived in Bogotá at the same time, having traveled from Venezuela via the Llanos. Rather than fight for supremacy, the three conquistadores decided to take their rival claims to arbitration at the Spanish court. In an unexpected turn of events, none of the three obtained title to the Muisca lands: When Bogotá became the administrative capital of New Granada, they came under the sway of the Spanish crown. Other expeditions swept across the Caribbean coast, through current-day Antioquia and the Santanderes.

COLONIAL NUEVA GRANADA (1550-1810)

For most of its colonial history, Nueva Granada was an appendage of the Viceroyalty of Peru. In 1717, Spain decided to establish a viceroyalty in Nueva Granada but changed its mind six years later because the benefits did not justify the cost. In 1739, the viceroyalty was reestablished, with Santa Fe de Bogotá as its capital. It was an unwieldy territory, encompassing present-day Colombia, Venezuela, Ecuador, and Panama. To make it more manageable, Venezuela and Panama were ruled by captains general and Ecuador by a president. At the local level, the viceroyalty was divided into *provincias* (provinces), each with a local assembly called a *cabildo*.

Settlement in Nueva Granada occurred primarily in three areas: where there were significant indigenous populations to exploit, as in the case of Tunja in the former Muisca territory; where there were gold deposits, as in Cauca, Antioquia, and Santander; and along trade routes, for example at Honda and Mompox on the Río Magdalena. Cartagena was the main port of call for the biennial convoys of gold and silver sent to Spain. Bogotá lived off of the official bureaucracy and sustained a fair number of artisans. Present-day Antioquia and Santander supported small-scale farming to provide provisions to the gold mining camps. Nueva Granada was one of the least economically dynamic of Spain's New World possessions. The mountainous topography and high transportation costs meant that agricultural production was primarily for local consumption and gold was the only significant export.

Colonial society was composed of a small Spanish and Creole (descendants of Spanish settlers) elite class governing a large mestizo (mixed indigenous-white) population. The Spanish had initially preserved indigenous communal lands known as *resguardos*, but the demographic collapse of the native population and intermarriage meant that, unlike in Peru or Mexico, there were relatively few people who were fully indigenous. There were also black slaves who were forced mostly to work in the mines and haciendas (plantations). Society was overwhelmingly Catholic and Spanish-speaking.

Culturally, Nueva Granada was also somewhat of a backwater. Though there was a modest flourishing of the arts, Bogotá could not compete with the magnificent architectural and artistic production of Quito, Lima, or Mexico City. The only truly notable event of learning that took place was the late 18th-century Expedición Botánica (Botanical Expedition), headed by Spanish naturalist José Celestino Mutis, the personal doctor to one of the viceroys. The aim of the expedition was to survey all the species of Nueva Granada—a rather tall order given that Colombia is home to 10 percent of the world's species. However, the expedition did some remarkable research and produced beautiful prints of the fauna and flora.

The late colonial period saw unrest in Nueva Granada. Starting in 1781, a revolt known as the Rebelión de los Comuneros took place in the province of Socorro (north of Bogotá) in present-day Santander as a result of an attempt by colonial authorities to levy higher taxes. It was not an antiroyalist movement, however, as its slogan indicates: *¡Viva el Rey, Muera el Mal Gobierno!* ("Long live the king, down with bad government!"). Rather it was a protest against unfair taxes, not much different from the Boston Tea Party. However, it gave the Spanish government a fright. A rebel army, led by José Antonio Galán, marched on Bogotá. Negotiations put an end to the assault, and later the authorities ruthlessly persecuted the leaders of the revolt.

STRUGGLE FOR INDEPENDENCE (1810-1821)

Though there was some ill feeling against the colonial government, as the Rebelión de los Comuneros attests, as well as rivalry between the Spanish- and American-born elites, it was an external event, the Napoleonic invasion of Spain, that set off the chain of events

that led to independence of Nueva Granada and the rest of the Spanish dominion in the New World.

In 1808, Napoleon invaded Spain, took King Ferdinand VII prisoner, and tried to impose his own brother, Joseph, as king of Spain. The Spaniards revolted, establishing a Central Junta in Seville to govern during the king's temporary absence from power. Faced with the issue of whether to recognize the new Central Junta in Spain, the colonial elites decided to take matters in their own hands and establish juntas of their own. The first such junta in Nueva Granada was established in Caracas in April 1810. Cartagena followed suit in May and Bogotá on July 20, 1810. According to popular myth, the revolt in Bogotá was the result of the failure of a prominent Spaniard merchant to lend a flower vase to a pair of Creoles.

Though they pledged alliance to Ferdinand VII, once the local elites had tasted power, there was no going back. Spanish authorities were expelled, and in 1811, a government of sorts, under the loose mantle of the Provincias Unidas de Nueva Granada (United Provinces of New Granada), was established with its capital at Tunja. Bogotá and the adjoining province of Cundinamarca stayed aloof from the confederation, arguing that it was too weak to resist the Spanish. Subsequently, various provinces of Nueva Granada declared outright independence, starting with Venezuela and Cartagena in 1811 and Cundinamarca in 1813.

Several cities remained loyal to the crown, namely Santa Marta and deeply conservative Pasto in the south. From 1812 to 1814 there was a senseless civil war between the Provincias Unidas and Cundinamarca—that is why this period is called the Patria Boba, or Foolish Fatherland. Ultimately, the Provincias Unidas prevailed with the help of a young Venezuelan captain by the name of Simón Bolívar.

After the restoration of Ferdinand VII, Spain attempted to retake its wayward colonies, with a military expedition and reign of terror known as the Reconquista—the

Reconquest. The Spanish forces took Cartagena by siege in 1815 and took control of Bogotá in May 1816. However, in 1819, a revolutionary army composed of Venezuelans, Nueva Granadans, and European mercenaries headed by Bolívar arrived across the Llanos from Venezuela and decisively defeated the Spanish army in the Batalla del Puente de Boyacá—the Battle of the Boyacá Bridge—on August 7, near Tunja. The rest of the country fell quickly to the revolutionary army. With support from Nueva Granada, Bolívar defeated the Spanish in Venezuela in 1821. Panama, which had remained under Spanish control, declared independence in the same year. Finally, Bolívar dispatched Antonio José de Sucre to take Quito in 1822, bringing an end to the Spanish rule of Nueva Granada.

GRAN COLOMBIA: A FLAWED UNION (1821-1830)

Shortly after the Battle of Boyacá, the Congress of Angostura, meeting in its namesake city on the Río Orinoco in Venezuela, proclaimed the union of Nueva Granada, Venezuela, and Ecuador under the name of the República de Colombia. Historians refer to this entity as Gran Colombia. In 1821, while the fight for independence was still raging in parts of Venezuela and Ecuador, a constitutional congress met in Cúcuta. An ongoing debate about whether a centralist or federalist scheme was preferable resulted in a curious compromise: the República de Colombia assumed a highly centralist form, considered necessary to finish the battle for independence, but left the issue of federalism open to review after 10 years. The document was generally liberal, enshrining individual liberties and providing for the manumission of slaves, meaning that the children of slaves were born free.

Bolívar, who was born in Venezuela, was named president. Francisco de Paula Santander, who was born near Cúcuta in Nueva Granada, was named vice president. Santander had fought alongside Bolívar in the battles for independence of Nueva Granada and was seen as an able administrator. While Bolívar continued south to liberate Ecuador and Peru, Santander assumed the reins of power in Bogotá. He charted a generally liberal course, instituting public education and a curriculum that included avant-garde thinkers such as Jeremy Bentham. However, the highly centralist structure was unsavory to elites in Venezuela and Ecuador, who disliked rule from Bogotá. Shortly after the Congress of Cúcuta, revolt broke out in Venezuela and Ecuador. In 1826, Bolívar returned from Bolivia and Peru, hoping for the adoption in Gran Colombia of the Bolivian Constitution, an unusual document he drafted that called for a presidency for life.

There had been a growing distance between Bolívar and Santander: Bolívar saw Santander as an overzealous liberal reformer while Santander disliked Bolívar's authoritarian tendencies. In 1828, after a failed constitutional congress that met in Ocaña in eastern Colombia, Bolívar assumed dictatorial powers. He rolled back many of Santander's liberal reforms. In September 1828 there was an attempt on Bolívar's life in Bogotá. This was famously foiled by his companion, Manuela Sáenz. The last years of Gran Colombia were marked by revolts in various parts of the country and a war with Peru. In 1830, a further constitutional assembly was convened in Bogotá, but by that point Gran Colombia had ceased to exist: Venezuela and Ecuador had seceded. In March 1830, a physically ill Bolívar decided to leave for voluntary exile in Europe and died on his way in Santa Marta.

CIVIL WARS AND CONSTITUTIONS (1830-1902)

After the separation of Venezuela and Ecuador, what is now Colombia adopted the name República de Nueva Granada. In 1832, it adopted a new constitution that corrected many of the errors of the excessively centralist constitution of Gran Colombia. There was a semblance of stability with the orderly succession of elected presidents. The elimination of some monasteries in Pasto sparked a short civil conflict known as the Guerra de los Supremos, which lasted 1839-1842. During this war, Conservative and Liberal factions coalesced for the first time, establishing the foundation of Colombia's two-party system. Generally, the Conservative Party supported the Catholic Church, favored centralization, and followed the ideas of Bolívar. The Liberal Party supported federalism and free trade and identified with the ideas of Santander.

The country's rugged topography meant that Nueva Granada was not very integrated into the world economy. Gold, extracted mostly in Antioquia, was the main export. Most of the country eked out its subsistence from agriculture, with trade restricted within regions. This period saw some economic development, such as steam navigation on the Magdalena and Cauca Rivers, and a contract for the construction of the trans-isthmian railroad in Panama, which had yet to secede.

Midcentury saw the rise of a new class of leaders who had grown up wholly under Republican governments. They ushered in a period of liberal reform. In 1851, Congress abolished slavery. In 1853, a new constitution established universal male suffrage, religious tolerance, and direct election of provincial governors. The government reduced tariffs and Nueva Granada experienced a short export-oriented tobacco boom.

Conflicts between radical reformers within the Liberal Party, moderates, and Conservatives led to unrest in various provinces. In 1859, discontented Liberals under Tomás Cipriano de Mosquera revolted, leading to generalized civil war in which the Liberals were ultimately victorious. Once in power, they pushed radical reform. Mosquera expropriated all nonreligious church property, partly in vengeance for church support of the Conservatives in the previous civil war.

The 1863 constitution was one of the world's most audacious federalist experiments. The country was renamed the Estados Unidos de Colombia (United States of Colombia), comprising nine states. The president had a two-year term and was not immediately reelectable. All powers that were not explicitly assigned to the central government were the responsibility of the states. Many of the states engaged in true progressive policies, such as establishing public education and promoting the construction of railroads. This period coincided with agricultural booms in quinine, cotton, and indigo that, for the first time, brought limited prosperity. This period saw the establishment of the Universidad Nacional (National University) and the country's first bank.

In 1880 and then in 1884, a coalition of Conservatives and moderate Liberals, who were dissatisfied with radical policies, elected Rafael Núñez as president. Núñez tried to strengthen the power of the central government, sparking a Liberal revolt. The Conservatives were ultimately victorious and, in 1886, enacted a new centralist constitution that lasted through most of the 20th century. The country was rechristened República de Colombia, the name it has conserved since then. During the period from 1886 through 1904, known as the Regeneración, the Conservative Party held sway, rolling back many of the previous reforms, especially anticlerical measures and unrestricted male suffrage. The Liberal Party, excluded from power, revolted in 1899. The ensuing Guerra de los Mil Días (Thousand Days' War), which raged through 1902, was a terribly bloody conflict. It is not clear how many died in the war, but some historians put the figure as high as 100,000, or an incredible 2.5 percent of the country's population of four million at the time.

One year after the end of the war, Panama seceded. During the late 19th century, there had been resentment in Panama about the distribution of revenues from the transit trade that mostly were sent to Bogotá. However, in 1902 the local Panamanian elites had become alarmed at the lackadaisical attitude of the government in Bogotá regarding the construction of an interoceanic canal. After the failure of the French to build a canal, Colombia had entered into negotiations with the United States. In the closing days of the Guerra de los Mil Días, Colombia and the United States signed the Hay-Herrán Treaty, which called for the construction of the canal, surrendering control over a strip of land on either side of the canal to the United States. The Americans threatened that if the treaty were not ratified, they would dig the canal in Nicaragua. Arguing that the treaty undermined Colombian sovereignty, the congress in Bogotá unanimously rejected it in August 1903. That was a big mistake: A few months later, Panama seceded with the support of the United States.

PEACE AND REFORM (1902-1946)

Under the leadership of moderate Conservative Rafael Reyes, who was president 1904-1909, Colombia entered a period of peace and stability. Reyes focused on creating a professional, nonpartisan army. He gave representation to Liberals in government, enacted a protective tariff to spur domestic industry, and pushed public works. During his administration, Bogotá was finally connected by railway to the Río Magdalena. He reestablished relations with the United States, signing a treaty that provided Colombia with an indemnity for the loss of Panama. During the 1920s and 1930s, Colombia was governed by a succession of Conservative Party presidents. Though there was often electoral fraud, constitutional reform that guaranteed minority representation ensured peace.

Expanding world demand for coffee spurred production across Colombia, especially in southern Antioquia and what is now known as the Coffee Region, creating a new class of independent farmers. Improved transportation, especially the completion of the railways from Cali to Buenaventura on the Pacific coast and from Medellín to the Río Magdalena, was key to the growth of coffee exports. In the Magdalena Medio region and in Norte de Santander, U.S.

companies explored and started producing petroleum. Medellín became a center of textile manufacturing. With the country's broken geography, air transportation developed rapidly. The Sociedad Colombo Alemana de Transportes Aéreos (Colombian German Air Transportation Society) or SCADTA, the predecessor of Avianca, was founded in Barranquilla in 1919, and is reputedly the second-oldest commercial aviation company in the world (the oldest is KLM).

In 1930, a split Conservative ticket allowed the Liberals to win the elections. After being out of power for 50 years, the Liberal Party was happy to regain control of the state apparatus. This led to strife with Conservatives long accustomed to power—presaging the intense interparty violence that was to erupt later.

From 1932 to 1933, Colombia and Peru fought a brief war in the Amazon over the control of the port city of Leticia. The League of Nations brokered a truce, the first time that this body, which was a precursor to the United Nations, actively intervened in a dispute between two countries.

Starting in 1934, Liberal president Alfonso López Pumarejo undertook major social and labor reforms, with some similarities to Roosevelt's New Deal. His policies included agrarian reform, encouragement and protection of labor unions, and increased spending on education. He reduced the Catholic Church's sway over education and eliminated the literacy requirement for male voters. Many of these reforms simply returned the country to policies that had been enacted by Liberals in the 1850s, 80 years prior. In opposition to these policies, a new radical right, with a confrontational style and strains of fascism and anti-Semitism, arose under the leadership of Laureano Gómez.

During World War II, Colombia closely allied itself with the United States and eventually declared war on the Axis powers in retaliation for German attacks on Colombian merchant ships in the Caribbean Sea. The government concentrated those of German descent in a hotel in Fusagasugá near Bogotá and removed all German influence from SCADTA.

LA VIOLENCIA (1946-1953)

In the 1946 elections, the Liberal Party split its ticket between establishment-backed Gabriel Turbay and newcomer Jorge Eliécer Gaitán. Gaitán was a self-made man who had scaled the ladders of power within the Liberal Party despite the opposition of the traditional Liberal elite. He had a vaguely populist platform and much charisma. The moderate Conservative Mariano Ospina won a plurality of votes and was elected to the presidency. As in 1930, the transfer of power from Liberals to Conservatives led to outbursts of violence.

On April 9, 1948, a deranged youth killed former presidential candidate Gaitán as he left his office in downtown Bogotá. His assassination sparked riots and bloodshed throughout the country, with severe destruction in the capital. The disturbance in Bogotá, known as El Bogotazo, occurred during the 9th Inter-American Conference, which had brought together leaders from all over the hemisphere. Young Fidel Castro happened to be in Bogotá that day, though he had no part in the upheaval.

The assassination of Gaitán further incited the violence that had started in 1946. Over the course of 10 years, an estimated 100,000-200,000 people died in what was laconically labeled La Violencia (The Violence). This conflict was comparable in destruction of human life with the Guerra de los Mil Días. The killing took place throughout the country, often in small towns and rural areas. Mostly it involved loyalists of the predominant party settling scores or intimidating members of the opposite party in order to extract land or secure economic gain. In some cases, the violence was sheer banditry. Numerous, horrific mass murders took place. The police often took sides with the Conservatives or simply turned a blind eye. In response, some Liberals resorted to armed resistance, giving birth to

Colombia's first guerrilla armies. The Liberal Party boycotted the 1950 elections, and radical Conservative Laureano Gómez was elected president. His government pursued authoritarian and highly partisan policies, further exacerbating the violence.

DICTATORSHIP (1953-1957)

In 1953, with the purported aim of bringing an end to fighting between Liberals and Conservatives, the Colombian army, under the command of General Gustavo Rojas Pinilla, staged a coup. Rojas was able to reduce, but not halt, the violence, by curtailing police support of the Conservatives and by negotiating an amnesty with Liberal guerrillas. In 1954, Rojas was elected for a four-term period by a handpicked assembly. Incidentally, it was this nondemocratically elected assembly that finally got around to extending suffrage to women, making Colombia one of the last countries in Latin America to do so. Rojas tried to build a populist regime with the support of organized labor, modeled after Perón in Argentina. His daughter, María Eugenia Rojas, was put in charge of social welfare programs. Though a majority of Colombians supported Rojas at first, his repressive policies and press censorship ended up alienating the political elites.

THE NATIONAL FRONT (1957-1974)

In May 1957, under the leadership of a coalition of Liberals and Conservatives, the country went on an extended general strike to oppose the dictatorship. Remarkably, Rojas voluntarily surrendered power and went into exile in Spain. As a way to put an end to La Violencia, Liberal and Conservative Party leaders proposed alternating presidential power for four consecutive terms while divvying up the bureaucracy on a 50-50 basis. The proposal, labeled the National Front, was ratified by a nationwide referendum and was in effect 1958-1974.

The National Front dramatically reduced

the level of violence. After years of fighting, both factions were ready to give up their arms. During this period, thanks to competent economic management, the economy prospered and incomes rose. The government adopted import substitution policies that gave rise to a number of new industries, including automobiles.

By institutionalizing the power of the two traditional parties, the National Front had the unintended consequence of squeezing out other political movements, especially from the left. As a result, during the 1960s a number of leftist guerrilla groups appeared. Some were simply the continuation, under a new name, of the guerrilla groups formed during La Violencia. The Fuerzas Armadas Revolucionarias de Colombia (FARC) was a rural, peasant-based group espousing Soviet Marxism. The Ejército de Liberación Nacional (ELN) was a smaller group inspired by the Cuban revolution. The even smaller Ejército Popular de Liberación (EPL) was a Maoist-inspired group. The Movimiento 19 de Abril (M-19) was a more urban group formed by middle-class intellectuals after alleged electoral fraud deprived the populist ANAPO Party (Alianza Nacional Popular; created by ex-dictator Rojas) of power. During the 1970s and 1980s, the M-19 staged flashy coups, such as stealing Bolívar's sword (and promising to return it once the revolution had been achieved) in 1974 and seizing control of the embassy of the Dominican Republic in Bogotá in 1980.

UNDER SIEGE (1974-1991)
The Drug Trade and the Rise of Illegal Armed Groups

Due to its relative proximity to the United States, treacherous geography, and weak government institutions, Colombia has been an ideal place for cultivation, production, and shipment of illegal drugs, primarily to the United States. During the 1970s, Colombia experienced a marijuana boom centered on the Sierra Nevada de Santa Marta. Eradication efforts by Colombian authorities and competition from homegrown marijuana produced in the United States quickly brought this boom to an end.

During the late 1970s, cocaine replaced marijuana as the main illegal drug. Though most of the coca cultivation at the time was in Peru and Bolivia, Colombian drug dealers based in Medellín started the business of picking up coca paste in Peru and Bolivia, processing it into cocaine in Colombia, and exporting the drug to the United States, where they even controlled some distribution at the local level. During its heyday in the mid-1980s, Pablo Escobar's Medellín Cartel controlled 80 percent of the world's cocaine trade. The rival Cali Cartel, controlled by the Rodríguez brothers, emerged in the 1980s and started to contest the supremacy of the Medellín Cartel, leading to a bloody feud.

During the 1980s and 1990s, coca cultivation shifted from Peru and Bolivia to Colombia, mainly to the Amazon regions of Putumayo, Caquetá, Meta, and Guaviare. Initially, leftist guerrillas such as the FARC protected the fields from the authorities in return for payment from the cartels. Eventually, they started processing and trafficking the drugs themselves. Though the guerrillas had other sources of income, such as kidnapping and extortion, especially of oil companies operating in the Llanos, the drug trade was a key factor in their growth. With these sources of income, they no longer needed popular support and morphed into criminal organizations. By the mid-1980s, the FARC had grown into a 4,000-person-strong army that controlled large portions of territory, especially in the south of the country.

During the 1980s and 1990s, the price of land was depressed as a result of the threat posed by the guerrillas. Using their vast wealth and power of intimidation, drug traffickers purchased vast swaths of land, mostly along the Caribbean coast of Colombia, at bargain prices. To defend their properties from extortion, they allied themselves with traditional landowners to create paramilitary groups. These groups often operated with the direct or tacit support of the army.

Colombian *campesinos* (small farmers), caught in the middle of the conflict between guerrillas and paramilitaries, suffered disproportionately. They were accused by both guerrillas and paramilitaries of sympathizing with the enemy, and the government was not there to protect them. The paramilitaries were particularly ruthless, often ordering entire villages to abandon their lands or massacring the population. The conflict between guerrillas and paramilitaries is at the source of the mass displacement of people in Colombia.

Peace Negotiations with the FARC and M-19

In 1982, President Belisario Betancur was elected with the promise of negotiating peace with the guerrillas. The negotiations with the guerrillas got nowhere, but the FARC did establish a political party, the Unión Patriótica (UP), which successfully participated in the 1986 presidential elections and 1988 local elections, managing to win some mayoralties. The paramilitaries and local elites did not want the political arm of the FARC to wield local power. As a result, the UP was subjected to a brutal persecution by the paramilitaries, who killed more than 1,000 party members. In the midst of this violence, Colombia suffered one of its worst natural disasters: the eruption of the Nevado del Ruiz in November 1985, which produced a massive mudslide that engulfed the town of Armero, killing more than 20,000 people.

In 1985, the M-19 brazenly seized the Palacio de Justicia in Bogotá. The Colombian army responded with a heavy hand, and in the ensuing battle, half of Colombia's Supreme Court justices were killed. Many people, including many cafeteria employees, disappeared in the army takeover of the building, and there is speculation that they were executed and buried in a mass grave in the south of Bogotá. Weakened by this fiasco, leaders of the M-19 took up President Virgilio Barco's offer to negotiate peace. The government set down clear rules, including a cease-fire on the part of the M-19, before talks could proceed. On March 19, 1990, Barco and the M-19's young leader, Carlos Pizarro, signed a peace agreement, the only major successful peace agreement to date between the authorities and a major guerrilla group. Unlike the FARC, the M-19 was still an ideological movement, and the leaders of the M-19 saw that by participating in civil life they could probably gain more than by fighting. They were right: In 2011 the people of Bogotá elected Gustavo Petro, a former M-19 guerrilla, as their mayor.

The Rise and Fall of the Medellín Cartel

Initially, the Colombian establishment turned a blind eye to the rise of the drug cartels and even took a favorable view of the paramilitaries, who were seen as an antidote to the scourge of the guerrillas. For a time, Escobar was active in politics and cultivated a Robin Hood image, funding public works such as parks and housing projects. Rather than stick to his business, as the Cali Cartel did, Escobar started to threaten any official who tried to check his power. In 1984, he had Rodrigo Lara Bonilla, the minister of justice, assassinated. When the government subsequently cracked down, Escobar declared outright war. He assassinated judges and political leaders, set off car bombs to intimidate the public, and paid a reward for every policeman that was murdered in Medellín—a total of 657. To take out an enemy, he planted a bomb in an Avianca flight from Bogotá to Cali, killing all passengers on board. The Medellín Cartel planted dozens of massive bombs in Bogotá and throughout the country, terrorizing the country's population. The cartel is allegedly responsible for the assassination of three presidential candidates in 1990: Luis Carlos Galán, the staunchly anti-mafia candidate of the Liberal Party; Carlos Pizarro, the candidate of the newly demilitarized M-19; and Bernardo Jaramillo, candidate of the Unión Patriótica.

There was really only one thing that Escobar feared—extradition to the United

States. Through bribery and intimidation, he managed to get extradition outlawed, and he negotiated a lopsided deal with the government of César Gaviria: In return for his surrender, he was allowed to control the jail where he was locked up. From the luxurious confines of La Catedral, as the prison was named, he continued to run his empire. In 1992 there was an outcry when it became known that he had interrogated and executed enemies within the jail. When he got wind that the government planned to transfer him to another prison, he fled. In December 1993, government intelligence intercepted a phone call he made to his family, located him in Medellín, and killed him on a rooftop as he attempted to flee. It is widely believed that the Cali Cartel actively aided the authorities in the manhunt.

A New Constitution

The 1990s started on a positive footing with the enactment of a new constitution in 1991. The Constitutional Assembly that drafted the charter was drawn from all segments of the political spectrum, including the M-19. The new constitution was very progressive, devolving considerable power to local communities and recognizing the rights of indigenous and Afro-Colombian communities to govern their communities and ancestral lands. The charter created a powerful new Constitutional Court, which has become a stalwart defender of basic rights, as well as an independent accusatory justice system, headed by a powerful attorney general, which was created to reduce impunity.

COLOMBIA ON THE BRINK (1992-2002)
New Cartels, Paramilitaries, and Guerrillas

Drug cultivation and production increased significantly during the 1990s. The overall land dedicated to coca cultivation rose from 60,000 hectares (148,300 acres) in 1992 to 165,000 hectares (407,700 acres) in 2002. As a result of the government's successful

crackdown first on the Medellín Cartel and then on the Cali Cartel, drug production split into smaller, more nimble criminal organizations. During the 1990s, the paramilitaries became stand-alone organizations that engaged in drug trafficking, expanding to more than 30,000 men in 2002. They created a national structure called the Autodefensas Unidas de Colombia, or AUC, under the leadership of Carlos Castaño. The AUC coordinated activities with local military commanders and committed atrocious crimes, often massacring scores of so-called sympathizers of guerrillas.

At the same time, the guerrillas expanded significantly during the 1990s. Strengthened by hefty revenues from kidnapping, extortion, and drug trafficking, they grew to more than 50,000 mostly peasant fighters in 2002. Their strategy was dictated primarily by military and economic considerations and they had little to no public support. At their heyday, the FARC covered the entire country, attacking military garrisons and even threatening major urban centers such as Cali. They performed increasingly large operations, such as attacking Mitú, the capital of the department of Vaupés, in 1998 or kidnapping 12 members of the Assembly of Valle del Cauca in Cali in 2002. The FARC commanders moved around the countryside unchecked. In the territories they controlled, they ruled over civilians, often committing heinous crimes. In 2002, they attacked a church in the town of Bojayá in Chocó, killing more than 100 unarmed civilians, including many children, who had sought refuge there.

Plan Colombia

The increasing growth of drug exports from Colombia to the United States in the 1990s became a source of concern for the U.S. government. From 1994 to 1998, the United States was reluctant to provide support to Colombia because the president at the time, Ernesto Samper, was tainted by accusations of having received campaign money from drug traffickers and because of evidence about human rights abuses by the Colombian army. When

Andrés Pastrana was elected president in 1998, the Colombian and U.S. administrations designed a strategy to curb drug production and counteract the insurgency called Plan Colombia. This strategy had both military and social components, and was to be financed jointly by the United States and Colombia. Ultimately, the United States provided Colombia, which was becoming one of its strongest and most loyal allies in Latin America, with more than US$7 billion, heavily weighted toward military aid, especially for training and for providing aerial mobility to Colombian troops. While the impact of Plan Colombia was not immediately visible, over time it changed the balance of power in favor of the government, allowing the Colombian army to regain the upper hand in the following years.

Flawed Peace Negotiations with the FARC

President Pastrana embarked on what is now widely believed to have been an ill-conceived, hurried peace process with the FARC. He had met Manuel Marulanda, the head of the FARC, before his inauguration in 1998 and was convinced that he could bring about a quick peace. Without a clear framework, in November 1998 he acceded to the FARC's request to grant them a demilitarized zone the size of Switzerland in the eastern departments of Meta and Caquetá. In hindsight, it seems clear that the FARC had no interest or need to negotiate because they were at the peak of their military power. Rather, the FARC commanders saw the grant of the demilitarized zone as an opportunity to strengthen their organization.

From the beginning, it became clear that the FARC did not take the peace process seriously. Marulanda failed to show up at the inaugural ceremony of the peace process, leaving a forlorn Pastrana sitting alone on the stage next to a now famous *silla vacilla* (empty seat). They ran the demilitarized zone as a mini-state, nicknamed Farclandia, using it to smuggle arms, hold kidnapped prisoners,

and process cocaine. During the peace negotiations, the FARC continued their attacks on the military and civilians. In February 2002, after the FARC kidnapped Eduardo Gechem, senator and president of the Senate Peace Commission, Pastrana declared the end of this ill-advised demilitarized zone and sent in the Colombian army.

A Failed State?

In 2002, the Colombian army was battling more than 50,000 guerrillas and 30,000 paramilitaries, with an estimated 6,000 child soldiers among those groups. The insurgents controlled approximately 75 percent of the country's territory. An estimated 100,000 antipersonnel mines covered 30 of 32 departments. More than 2.5 million people had been internally displaced between 1985 and 2003, with 300,000 people displaced in 2002 alone. Not surprisingly, prestigious publications such as *Foreign Policy* described Colombia at the time as failed state.

REGAINING ITS FOOTING (2002-PRESENT)
Álvaro Uribe's Assault on the Guerrillas

In the 2002 elections, fed-up Colombians overwhelmingly elected Álvaro Uribe, a former governor of Antioquia who promised to take the fight to the guerrillas. Uribe had a real grudge against the FARC, who had assassinated his father. The FARC were not fans of his, either. In a brazen show of defiance, during Uribe's inauguration ceremony in Bogotá on August 7, 2002, the guerrilla group fired various rockets aimed at the presidential palace during a post-swearing-in reception. Several rockets struck the exterior of the palace, causing minor damage (attendees were unaware of the attack), but many more fell on the humble dwellings in barrios nearby, killing 21.

During his first term, Uribe embarked on a policy of Seguridad Democrática, or Democratic Security, based on strengthening the army, eradicating illicit crops to deprive the guerrillas of revenues, and creating a controversial network of civilian collaborators who were paid for providing tips that led to successful operations against the insurgents. The government increased military expenditure and decreed taxes on the rich totaling US$4 billion to finance the cost of the war. Colombian military personnel grew from 300,000 in 2002 to 400,000 in 2007.

From 2002 to 2003, the army evicted the FARC from the central part of the country around Bogotá and Medellín, although that did not prevent them from causing terror in the cities. In February 2003, a car bomb attributed to the FARC exploded in the parking lot of the exclusive social club El Nogal, killing more than 30 people—mostly employees of the club. From 2004 to 2006, the army pressed the FARC in its stronghold in the southern part of the country. Aerial spraying of coca crops brought down cultivated areas from 165,000 hectares (407,700 acres) in 2002 to 76,000 hectares (187,800 acres) in 2006.

In 2006, Uribe was reelected by a landslide, after Congress amended the constitution to allow for immediate presidential reelection. There is clear evidence that the government effectively bribed two congressmen whose votes were necessary for passage of the measure. Uribe interpreted the election results as a mandate to continue single-mindedly pursuing the guerrillas. The FARC came under severe stress, with thousands of guerrillas deserting, and for the first time, the FARC was subjected to effective strikes against top commanders. No longer safe in their traditional jungle strongholds in Colombia, many FARC operatives crossed the border into Venezuela and Ecuador, causing tension between Colombia and the governments of those countries.

In early 2008, the Colombian military bombed and killed leading FARC commander Raúl Reyes in a camp in Ecuador, causing a diplomatic crisis with that country. Later that year, the military executed Operación Jaque (Operation Checkmate), a dramatic rescue operation in which they duped the FARC into handing over their most important hostages. The hostages released included three U.S. defense contractors and Ingrid Betancur, a French-Colombian independent presidential candidate who was kidnapped by the FARC during the 2002 presidential election as she proceeded by land, against the advice of the military, toward the capital of the former FARC demilitarized zone. In 2008, Manuel Marulanda, founder of the FARC, died a natural death. At that time, it was estimated that the FARC forces had plummeted to about 9,000 fighters, half of what they had been eight years before.

The Colombian army has been implicated in serious human rights abuses. Pressure from top brass to show results in the war against the guerrillas and the possibility of obtaining extended vacation time led several garrisons to execute civilians and present them as guerrillas killed in combat. In 2008, it was discovered that numerous young poor men from the city of Soacha, duped by false promises of work, had been taken to rural areas, assassinated by the army, and presented as guerrillas killed in anti-insurgency operations. This macabre episode—referred to as the scandal of *falsos positives* (false positives)—was done under the watch of Minister of Defense Juan Manuel Santos, who was later elected president of Colombia.

Peace Process with the AUC

From 2003 to 2008, the Uribe government pursued a controversial peace process with the right-wing paramilitaries, the Autodefensas Unidas de Colombia (AUC). As part of that process, an estimated 28,000 paramilitary fighters demobilized, including most of the high-level commanders. In 2005, the Colombian Congress passed the Justice and Peace Law to provide a legal framework for the process. Unlike previous peace laws that simply granted an amnesty to the insurgents, this law provided for reduced sentences for paramilitaries who had committed serious crimes in exchange for full confessions and reparation of victims. Domestic and international observers were extremely skeptical about the process, worrying that the paramilitaries would use their power to pressure for lenient terms. These misgivings were justified by evidence that they used their power of coercion to influence the results of the 2006 parliamentary elections, a scandal referred to as *parapolítica.* Many congresspersons, including a first cousin of Uribe, ended up in prison.

It soon became clear that the paramilitary commanders were not sincere in their commitment to peace. Many refused to confess crimes and transferred their assets to front men. Covertly, they continued their drug-trafficking operations. The government placed scant importance on the truth and reparation elements of the Justice and Peace Law, severely underfunding the effort to redress crimes committed against more than 150,000 victims who had signed up as part of the process. Through 2008, the paramilitaries had confessed to a mere 2,700 crimes, a fraction of the estimated total, and refused to hand over assets. Fed up with their lack of cooperation, in 2008 Uribe extradited 14 top-ranking paramilitary commanders to the United States, where they were likely to face long sentences. However, the extradition severely hampered the effort to obtain truth and reparation for the victims of their crimes.

The difficulty in redressing the crimes against victims has been further troubled by the growth of the dozens of small *bacrim (bandas criminals,* or illegal armed groups) who have taken territorial control of former paramilitary areas, intimidating victims who have returned to their rightful lands under the peace process. Many of these *bacrim* inherited the structures of the former AUC groups and employ former paramilitaries.

Social and Economic Transformation

During the past decades, Colombia has made some remarkable strides in improving social and economic conditions. Due to improved security conditions, investment, both domestic and international, boomed. Economic growth averaged 3.6 percent 2010-2019, a significant increase over the prior decades. The number of people below poverty, as measured by the ability to buy a wide selection of basic goods and services, has declined from 59.7 percent in 2002 to 27 percent in 2019. In Colombia's 13 largest cities, which represent 45 percent of the population, poverty has fallen to 16 percent. In terms of basic needs, most urban areas are well served in terms of education, health, electricity, water, and sewage. However, there is a wide gap between the cities and rural areas, where 30 percent of the country's population lives. As of 2018, rural poverty stood at 37 percent. Though income inequality has been slowly falling, Colombia still has one of the most unequal distributions of income in the world.

Peace with the FARC

In the 2010 elections, Uribe's former minister of defense, Juan Manuel Santos, was elected president by a large majority. Santos continued to pursue an aggressive strategy against the FARC. Army operations killed Alfonso Cano, the new leader of the FARC, as well as Víctor Julio Suárez Rojas, the guerrillas' military strategist. As evidenced in the diary of Dutch FARC member Tanya Nijmeijer, found by the Colombian army after an attack on a rebel camp, morale within the FARC had sunk to an all-time low.

At the same time, Santos recognized the need to address nonmilitary facets of the violence. In 2011, Congress passed the comprehensive Victims and Land Restitutions Law, meant to rectify Uribe's Justice and Peace Law. This law provides a framework to redress the crimes committed against all victims of violence since 1985.

After a year of secret negotiations, Santos announced the start of peace dialogues with the FARC in October 2012, first in Oslo, Norway, and then in Havana, Cuba. These proceeded at a slow pace and covered a large number of topics, including agrarian development and drug trafficking. Former president Uribe and his allies opposed this initiative, claiming that a military defeat of the FARC was the best path forward.

In 2016, after four years of arduous negotiations, the government and the FARC agreed to comprehensive terms, which covered rural development, political participation, illegal drugs, justice for victims, and ending the armed conflict, among other topics. On September 26, 2016, the government and the FARC signed the agreement, only to have it rejected by a slim majority in a national vote. The government and the guerillas renegotiated the agreement, which was ratified on November 30, 2016, by Congress. Demobilization began in December 2016 and the guerillas began handing over their weapons to the UN during the first half of 2017.

President Juan Manuel Santos won the 2016 Nobel Peace Prize in honor of his efforts.

In 2018, however, Iván Duque Márquez rose from the ranks of right-wing policy makers to become Colombia's youngest president. Backed by former president Uribe, he took a confrontational stance against FARC and the peace process began stumbling. In 2019, several FARC leaders called for picking up arms again. Duque responded by calling for their arrest. Duque has also initiated a series of repressive austerity measures, including public transit cuts and university tuition hikes, leading to large student-led demonstrations in Bogotá and other major cities. In 2020, the country continues to experience frequent *paros* (large marches and walkouts from school and work).

Government and Economy

Under the 1991 constitution, Colombia is organized as a republic, with three branches of power—the executive, the legislative, and the judicial. The country is divided into 32 *departamentos* (departments or provinces) and the Distrito Capital (Capital District), where Bogotá is located. The departments are in turn divided into *municipios* (municipalities). These *municipios* include towns and rural areas.

The president of the republic, who is both head of state and head of government, is elected for a four-year term. With the exception of the military dictatorship of Gen. Gustavo Rojas Pinilla from 1953 to 1957, presidents have been elected by the people since 1914. In 2005, then-president Álvaro Uribe succeeded in changing the constitution to allow for one immediate presidential reelection. In 2009, he attempted to get the constitution changed once more to allow for a second reelection but was thwarted by the powerful Constitutional Court, which decreed that this change would break the necessary checks and balances of the constitutional framework.

Presidential elections are held every four years in May. If no candidate receives more than 50 percent of the votes, there will be a runoff election. Inauguration of the president takes place on August 7, the anniversary of the Batalla del Puente de Boyacá, which sealed Colombia's independence from Spain.

The legislative branch is made up of a bicameral legislature: the Senado (102 members) and the Cámara de Representantes (162 members). These representatives are elected every four years. Senators are voted for on a nationwide basis, while representatives are chosen for each department and the Distrito Capital. In addition, two seats in the Senate are reserved for indigenous representation. In the Cámara de Representantes, there are seats reserved for indigenous and Afro-Colombian communities as well as for Colombians who live abroad. As negotiated in 2016, the FARC will be assured 10 seats in Congress until 2022: 5 in the Senado and 5 in the Cámara de Representantes.

All Colombians over the age of 18—with the exception of active-duty military and police as well as those who are incarcerated—have the right to vote in all elections. Women only gained the right to vote in 1954.

POLITICAL PARTIES

Historically Colombia has had a two-party system: the Conservative Party and the Liberal Party. The Conservative Party has traditionally been aligned with the Catholic Church and has favored a more centralized government, and followed the ideas of Simón Bolívar. The Liberal Party favored a federal system of governing, has opposed church intervention in government affairs, and was aligned with the ideas of Gen. Francisco Paula Santander.

The hegemony of the two largest political parties came to a halt in the 2002 presidential election of rightist candidate Álvaro Uribe, who registered his own independent movement and then established a new party called El Partido de la Unidad. Since then, traditional parties have lost some influence. A third party, the Polo Democrático, became a relatively strong force in the early 2000s, capturing the mayorship of Bogotá, but has since faded, leaving no clear representative of the left.

Political parties today have become personality-oriented, and many candidates have been known to shop around for a party—or create their own—rather than adhere to the traditional parties.

ECONOMY

Colombia has a thriving market economy based primarily on oil, mining, agriculture, and manufacturing. The country's GDP in 2019 was US$370 billion and per capita GDP was US$7,698, placing it as a middle-income country. After a decade of economic growth, the economy started to stumble in late 2019 and early 2020, with the peso hitting a record low against the U.S. dollar: COP$4,000 to US$1 in March 2020. Inflation has averaged 3.7 percent in the past five years and unemployment as of 2019 was about 13 percent.

During the colonial period and up until the early 20th century, small-scale gold mining and subsistence agriculture were the mainstays of Colombia's economy. Starting in the 1920s, coffee production spread throughout the country and rapidly became Colombia's major export good. The coffee is of the mild arabica variety and is produced at elevations of 1,000 to 1,900 meters (roughly 3,000-6,000 ft), mostly by small farmers. During most of the 20th century, Colombia emphasized increasing the volume of production, using the Café de Colombia name and mythical coffee farmer Juan Valdez and his donkey Paquita to brand it. A severe global slump in coffee prices during the past decade has led to a reassessment of this strategy and an increasing focus on specialty coffees. Today, coffee represents only 3 percent of all Colombian exports.

Colombia's wide range of climates, from hot on the coast to temperate in the mountains, means that the country produces a wide range of products. Until recently, sugarcane production, fresh flowers, and bananas were the only major export-driven agribusiness. However, improvements in security in recent years have resulted in a boom in large-scale agricultural projects in palm oil, rubber, and soy. Cattle ranching occupies an estimated 25 percent of the country's land. Commercial forestry is relatively underdeveloped, though there is considerable illegal logging, especially on the Pacific coast.

In recent decades, oil production and mining have become major economic activities. The main center of oil production is the Llanos, the eastern plains of Colombia, with oil pipelines extending from there over the Cordillera Oriental to Caribbean ports. Oil currently represents roughly half of all Colombian exports. There are also significant natural gas deposits, mostly dedicated to residential use. Large-scale mining has been focused on coal and nickel, with large deposits in the Caribbean coastal region. With the improvement of security conditions in the past decade, many international firms, such as Anglogold Ashanti, have requested concessions for large-scale gold mining, often with opposition from the community. Illegal gold mining, often conducted with large machinery, is a severe threat to fragile ecosystems, especially in the Pacific coast rainforest.

During the postwar period, Colombia pursued an import substitution policy, fostering the growth of domestic industries such as automobiles, appliances, and petrochemical goods. Since the early 1990s, the government has been gradually opening the economy to foreign competition and tearing down tariffs. In recent years, the country has signed free-trade agreements with the United States and the European Union. Today, the country has a fairly diversified industrial sector. The country is self-sufficient in energy, with hydropower supplying the bulk of electricity needs.

Until recently, tourism was minimal because of widespread insecurity and a negative image. Things started to change in the mid-2000s, and the annual number of international visitors has increased from 600,000 in 2000 to 4.5 million in 2019. While Bogotá and Cartagena still receive the bulk of visitors, almost the entire country has opened up for tourism, though there are still pockets of no-go zones. This boom in tourism has fostered a growth of community and ecotourism options, often with the support from government. The network of *posadas nativas* (guesthouses owned and operated by locals) is one initiative to foment tourism at the community level, particularly among Afro-Colombians. In recent years, Parques Nacionales has transferred local operation of ecotourism facilities in the parks to community-based associations.

The economy of Colombia has also historically relied on the production of illicit drugs like cocaine and marijuana. While it suffered greatly for this in the 1900s and 2000s as the target of the U.S.-funded War on Drugs, in recent times—as cannabis legalization has been sweeping the world—the potential for Colombia to emerge as a major exporter of medicinal-grade marijuana at a price point that cannot be beat on the global market is getting some attention. The country is home to at least three major historic cultivation areas with roots back to the 1960s and 1970s including Cauca, Huila, and the Sierra Nevada mountains of the Caribbean coast. Some estimates indicate that Colombia could produce over 40 percent of the worldwide cannabis supply by 2025.

People and Culture

DEMOGRAPHY

Colombia was estimated to have had a population of a little over 50 million in 2020 and has the third-highest population in Latin America, behind Brazil and Mexico and slightly higher than Argentina. Around four million Colombians live outside of Colombia, mostly in the United States, Venezuela, Spain, and Ecuador. The population growth rate has fallen significantly in the past two decades and was estimated at 1.08 percent in 2020. The population of the country is relatively young, with a median age of 29.3 years. Average life expectancy is 75.5 years.

Sixty percent of the Colombian population lives in the highland Andean interior of the country, where the largest metropolitan areas are located: Bogotá (9.8 million), Medellín (3.9 million), and Cali (3.4 million). On the Caribbean coast, Barranquilla is the largest metropolitan area (2.3 million), followed by Cartagena (1.2 million).

It is increasingly an urban country, with around 81 percent of the population living in urban areas. This trend began during La Violencia and accelerated in the 1970s and 1980s. Around 7 million persons have been internally displaced due to the armed conflict in Colombia, leaving their homes in rural areas and seeking safety and economic opportunity in large cities.

Most of the population (over 84 percent)

BACKGROUND
PEOPLE AND CULTURE

is either mestizo (having both Amerindian and European ancestry) or European. People of African (10.4 percent) and indigenous or Amerindian (over 3.4 percent) origin make up the rest of the Colombian population. There is a tiny Romani or Roma population of well under 1 percent of the population, but nonetheless they are a protected group according to the constitution.

There are more than 80 indigenous groups, with some of the largest being the Wayúu, who make up the majority in La Guajira department; the Nasa, from Cauca; the Emberá, who live in the isolated jungles of the Chocó department; and the Pastos, in Nariño. Departments in the Amazon region have the highest percentages of indigenous residents. In Vaupés, for example, 66 percent of the population is of indigenous background. Many indigenous people live on *resguardos*, areas that are collectively owned and administered by the communities.

Afro-Colombians, descendants of slaves who arrived primarily via Spanish slave trade centers in the Caribbean, mostly live along both Pacific and Caribbean coasts and in the San Andrés Archipelago. Chocó has the highest percentage of Afro-Colombians (83 percent), followed by San Andrés and Providencia (57 percent), Bolívar (28 percent), Valle del Cauca (22 percent), and Cauca (22 percent). Cali, Cartagena, and Buenaventura have particularly large Afro-Colombian populations. In the Americas, Colombia has the third-highest number of citizens of African origin, behind Brazil and the United States.

While Colombia has not attracted large numbers of immigrants, there have been periods in which the country opened its doors to newcomers. In the early 20th century, immigrants from the Middle East—specifically from Lebanon, Syria, and Palestine—arrived, settling mostly along the Caribbean coast, especially in the cities of Barranquilla, Santa Marta, Cartagena, and Maicao in La Guajira. From 1920 to 1950, a sizable number of Sephardic and Ashkenazi Jews immigrated. Colombia has not had a large immigration

from Asia, although in the early 20th century there was a small immigration of Japanese to the Cali area.

RELIGION

Over 90 percent of Colombians identify as Roman Catholics, and it has been the dominant religion since the arrival of the Spaniards. The numbers of evangelical Christians, called simply *cristianos,* continue to grow, and there are other Christian congregations, including Mormons and Jehovah's Witnesses, but their numbers are small. In San Andrés and Providencia, the native Raizal population—of African descent—is mostly Baptist.

The Jewish community—estimated at around 5,000 families—is concentrated in the large cities, such as Bogotá, Medellín, Cali, and Barranquilla. There are significant Muslim communities, especially along the Caribbean coast, and there are mosques in Barranquilla, Santa Marta, Valledupar, Maicao (La Guajira), San Andrés, and Bogotá.

Semana Santa—Holy or Easter Week—is the most important religious festival in the country, and Catholics in every village, town, and city commemorate the week with a series of processions and masses. The colonial cities of Popayán, Mompox, Tunja, and Pamplona are known for their elaborate Semana Santa processions. Popayán and Mompox in particular attract pilgrims and tourists from Colombia and beyond. In cities such as Bogotá, Cali, and Cartagena, there are multitudinous processions to mountaintop religious sites, such as Monserrate, the Cerro de la Cruz, and El Monasterio de la Popa, respectively.

LANGUAGE

Spanish is the official language in Colombia. In the San Andrés Archipelago, English is still spoken by native islanders who arrived from former English colonies after the abolition of slavery, but Spanish has gained prominence.

According to the Ministry of Culture, there are at least 68 native languages, which

Happy Monday!

Colombians enjoy a long list of holidays (over 20). With a few exceptions, such as the independence celebrations on July 20 and August 7, Christmas, and New Year's Day, holidays are celebrated on the following Monday, creating a *puente* (literally bridge, or three-day weekend).

During Semana Santa and between Christmas Day and New Year's, interior cities such as Bogotá and Medellín become ghost towns as locals head to the nearest beach or to the countryside. Conversely, beach resorts, natural reserves and parks, and pueblos fill up. Along with that, room rates and airfare can increase substantially.

The following is a list of Colombian holidays, but be sure to check a Colombian calendar for precise dates. Holidays marked with an asterisk are always celebrated on the Monday following the date of the holiday.

- Año Nuevo (New Year's Day): January 1
- Día de los Reyes Magos (Epiphany)*: January 6
- Día de San José (Saint Joseph's Day)*: March 19
- Jueves Santo (Maundy Thursday): Thursday before Easter Sunday
- Viernes Santo (Good Friday): Friday before Easter Sunday
- Día de Trabajo (International Workers' Day): May 1
- Ascensión (Ascension)*: Six weeks and one day after Easter Sunday
- Corpus Christi*: Nine weeks and one day after Easter Sunday
- Sagrado Corazón (Sacred Heart)*: Ten weeks and one day after Easter Sunday
- San Pedro y San Pablo (Saint Peter and Saint Paul)*: June 29
- Día de la Independencia (Independence Day): July 20
- Batalla de Boyacá (Battle of Boyacá): August 7
- La Asunción (Assumption of Mary)*: August 15
- Día de la Raza (equivalent of Columbus Day)*: October 12
- Todos Los Santos (All Saints' Day)*: November 1
- Día de la Independencia de Cartagena (Cartagena Independence Day)*: November 11
- La Inmaculada Concepción (Immaculate Conception): December 8
- Navidad (Christmas): December 25

are spoken by around 850,000 people. These include 65 indigenous languages, two Afro-Colombian languages, and Romani, which is spoken by the small Roma population.

Three indigenous languages have over 50,000 speakers: Wayúu, primarily spoken in La Guajira; Páez, primarily spoken in Cauca; and Emberá, primarily spoken in Chocó.

Essentials

Getting There

AIR

Visitors to Cartagena arrive by air at the **Rafael Núñez International Airport** (CTG). There are also nonstop international flights to the **Aeropuerto Internacional El Dorado** (BOG) in Bogotá and the **Aeropuerto Internacional José María Córdova** (MDE) in Medellín and to airports in Cali, Barranquilla, and Armenia.

From North America
Avianca (www.avianca.com) has nonstop flights between Bogotá

and Miami, Fort Lauderdale, Orlando, Washington, Los Angeles, and New York-JFK. From Miami there are also nonstops to Medellín, Cali, Barranquilla, and Cartagena.

Viva Air (www.vivaair.com) has nonstop budget flights between Miami and Bogotá and Medellín.

American (www.american.com) flies between Miami and Dallas and Bogotá; Miami and Medellín; and Cali and Medellín. **Delta** (www.delta.com) flies from Atlanta and New York-JFK to Bogotá; it also flies between Atlanta and Cartagena. **United** (www.united.com) has flights from Newark and Houston to Bogotá.

JetBlue (www.jetblue.com) has nonstop service to Bogotá from Orlando and Fort Lauderdale; to Cartagena from New York and Fort Lauderdale; and to Medellín from Fort Lauderdale. **Spirit** (www.spirit.com) has flights from Fort Lauderdale to Bogotá, Medellín, Cartagena, and Armenia.

Air Canada (www.aircanada.com) operates nonstop flights from Toronto to Bogotá. **Air Transat** (www.airtransat.com) provides seasonal service to Cartagena and San Andrés from Montreal.

From Europe

Avianca (www.avianca.com) has service to Bogotá and Medellín from Madrid and Barcelona, and between Bogotá and London. **Air France** (www.airfrance.com) flies from Paris to Bogotá. **Iberia** (www.iberia.com) serves Bogotá from Madrid, as does **Air Europa** (www.aireuropa.com). **Lufthansa** (www.lufthansa.com) offers service between Bogotá and Frankfurt. **Turkish Airlines** (www.turkishairlines.com) flies between Bogotá and Istanbul. **KLM** (www.klm.com) serves Amsterdam from Bogotá with a stopover in Cali, as well as offers several direct flights per week to Cartagena.

From Latin America

Avianca (www.avianca.com) flies to Bogotá from many capitals in Latin America, including Buenos Aires, São Paulo, Rio de Janeiro, Valencia, Caracas, Lima, Santiago, and La Paz in South America; Cancún, Guatemala City, Mexico City, San José, San Juan, San Salvador, and Panama City in Central America; and Havana, Santo Domingo, Punta Cana, Aruba, and Curaçao in the Caribbean. **Interjet** (www.interjet.com), a low-cost Mexican carrier, offers direct flights from Mexico City to Cartagena as well as Bogotá and Medellín. **Viva Air** (www.vivaair.com) runs low-cost flights to both Bogotá and Medellín from Cancun, Mexico, and Lima, Arequipa, and Iquitos in Peru. Aerolíneas Argentinas, AeroGal, Aeromexico, Air Insel, Conviasa, Copa, Cubana, LATAM, Gol, TACA, and Tiara Air Aruba also have connections to Colombia. **Copa Airlines** (www.copaair.com) flies directly to many Colombian cities—including Cartagena, Santa Marta, Barranquilla, and San Andrés—from Panama City.

CAR OR MOTORCYCLE

A growing number of travelers drive into Colombia in their own car or with a rented vehicle. The most common point of entry is the Rumichaca border crossing with Ecuador, at the city of Ipiales (Tulcán on the Ecuador side) on the Pan-American Highway. This entry point is open 5am-10pm daily.

On the Venezuelan side, the border at Cúcuta and San Antonio del Táchira is open 24 hours a day. Although there are other border crossings with Venezuela, this is the recommended overland point of entry.

For those taking the Pan-American Highway southbound, note that you will run out of pavement in Panama. In the Darién Gap, the road is interrupted by the Darién mountain range. The road picks up again in the town of Turbo on the Golfo de Urabá. Many travelers ship their vehicle from Panama City to Cartagena, which is not difficult to arrange, and will set you back about US$1,000. It takes about 10 days before you can retrieve your vehicle in Cartagena.

BUS

Frequent buses depart Quito bound for Cali (20 hours) or Bogotá (30 hours). You can also take a taxi from the town of Tulcán to the border at Ipiales and from there take an onward bus to Pasto, Popayán, Cali, or beyond. In Quito contact **Líneas de los Andes** (www.lineasdelosandes.com.co).

BOAT

It is possible to enter the country from Panama, usually via the San Blas Islands.

Blue Sailing (U.S. tel. 203/660-8654, www.bluesailing.net) offers sailboat trips between various points in Panama to Cartagena. The trip usually takes about 5-6 days and costs around US$500-700 per person. Sometimes, particularly during the windy season November-March, boats stop in Sapzurro, Colombia, near the border. **San Blas Adventures** (www.sanblasadventures.com, contact@sanblasadventures.com) offers multiday sailboat tours to the San Blas Islands that usually depart from Cartí and end up in the Panamanian border village of La Miel. From there you can walk over the border to Sapzurro and take a *lancha* (boat) from there to Capurganá. There are regular morning boats from Capurganá to Turbo. During the windy season, especially December-March, this trip can be quite rough.

Getting Around

AIR

Air travel is an excellent, quick, and, thanks to discount airlines such as VivaColombia, economical way to travel within Colombia. Flying is the best option for those looking to avoid spending double-digit hours in a bus or for those with a short amount of time—and sometimes it's cheaper than taking a bus, as well. Airlines have excellent track records and maintain modern fleets.

Bogotá is the major hub in the country, with the majority of domestic **Avianca** (tel. 1/401-3434, www.avianca.com) flights departing from the Puente Aéreo terminal (not the main terminal of the adjacent international airport). Other domestic carriers **LATAM Airlines** (Colombian toll-free tel. 01/800-094-9490, www.latam.com), **VivaColombia** (tel. 1/489-7989, www.vivacolombia.co), **EasyFly** (tel. 1/414-8111, www.easyfly.com.co), **Satena** (Colombian toll-free tel. 01/800-091-2034, www.satena.com), and **Copa Airlines** (Colombian toll-free tel. 01/800-011-0808,

www.copaair.com) depart from the domestic wing of the international airport.

To fly to Caribbean destinations such as Cartagena, San Andrés, Providencia, and Santa Marta during high tourist season, be sure to purchase your ticket well in advance, as seats quickly sell out and prices go through the roof. If your destination is Cartagena or Santa Marta, be sure to check fares to Barranquilla; these may be less expensive, and that city is only about an hour away. Similarly, if you plan to go to the Carnaval de Barranquilla in February, check fares to both Cartagena and Santa Marta. If you are flying to the Coffee Region, inquire about flights to Pereira, Armenia, and Manizales, as the distances between these cities are short. The Manizales airport, however, is often closed due to inclement weather.

For Leticia in the Amazon, the Pacific coast destinations of Bahía Solano and Nuquí, La Macarena (Caño Cristales) in Los Llanos, and San Andrés and Providencia in the Caribbean, the only viable way to get there is by air.

There are strict weight restrictions for flights to Providencia from San Andrés, which are generally on small planes such as those used by the military-owned Satena airline. These island flights sell out fast.

Medellín has two airports: **Aeropuerto Internacional José María Córdova** (in Rionegro) and **Aeropuerto Olaya Herrera.** All international flights and most large airplane flights depart from Rionegro, a town about an hour away from Medellín. The airport is simply referred to as "Rionegro." **Satena** (Colombian toll-free tel. 01/800-091-2034, www.satena.com) and **Aerolíneas de Antioquia-ADA** (Colombian toll-free tel. 01/800-051-4232, www.ada-aero.com) use the Olaya Herrera airport, which is conveniently located in town. This is a hub for flights to remote communities in the Pacific region.

Cali, the country's third-largest city, is much less of an air hub, but with the opening of **GCA Air** (www.gcaair.com), which offers direct low-cost flights to and from Cartagena, it's another option for getting to the Caribbean coast from the southern part of the country.

LONG-DISTANCE BUS

In order to thoroughly cover the country, you will have to hop on a bus at some point—just like the vast majority of Colombians. This is the money-saving choice and often the only option for getting to smaller communities. There are different types of buses, from large coaches for long-distance travel to *colectivos* for shorter distances. *Colectivos* (minivans) are often much quicker, although you won't have much legroom. There are also shared taxis that run between towns, a cramped but quick option. During major holidays, purchase bus tickets in advance if you can, as buses can quickly fill up.

When you arrive at a bus station with guidebook in hand and backpack on, you will be swarmed by touts barking out city names to you, desperately seeking your business on their bus. You can go with the flow and follow them, or, if you prefer a little more control

and calm, you can instead walk past them to the ticket booths. Forge ahead and shake your head while saying *gracias.* You can try to negotiate better fares at the ticket booths, as there are often various options for traveling the same route. Find out what time the bus is leaving, if the vehicle is a big bus, a *buseta,* or minivan, and where your seat is located (try not to get stuck in the last row).

Be alert and aware of your surroundings and of your possessions when you arrive at bus stations, are waiting in the bus terminal, and are aboard buses. Try to avoid flashing around expensive gadgets and cameras while on board. If you check luggage, request a receipt. During pit stops along the way, be sure to keep your valuables with you at all times.

During most bus rides of more than a few hours' length, you will be subjected to loud and/or violent films. Earplugs, eye masks, and even sleeping pills available at most pharmacies may come in handy for those long journeys, but make sure your possessions are well guarded. Expect the air-conditioning to be cranked to full blast, so have a layer or two at the ready. Pick up some provisions like apples or nuts before departing, because food options are generally unhealthy.

Bus drivers like to drive as fast as possible, and generally have few qualms about overtaking cars even on hairpin curves. Large buses tend to be safer than smaller ones, if only because they can't go as fast.

Buses may be stopped by police, and you may be required to show or temporarily hand over your passport (keep it handy). Sometimes passengers may be asked to disembark from the bus so that the police can search it for illegal drugs or other contraband. Young males may be given a pat-down. Even if it annoys you, it is always best to keep cool and remain courteous with police officers who are just doing their job.

PUBLIC TRANSPORTATION

For visitors, public transportation networks are most useful in Bogotá, Medellín, and Cali.

Many cities, such as Medellín, Cali, Armenia, Bucaramanga, Pereira, Barranquilla, and Cartagena have adopted the Bogotá rapid bus system (BRT) model of the TransMilenio.

Today, buses, such as the SITP bus network in Bogotá, are clean, safe, and only pick up passengers at designated stops. In large cities, you will need to purchase an electronic refillable bus card. These can be purchased at *papelerías* (stationery shops), which are often close to bus stops and stations.

The free app **Moovit** provides route information for public transportation options in many Colombian cities.

CAR, MOTORCYCLE, OR BICYCLE

Roads in Colombia are in good condition for the most part, but for many areas of the country, renting a car isn't necessary or recommended for international travelers since public transit is fast and easy and parking often presents a problem.

The areas you may want to consider a car for would be a road trip from Santa Marta to La Guajira along the Caribbean coast, or in the Coffee Region, which has excellent four-lane roads and manageable distances and traffic.

Another region where renting a car may make sense is in Boyacá. Here the countryside is beautiful and traffic is manageable.

There are car rental offices in all the major airports in the country. **Hertz** (tel. 1/756-0600, www.rentacarcolombia.co) and the national **Colombia Car Rental** (U.S. tel. 913/368-0091, www.colombiacarsrental.com) are two with various offices nationwide.

Touring Colombia on motorcycle is an increasingly popular option. One of the best motorcycle travel agencies in the country is **Motolombia** (tel. 2/665-9548, www.motolombia.com), based in Cali. A growing number of travelers are motoring the Pan-American Highway, shipping their bikes from Panama or the United States to Cartagena, or vice versa.

Bicyclists will not get much respect on Colombian roads, and there are rarely any bike lanes of significance. In Santander and in Boyacá the scenery is absolutely spectacular, but, especially in Santander, it is often quite mountainous. In the Valle del Cauca, around Buga and toward Roldanillo, the roads are good and flat. Staff at **Colombian Bike Junkies** (San Gil cell tel. 316/327-6101, Medellín cell tel. 318/808-6769, www.colombianbikejunkies.com), based in San Gil, are experts on biking throughout the country, with an emphasis on mountain biking. Another outfitter is **Colombia en Bicicleta** (www.colombiaenbicicleta.com), catering mostly to bike enthusiasts living in Bogotá.

Every Sunday in cities across Colombia thousands of cyclists (joggers, skaters, and dog walkers, too) head to the city streets for some fresh air and exercise. This is the **Ciclovía,** an initiative that began in Bogotá in which city streets are closed to traffic. Except in Bogotá, it may be difficult to find a bike rental place, but you can still head out for a jog. *Ciclorutas* (bike paths) are being built in the major cities as well, and Bogotá has an extensive *cicloruta* network. Again, cyclists don't get much respect from motorists, so be careful!

BOAT

In some remote locations in Colombia the most common way to get around is by *lancha,* or boat.

Capurganá and Sapzurro are currently accessible only by boat. To get to the towns, you must take a *lancha* to Capurganá from the coastal town of Necoclí or rough port city of Turbo, both on the Golfo de Urabá. Waters can be rough, especially November-March. Don't risk this trip if you have a bad back, as the boat ride can be jarring.

The fabulous beaches of Islas del Rosario, off the coast of Cartagena, are accessed only by boat from the Muelle Turístico de la Bodeguita.

Many of the isolated villages and beaches and the Parque Nacional Natural Utría along the Pacific coast are accessed only by boat from either Bahía Solano or Nuquí. The same goes for Isla Gorgona. To get to this island park, you normally have to take a boat from Guapi or from Buenaventura. All hotels or travel agencies can organize these trips for you.

In the Amazon region, the only way to get from Leticia to attractions nearby, including Puerto Nariño and the eco-lodges on the Río Javari, is by a boat on the Amazon, which is a memorable experience. All boats leave from the *malecón* (wharf) in Leticia.

TAXI AND RIDE-HAILING APP

Taxis are prevalent and cheap all over Colombia and can usually simply be hailed on the street, even in the smallest of towns. Airports and bus terminals use a registration system where travelers are matched with taxis, and their license plate recorded for security. In general, taxis are safe to use throughout the country. Overcharging remains rampant in very touristed areas of Cartagena, however, where taxis aren't metered; establish the fare before getting in the taxi. Taxis are also unmetered in Barranquilla and Santa Marta, but overcharging isn't as much of an issue in these cities. In most of the rest of the country outside of the Caribbean coast, taxis are metered. Tipping isn't customary.

A useful app is **Easy Taxi** (http://cabify.com), run by Cabify, which allows you call a taxi to your location and gives you the price upfront, a good defense against gouging. As of 2020, **Uber** (www.uber.com) is in litigation against the government of Colombia, which banned the app in 2019, so check on the status before you travel.

Visas and Officialdom

PASSPORTS AND VISAS

U.S. and Canadian citizens do not need a visa for visits to Colombia of fewer than 90 days. You may be asked to show a return ticket.

There is an exit tax (Tasa Aeroportuaria Internacional) of around US$37 (COP$122,000). This is often automatically tacked onto your ticket price, but the airline agents will let you know upon check-in. If you are visiting for fewer than 60 days, you are exempt. Prior to check-in, inquire with the airline if you qualify for an exemption. You may be directed to the Aeronáutica Civil booth across from the airline check-in counter, where you'll show your passport to get an exemption stamp.

To renew a tourist visa, you must go to an office of **Migración Colombia** (www.migracioncolombia.gov.co) to request an extension of another 90 days. Tourists can stay a maximum of 180 days out of a calendar year.

CUSTOMS

Upon arrival in Colombia, bags will be spot-checked by customs authorities. Duty-free items up to a value of US$1,500 can be brought into Colombia. Firearms are not allowed into the country, and many animal and vegetable products are not allowed. If you are carrying over US$10,000 in cash you must declare it.

Departing Colombia, expect a smooth process, but luggage may be screened for drugs, Colombian art, and exotic animals.

EMBASSIES AND CONSULATES

The **United States Embassy** (Cl. 24 Bis No. 48-50, tel. 1/275-2000, http://bogota.usembassy.gov) is in Bogotá, near the airport. In case of an emergency, during business hours contact the **U.S. Citizen Services Hotline** (business hours tel. 1/275-2000, after-hours and weekends tel. 1/275-4021). Nonemergency calls are answered at the American Citizen Services Section Monday-Thursday 2pm-4pm. To be informed of security developments or emergencies during your visit, you can enroll in the Smart Traveler Enrollment Program (STEP) on the U.S. Embassy website. In Barranquilla, there is a **Consular Agency Office** (Cl. 77B No. 57-141, Suite 511, tel. 5/353-2001 or tel. 5/353-2182), but its hours and services are limited.

The **Canadian Embassy** (Cra. 7 No. 114-33, Piso 14, tel. 1/657-9800, www.canadainternational.gc.ca) is in Bogotá. There is a **Canadian Consular Office** (Bocagrande Edificio Centro Ejecutivo Oficina 1103, Cra. 3, No. 8-129, tel. 5/665-5838) in Cartagena. For emergencies, Canadian citizens can call the **emergency hotline** (Can. tel. 613/996-8885) in Canada collect.

Accommodations and Food

Many hotels include free wireless Internet and breakfast (although food quality will vary). While all the fancy hotels and backpacker places have English-speaking staff—at least at the front desk—smaller hotels may not. Room rates usually depend on the number of occupants, not the size of the room. Except for some international chains and upper-end hotels, most hotels will not have heating or air-conditioning in their rooms.

Note that *moteles* are always, *residencias* are usually, and *hospedajes* are sometimes Colombian love hotels.

HOTELS

Midrange hotels are often harder to find and their quality can be unpredictable. Beds can be uncomfortable, rooms may be small, views might be unappealing, and service hit-or-miss. Spanish is the most prevalent language spoken at these types of accommodations.

High-end hotels, including international brands, are in all large cities. In tourist centers such as Cartagena and Santa Marta, boutique hotels are good options for those seeking charm. Expect courteous service and comfort. The only place to expect international television channels and access for travelers with disabilities are at high-end international hotels.

HOSTELS

Hostels catering to backpackers are found everywhere, many run by young, globally minded Colombians. Most of these offer private rooms for those not interested in sharing a dorm room with strangers. Young people are drawn to hostels, but an increasing number of older travelers opt for hostels, as these, in addition to offering budget accommodations, are also the best places for information on activities. Most hostel staff speak English. **Hostel Trail** (www.hosteltrail.com) is a good resource for information on Colombian hostels. Hostels generally maintain updated information on their Facebook pages.

VALUE-ADDED TAX EXEMPTION

Non-Colombian visitors are exempt from IVA, a sales tax, which is around 16 percent. To qualify for the exemption, you must make your hotel reservation by email or phone from abroad, there must be at least two services included (such as the room fee and an included breakfast), and you must show proof of being in Colombia for less than six months.

FOOD AND DRINK

In Bogotá and Cartagena especially, Colombian foodie culture is alive and well, and visitors will have a wealth of excellent dining options—if they don't mind the occasional Manhattan prices.

While seafood, especially *pescado frito* (fried fish), is de rigueur in the Caribbean and along the Pacific, in the interior beef and chicken rule. In the Medellín area, the famed and hearty *bandeja paisa* is a dish made of red beans cooked with pork, white rice, ground meat, *chicharrón* (fried pork rinds), fried egg, plantains (*patacones*), chorizo, *hogao* sauce, *morcilla* (black pudding), avocado, and lemon. In Bogotá, the dish for cool evenings is *ajiaco*, a chicken and potato soup. In rural areas, the typical lunchtime meal will include soup and a main dish (*seco*) such as *arroz con pollo* (chicken with rice). Eat what you can, but foreigners are forgiven if they can't finish a plate.

Vegetarians have decent options available to them, especially in tourist centers. A can of lentils can be a helpful travel companion in rural areas. In coastal areas it will be hard to avoid eating fish.

Be sure to try the many unusual fruits and juices in Colombia. Juice is either served in water or in milk, and sometimes has a lot of sugar. The same goes for freshly squeezed lemonade.

Tinto (percolated coffee) can be downright dismal in rural areas, where it is served very sweet. For a good cup of coffee, head to a national brand like Juan Valdez or Oma. Non-coffee drinkers will enjoy *aromatica,* herbal tea that is typically served after dinner.

Colombia is a major chocolate producer and has some award-winning local brands, such as Cacao Hunter's Chocolate, which works with small farmers in different regions including the Sierra Nevada and near Tumaco.

Breakfast almost universally consists of eggs, bread or arepas, juice, and coffee. Fresh fruit is not that common at breakfast. Arepas are important in Colombia: Every region has its own take on these starchy corn cakes. Arepas in Medellín are large, thin, and bland, while arepas in other parts of the country can be cheese-filled.

Travel Tips

ALCOHOL AND CANNABIS

The legal drinking age in Colombia is 18 years old, and many bars and clubs will request ID. Public alcohol consumption is part of Colombian culture and legal in most parts of the country. In Cartagena, outdoor drinking is everywhere and part of the experience. In some parts of the country, however, notably Bogotá and Medellín, public consumption is restricted to certain areas. However, police seldom do more than ask you to take it somewhere else.

Travelers will receive many mixed messages in regard to cannabis use in Colombia. Cannabis products are sold openly in both the streets and in shops throughout the country, particularly in the northern Caribbean coast's Santa Marta-Minca region, one of the traditional growing areas. Colombia is also expected to eventually become the world's largest producer in the new legal cannabis market opening up around the world. But recreational cannabis use has not yet been legalized in the country—although in 2019 congress drafted legislation to do so. While the country's Constitutional Court decriminalized a "personal dose" of recreational drugs for adults in 1994, upheld again—and deemed a "human right"—after being challenged in 2018 by President Iván Duque Márquez, in practice police may harass those caught with cannabis, confiscate it, and solicit bribes under threat of arrest. Especially in certain backpacker areas, such as Cartagena's Getsemaní neighborhood and the Caribbean coast's Taganga, corrupt police take advantage of the cannabis confusion and try to shake down unsuspecting tourists.

ACCESS FOR TRAVELERS WITH DISABILITIES

Only international and some national hotel chains offer rooms (usually just one or two) that are wheelchair-accessible. Hostels and small hotels in secondary cities or towns will not. Airport and airline staff will usually bend over backwards to help those with disabilities, if you ask.

Getting around cities and towns is complicated, as good sidewalks and ramps are the exception, not the rule. Motorists may not stop—or even slow down—for pedestrians.

WOMEN TRAVELING ALONE

Along the Caribbean and Pacific coasts especially, women traveling alone should expect to be on the receiving end of flirting and various friendly offers by men and curiosity by everyone. Women should be extra cautious in taxis and buses. Always order taxis by phone or through the Easy Taxi app, and avoid taking them alone at night. While incidents are unlikely, it is not a fantastic idea to go out for a jog, a walk on a remote beach, or a hike through the jungle on your own. Walking about small towns at night alone may elicit looks or comments. Don't reveal personal information, where you are staying, or where you are going to inquisitive strangers. There have been incidents in the past with single women travelers in remote areas of La Guajira.

GAY AND LESBIAN TRAVELERS

Colombia has some of the Western Hemisphere's most progressive laws regarding the rights of LGBTQ people. The Constitutional Court legalized same-sex marriage and adoption in 2016 after a torturous, decades-long struggle marked by court victories, legislative defeats, and much debate.

Colombia is a fairly tolerant country, especially in its large cities. Bogotá is one of the most gay-friendly cities on the continent, with a large gay nightlife scene and city-supported LGBTQ community centers. In many neighborhoods, passersby don't blink an eye when they see a gay couple holding hands on the sidewalk.

The Caribbean region is generally less open to homosexuality, and this is especially true in rural areas. Nevertheless, the main cities of the region—Cartagena, Barranquilla, and Santa Marta—have gay clubs and are home to active LGBT communities. All bars and clubs, while catering to men, are welcoming to gay women and to straight people. In the San Andrés Archipelago, homophobia is the norm among the native islanders, although violence against gay travelers is unheard of. The online guide **Guia GAY Colombia** (www.guiagaycolombia.com) has a listing of meeting places for LGBT people throughout the country.

Discrimination, especially against transgender people and even more so against trans sex workers, continues to be a problem in many cities and towns, in particular in Cali and the Caribbean. The award-winning nonprofit group **Colombia Diversa** (www.colombiadiversa.org) is the main advocate for LGBTQ rights in the country, with **Caribe Afirmativo** (www.caribeafirmativo.lgbt) focusing its efforts on the Caribbean region.

Gay men in particular should be cautious using dating apps, keep an eye on drinks at nightclubs, and avoid cabs off the street when departing clubs.

Same-sex couples should not hesitate to insist on *matrimonial* (double) beds at hotels. Most hotels in cities and even in smaller towns and rural areas are becoming more clued in on this. At guesthouses, hostels, and at some midsized hotels, front desk staff may charge if you invite a guest to the room. At large international hotels and at apartments for rent, this is never the case.

CONDUCT AND CUSTOMS

Colombians are generally friendly to visitors and are often inquisitive about where you are from and how you like Colombia so far. This is most often the case in rural areas. Colombians are also quite proud of their country, after emerging from decades of armed conflict.

With acquaintances and strangers alike, it is customary to ask how someone is doing before moving on to other business. You're even expected to issue a blanket *buenos días* ("Good morning") in the elevator. When greeting an acquaintance, it's customary to shake hands (between men) or give an air kiss on the cheek (for women), although this is mostly the case in urban areas, especially with the upper crust.

Colombians are comfortable with noise—expect the TV to always be on and music blasting almost everywhere. Many Colombians you meet will ask about your family. Family ties are very important to Colombians.

Sundays often mean lunch in the countryside with nuclear and extended family members.

While tourists get a pass on appearance, it's preferred that men avoid wearing shorts, especially at restaurants, except on the Caribbean coast. Dress up, like the locals do, when going out on the town.

Indigenous cultures are much more conservative, and women are expected to refrain from showing much skin.

Health and Safety

VACCINATIONS

There are no vaccination requirements for travel to Colombia. However, having proof of vaccination may make life easier, especially if you plan on traveling onward to Brazil or other countries.

The Centers for Disease Control (CDC) recommends that travelers to Colombia get up-to-date on the following vaccines: measles-mumps-rubella (MMR), diphtheria-tetanus-pertussis, varicella (chicken pox), polio, and the yearly flu shot.

DISEASES AND ILLNESSES
Malaria, Zika, Chikungunya, and Dengue Fever

In low-lying tropical areas of Colombia, mosquito-borne illnesses such as malaria, dengue fever, chikungunya, and Zika are common. It is best to assume that there is a risk, albeit quite small, in all areas of the country.

Malaria is a concern in the entire Amazon region and in the lowland departments of Antioquia, Chocó, Córdoba, Nariño, and Bolívar. There is low to no malarial risk in Cartagena and in areas above 1,600 meters (5,000 ft). The Colombian Ministry of Health estimates that there are around 63,000 annual cases of malaria in the country, 20 of which result in death. Most at risk are children under the age of 15. Malaria symptoms include fever,

headache, chills, vomiting, fatigue, and difficulty breathing. Treatment involves the administration of various antimalarial drugs. If you plan on spending a lot of time outdoors in lowland tropical areas, consider taking an antimalarial chemoprophylaxis.

The number of cases of **dengue fever** in Colombia has grown from 5.2 cases per 100,000 residents in the 1990s to around 18.1 cases per 100,000 in the 2000s. It is another mosquito-borne illness. The most common symptoms of dengue fever are fever; headaches; muscle, bone, and joint pain; and pain behind the eyes. It is fatal in less than 1 percent of the cases. Treatment usually involves rest and hydration and the administration of pain relievers for headache and muscle pain. **Chikungunya virus** has similar symptoms to dengue, and an infection, involving painful aches, can last for several months. It is spread, like dengue, by the *Aedes aegypti* mosquito, often during daytime.

Zika virus is a concern to pregnant women, as there is a link between the virus and birth defects. Pregnant women should avoid traveling to low-lying areas (under 2,000 m/6,000 ft) where Zika is present. This includes much of Colombia. Symptoms include fever, rash, joint pains, and conjunctivitis.

The Centers for Disease Control (www.cdc.gov) remains the best resource on health concerns for worldwide travel.

PREVENTION

Use mosquito nets over beds when visiting tropical areas of Colombia. Examine them well before using, and if you notice large holes in the nets request replacements. Mosquitoes tend to be at their worst at dawn, dusk, and in the evenings. Wear lightweight, long-sleeved, and light-colored shirts, long pants, and socks, and keep some insect repellent handy.

DEET is considered effective in preventing mosquito bites, but there are other, less-toxic alternatives, most available from online retailers.

If you go to the Amazon region, especially during rainy seasons, take an antimalarial prophylaxis starting 15 days before arrival, and continuing 15 days after departing the region. According to the CDC, the recommended chemoprophylaxis for visitors to malarial regions of Colombia is atovaquone-proguanil, doxycycline, or mefloquine. These drugs are available at most pharmacies in Colombia with no prescription necessary.

Altitude Sickness

The high altitudes of the Andes, including in Bogotá (2,625 meters/8,612 ft), can be a problem for some. If arriving directly in Bogotá, or if you are embarking on treks in the Sierra Nevada del Cocuy or in Los Nevados, where the highest peaks reach 5,300 meters (over 17,000 ft), take it easy and avoid drinking alcohol for the first couple of days. Make mountain ascents gradually if possible. You can also take the drug acetazolamide to help speed up your acclimatization. Drinking coca tea or chewing on coca leaves may help prevent *soroche,* as altitude sickness is called in Colombia.

Traveler's Diarrhea

Stomach flu or traveler's diarrhea is a common malady when traveling through Colombia. These are usually caused by food contamination resulting from the presence of *E. coli* bacteria. Street foods, including undercooked meat, raw vegetables, dairy products, and ice, are some of the main culprits. If you get a case

of traveler's diarrhea, be sure to drink lots of clear liquids, avoid caffeine, and take an oral rehydration solution of salt, sugar, and water.

Tap Water

Tap water is fine to drink in Colombia's major cities, but you should drink bottled, purified, or boiled water in the Amazon, the Pacific coast, the Darién Gap, La Guajira, and San Andrés and Providencia. As an alternative to buying plastic bottles, look for *bolsitas* (bags) of water. They come in a variety of sizes and use less plastic.

MEDICAL SERVICES

Colombia has excellent health services, particularly in its major cities, and has been ranked highly in terms of quality of healthcare by the World Health Organization, among others. Over 20 hospitals in Colombia (in Bogotá, Medellín, Bucaramanga, and Cali) have been listed in the *América Economía* magazine listing of the top 40 hospitals of Latin America. Four hospitals were in the top 10. Those were the **Fundación Santa Fe de Bogotá** (www. fsfb.org.co), the **Fundación Valle del Lili** (www.valledellili.org) in Cali, the **Fundación Cardioinfantil** (www.cardioinfantil. org) in Bogotá, and the **Fundación Cardiovascular de Colombia** (www.fcv. org) in Floridablanca, near Bucaramanga. For sexual and reproductive health issues, **Profamilia** (www.profamilia.org.co) has a large network of clinics that provide walk-in and low-cost services throughout the country.

Both Cartagena and Barranquilla, and to a lesser extent Santa Marta and Riohacha, are home to both public and private hospitals as well as clinics. Right on the beach on Cartagena's Bocagrande peninsula, the **Clinica MediHelp** (Cra. 6 No. 5-101, 5/647-5290, www.clinicamedihelp.com, 24 hours daily) specializes in urgent medical problems for visitors.

Aerosanidad SAS (tel. 1/439-7080, 24-hour hotline tel. 1/266-2247 or tel. 1/439-7080, www.aerosanidadsas.com) provides transportation services for ill or injured persons in remote locations of Colombia to medical facilities in the large cities.

Travel insurance is a good idea to purchase before arriving in Colombia, especially if you plan on doing a lot of outdoor adventures. One recommended provider of travel insurance is **Assist Card** (www.assist-card.com). Before taking a paragliding ride or white-water rafting trip inquire to see whether insurance is included in the price of the trip—it should be.

CRIME

Colombia is safe to visit, and the majority of visitors have a wonderful experience in the country. For international travelers, there is little to worry about when it comes to illegal armed groups today. The threat of kidnapping of civilians and visitors has been almost completely eliminated.

Even in the worst of times, places like Cartagena and Bogotá have always been less affected by violence from the armed conflict plaguing the rest of the country. Now, with implementation of a peace deal between FARC guerrillas and the Colombian government, the outlook is brighter than ever. However, uncertainty remains and smaller groups of former paramilitaries (*bacrim*) and guerrillas operate in some cities and towns, while drug lords and dangerous gangs rule marginalized urban areas.

There are still places to avoid, even along the peaceful Caribbean coast. In the northwest, avoid the jungle and rural areas in and around Parque Nacional Natural Los Katios in the Darién region, as well as the Parque Nacional Natural Paramillo in Córdoba. On the eastern side of the country, the Catatumbo region, along the Venezuelan border, remains volatile. In the rest of the country, hot spots include much of the Amazonian rainforest (with the notable exception of Leticia and Puerto Nariño), areas near La Macarena in Meta (but Caño Cristales is safe), rural areas of Cauca (Popayán and Tierradentro are fine), rural areas near Tumaco and Buenaventura on the Pacific coast, and much of the Chocó jungle (except for tourist areas of Bahía Solano, Nuquí, and the capital city of Quibdó).

For updated travel advisories, check the website of the **U.S. Embassy** (http://bogota.usembassy.gov) in Bogotá. The embassy always errs on the side of caution.

Street Crime

Street theft is problematic in major cities and heavily touristed areas, so always keep an eye on belongings.

Cell phone theft plagues much of the country. Keep wallets in front pockets, be aware of your surroundings, and keep shopping bags and backpacks near you at all times. Muggings in major cities are not unheard of, but are quite rare. Be alert to your surroundings late at night.

Police

From just about anywhere in the country, the police can be reached by dialing 123 on any phone. Otherwise, many parks are home to neighborhood police stations, called CAI (Centros de Atención Inmediata). Authorities may not be able to do much about petty theft, however.

Information and Services

MONEY

Currency

Colombia's official currency is the peso, which is abbreviated as COP. Prices in Colombia are marked with a dollar sign, but remember that you're seeing the price in Colombian pesos. COP$1,000,000 isn't enough to buy a house in Colombia, but it will usually cover a few nights in a nice hotel!

Bills in Colombia are in denominations of $1,000, $2,000, $5,000, $10,000, $20,000, $50,000, and $100,000. Some of the bills got a makeover in 2016, so you may see two different versions of the same amount. Coins in Colombia are in denominations of $50, $100, $200, $500, and $1,000. The equivalent of cents is *centavos* in Colombian Spanish.

Due to dropping oil prices, the Colombian peso has devalued to record levels, making the country a bargain for international visitors. In early 2020, one U.S. dollar was the equivalent of COP$4,000.

Most banks in Colombia do not exchange money. For that, you'll have to go to a money exchange, located in all major cities. There are money changers on the streets of Cartagena, but the street is not the best place for safe and honest transactions.

Travelers checks are not worth the hassle, as they are hard to cash. Dollars are sometimes accepted in Cartagena and other major tourist destinations. To have cash wired to you from abroad, look for a Western Union office. These are located only in major cities.

Counterfeit bills are a problem in Colombia, and unsuspecting international visitors are often the recipients. Bar staff, taxi drivers, and street vendors are the most common culprits. It's good to always have a stash of small bills to avoid getting large bills back as change. Tattered and torn bills will also be passed off to you, which could pose a problem. Try not to accept those.

Consignaciones

Consignaciones (bank transfers) are a common way to pay for hotel reservations (especially in areas such as Providencia and remote resorts), tour packages or guides, or entry to national parks. It's often a pain to make these deposits in person, as the world of banking can be confusing for non-Colombians. On the plus side, making a deposit directly into the hotel's bank account provides some peace of mind because it will diminish the need to carry large amounts of cash. To make a *consignación* you will need to know the recipient's bank account and whether that is a *corriente* (checking) or *ahorros* (savings) account, and you will need to show some identification and probably have to provide a fingerprint. Be sure to hold onto the receipt to notify the recipient of your deposit.

ATMs

The best way to get cash is to use your bank ATM card. These are almost universally accepted at *cajeros automáticos* (ATMs) in the country. *Cajeros* are almost everywhere except in the smallest of towns or in remote areas. Withdrawal fees are relatively expensive, although they vary. You can usually take out up to around COP$300,000-500,000 (the equivalent of around US$150-250) per transaction. Many banks place limits on how much one can withdraw in a day (COP$1,000,000).

Credit and Debit Cards

Credit and debit card use is becoming more prevalent in Colombia; however, online credit card transactions are still not so common except for the major airlines and some of the event ticket companies, such as www.tuboleta.com or www.colboletos.com. When you use your plastic, you will be asked if it's *credito* (credit) or *debito* (debit). If using a *tarjeta de crédito* (credit card) in restaurants and stores, you will be asked something like, "*¿Cuantas* *cuotas?"* or *"¿Numero de cuotas?"* ("How many installments?"). Most visitors prefer one *cuota* (*"Una, por favor"*). But you can have even your dinner bill paid in up to 24 installments! If using a *tarjeta de débito,* you'll be asked if it is a *corriente* (checking) or *ahorros* (savings) account.

Tipping

In most sit-down restaurants in larger cities, a 10 percent service charge is automatically included in the bill. Waitstaff are required to ask you, *"¿Desea incluir el servicio?"* ("Would you like to include the service in the bill?"). Many times restaurant staff neglect to ask international tourists about the service inclusion. If you find the service to be exceptional, you can leave a little extra in cash. Although tipping is not expected in bars or cafés, tip jars are becoming more common. International visitors are often expected to tip more than Colombians. In small-town restaurants throughout the country, tipping is not the norm.

It is not customary to tip taxi drivers. But if you feel the driver was a good one who drove safely and was honest, or if he or she made an additional stop for you, waited for you, or was just pleasant, you can always round up the bill (instead of COP$6,200 give the driver COP$7,000 and say *"Quédese con las vueltas por favor"* ("Keep the change"). Note that sometimes a "tip" is already included in the fare for non-Colombian visitors!

In hotels, usually a tip of COP$5,000 will suffice for porters who help with luggage, unless you have lots of stuff. Tips are not expected, but are certainly welcome, for housekeeping staff.

Value-Added Tax

Non-Colombian visitors are entitled to a refund of value-added taxes for purchases on clothing, jewelry, and other items if their purchases total more than COP$300,000. Save all credit card receipts and fill out Form 1344 (available online at www.dian.gov.co). Submit this to the **DIAN office** (tel. 1/607-9999) at the airport before departure. You may have several hoops to go through to achieve success. Go to the DIAN office before checking your luggage, as you will have to present the items you purchased.

INTERNET AND TELEPHONES

Being connected makes travel throughout Colombia so much easier. Free Wi-Fi is available at most hotels, restaurants, and cafés in major cities. An important Spanish phrase to learn is *"Como es la contraseña para el wifi?"* ("What's the password for the Wi-Fi?")

Obtaining a SIM card for your cell phone will ensure connectivity in all but the most remote locations. Sometimes low-tech phones work better than smartphones in very rural or remote locations like Providencia. SIM cards (*datos de prepago*) are available at mobile-phone carriers in all major towns and cities. Three main cell phone companies are Claro, Movistar, and Tigo.

Facebook and Whatsapp are often the best bets for contacting hotels, restaurants, and shops.

The telephone country code for Colombia is 57. Cell phone numbers are 10 digits long, beginning with a 3. To call a Colombian cell phone from abroad, you must use the country code followed by that 10-digit number. Landline numbers in Colombia are seven digits long. An area code is necessary when calling from a different region. To call a landline from a cell phone, dial 03 + area code + 7-digit number. To reach a cell phone from a landline, dial 03 + 10-digit number.

Resources

Spanish Phrasebook

Knowing some Spanish is essential to visit Colombia, as relatively few people outside the major cities speak English. Colombian Spanish is said to be among the clearest in Latin America. However, there are many regional differences.

Spanish commonly uses 30 letters—the familiar English 26, plus four straightforward additions: ch, ll, ñ, and rr, which are explained in "Consonants," below.

PRONUNCIATION

Once you learn them, Spanish pronunciation rules—in contrast to English—don't change. Spanish vowels generally sound softer than in English. (*Note:* The capitalized syllables below receive stronger accents.)

Vowels

a   like ah, as in "hah": *agua* AH-gooah (water), *pan* PAHN (bread), and *casa* CAH-sah (house)

e   like ay, as in "may": *mesa* MAY-sah (table), *tela* TAY-lah (cloth), and *de* DAY (of, from)

i   like ee, as in "need": *diez* dee-AYZ (ten), *comida* ko-MEE-dah (meal), and *fin* FEEN (end)

o   like oh, as in "go": *peso* PAY-soh (weight), *ocho* OH-choh (eight), and *poco* POH-koh (a bit)

u   like oo, as in "cool": *uno* OO-noh (one), *cuarto* KOOAHR-toh (room), and *usted* oos-TAYD (you); when it follows a "q" the u is silent; when it follows an "h" or has an umlaut, it's pronounced like "w"

Consonants

b, d, f, k, l, m, n, p, q, s, t, v, w, x, y, z, and

ch   pronounced almost as in English; h occurs, but is silent—not pronounced at all

c   like k as in "keep": *cuarto* KOOAR-toh (room), *casa* KAH-sah (house); when it precedes "e" or "i," pronounce c like s, as in "sit": *cerveza* sayr-VAY-sah (beer), *encima* ayn-SEE-mah (atop)

g   like g as in "gift" when it precedes "a," "o," "u," or a consonant: *gato* GAH-toh (cat), *hago* AH-goh (I do, make); otherwise, pronounce g like h as in "hat": *giro* HEE-roh (money order), *gente* HAYN-tay (people)

j   like h, as in "has": *Jueves* HOOAY-vays (Thursday), *mejor* may-HOR (better)

ll   like y, as in "yes": *toalla* toh-AH-yah (towel), *ellos* AY-yohs (they, them)

ñ   like ny, as in "canyon": *año* AH-nyo (year), *señor* SAY-nyor (Mr., sir)

r   is lightly trilled, with tongue at the roof of your mouth like a very light English d, as in "ready": *pero* PAY-roh (but), *tres* TRAYS (three), *cuatro* KOOAH-troh (four)

rr   like a Spanish r, but with much more emphasis and trill. Let your tongue flap. Practice with *burro* (donkey), *carretera* (highway), and Carrillo (proper name), then really let go with *ferrocarril* (railroad)

Note: The single small but common exception to all of the above is the pronunciation of Spanish y when it's being used as the Spanish word for "and," as in "Ron y Kathy." In such case, pronounce it like the English ee, as in "keep": Ron "ee" Kathy (Ron and Kathy).

Accent

The rule for accents, the relative stress given to syllables within a given word, is straightforward: If a word ends in a vowel, an n, or an s, accent the next-to-last syllable; if not, accent the last syllable.

Pronounce *gracias* GRAH-seeahs (thank you), *orden* OHR-dayn (order), and *carretera* kah-ray-TAY-rah (highway) with stress on the next-to-last syllable. Otherwise, accent the last syllable: *venir* vay-NEER (to come), *ferrocarril* fay-roh-cah-REEL (railroad), and *edad* ay-DAHD (age).

Exceptions to the accent rule are always marked with an accent sign: (á, é, í, ó, or ú), such as *teléfono* tay-LAY-foh-noh (telephone), *jabón* hah BON (soap), and *rápido* RAH-pee-doh (rapid).

BASIC AND COURTEOUS EXPRESSIONS

Colombians use many courteous formalities. Whenever approaching anyone for information or some other reason, do not forget the appropriate salutation—good morning, good evening, etc. Standing alone, the greeting *hola* (hello) can sound brusque.

Hello. *Hola.*
Good morning. *Buenos días.*
Good afternoon. *Buenas tardes.*
Good evening. *Buenas noches.*
How are you? Colombians have many ways of saying this: *¿Cómo estás/como está? ¿Qué hubo/Qu'hubo? ¿Cómo va/vas? ¿Que tal?*
Very well, thank you. *Muy bien, gracias.*
Okay; good. *Bien.*
Not okay; bad. *Mal.*
So-so. *Más o menos.*
And you? *¿Y Usted?*
Thank you. *Gracias.*
Thank you very much. *Muchas gracias.*
You're very kind. *Muy amable.*
You're welcome. *De nada.*
Goodbye. *Adiós.*
See you later. *Hasta luego. Chao.*
please *por favor;* (slang) *por fa*
yes *sí*
no *no*
I don't know. *No sé.*

Just a moment, please. *Un momento, por favor.*
Excuse me, please (when you're trying to get attention). *Disculpe.*
Excuse me (when you've made a mistake). *Perdón. Que pena.*
I'm sorry. *Lo siento.*
Pleased to meet you. *Mucho gusto.*
How do you say . . . in Spanish? *¿Cómo se dice . . . en español?*
What is your name? *¿Cómo se llama (Usted)? ¿Cómo te llamas?*
Do you speak English? *¿Habla (Usted) inglés? ¿Hablas inglés?*
Does anyone here speak English? *¿Hay alguien que hable inglés?*
I don't speak Spanish well. *No hablo bien el español.*
Please speak more slowly. *Por favor hable más despacio.*
I don't understand. *No entiendo.*
Please write it down. *Por favor escríbalo.*
My name is . . . *Me llamo . . . Mi nombre es . . .*
I would like . . . *Quisiera . . . Quiero . . .*
Let's go to . . . *Vamos a . . .*
That's fine. *Está bien.*
All right. *Listo.*
cool, awesome *chévere, rico, super*
Oh my god! *¡Dios mío!*
That's crazy! *¡Qué locura!*
You're crazy! *¡Estás loca/o!*

TERMS OF ADDRESS

When in doubt, use the formal *Usted* (you) as a form of address.

I *yo*
you (formal) *Usted*
you (familiar) *tú*
he/him *él*
she/her *ella*
we/us *nosotros*
you (plural) *Ustedes*
they/them *ellas* (all females); *ellos* (all males or mixed gender)
Mr., sir *señor*
Mrs., madam *señora*
miss, young lady *señorita*
wife *esposa*

husband *esposo*
friend *amigo/a*
girlfriend/boyfriend *novia* (female); *novio* (male)
partner *pareja*
daughter; son *hija; hijo*
brother; sister *hermano; hermana*
mother; father *madre; padre*
grandfather; grandmother *abuelo; abuela*

TRANSPORTATION

Where is ...? *¿Dónde está ...?*
How far is it to ...? *¿A cuánto queda ...?*
from ... to ... *de ... a ...*
How many blocks? *¿Cuántas cuadras?*
Where (Which) is the way to ...? *¿Cuál es el camino a ...? ¿Por dónde es ...?*
bus station *la terminal de buses/terminal de transportes*
bus stop *la parada*
Where is this bus going? *¿A dónde va este bús?*
boat *el barco, la lancha*
dock *el muelle*
airport *el aeropuerto*
I'd like a ticket to ... *Quisiera un pasaje a ...*
round-trip *ida y vuelta*
reservation *reserva*
baggage *equipaje*
next flight *el próximo vuelo*
Stop here, please. *Pare aquí, por favor.*
the entrance *la entrada*
the exit *la salida*
(very) near; far *(muy) cerca; lejos*
to; toward *a*
by; through *por*
from *de*
right *la derecha*
left *la izquierda*
straight ahead *derecho*
in front *en frente*
beside *al lado*
behind *atrás*
corner *la esquina*
stoplight *el semáforo*
turn *una vuelta*

here *aquí*
somewhere around here *por aquí*
there *allí*
somewhere around there *por allá*
road *camino*
street *calle, carrera*
avenue *avenida*
block *la cuadra*
highway *carretera*
kilometer *kilómetro*
bridge; toll *puente; peaje*
address *dirección*
north; south *norte; sur*
east; west *oriente (este); occidente (oeste)*

FOOD

I'm hungry. *Tengo hambre.*
I'm thirsty. *Tengo sed.*
Table for two, please. *Una mesa para dos, por favor.*
menu *carta*
order *orden*
glass *vaso*
glass of water *vaso con agua*
fork *tenedor*
knife *cuchillo*
spoon *cuchara*
napkin *servilleta*
soft drink *gaseosa*
coffee *café, tinto*
tea *té*
drinking water *agua potable*
bottled carbonated water *agua con gas*
bottled uncarbonated water *agua sin gas*
beer *cerveza*
wine *vino*
glass of wine *copa de vino*
red wine *vino tinto*
white wine *vino blanco*
milk *leche*
juice *jugo*
cream *crema*
sugar *azúcar*
cheese *queso*
breakfast *desayuno*
lunch *almuerzo*
daily lunch special *menú del día*

dinner *comida*
the check *la cuenta*
eggs *huevos*
bread *pan*
salad *ensalada*
lettuce *lechuga*
tomato *tomate*
onion *cebolla*
garlic *ajo*
hot sauce *ají*
fruit *fruta*
mango *mango*
watermelon *patilla*
papaya *papaya*
banana *banano*
apple *manzana*
orange *naranja*
lime *limón*
passion fruit *maracuyá*
guava *guayaba*
grape *uva*
fish *pescado*
shellfish *mariscos*
shrimp *camarones*
(without) meat *(sin) carne*
chicken *pollo*
pork *cerdo*
beef *carne de res*
bacon; ham *tocino; jamón*
fried *frito*
roasted *asado*
Do you have vegetarian options? *¿Tienen opciones vegetarianas?*
I'm vegetarian. *Soy vegetarian(o).*
I don't eat ... *No como ...*
to share *para compartir*
Check, please. *La cuenta, por favor.*
Is the service included? *¿Está incluido el servicio?*
tip *propina*
large *grande*
small *pequeño*

ACCOMMODATIONS

hotel *hotel*
Is there a room available? *¿Hay un cuarto disponible?*

May I (may we) see it? *¿Puedo (podemos) verlo?*
How much is it? *¿Cuánto cuesta?*
Is there something cheaper? *¿Hay algo más económico?*
single room *un cuarto sencillo*
double room *un cuarto doble*
double bed *cama matrimonial*
single bed *cama sencilla*
with private bath *con baño propio*
television *televisor*
window *ventana*
view *vista*
hot water *agua caliente*
shower *ducha*
towels *toallas*
soap *jabón*
toilet paper *papel higiénico*
pillow *almohada*
blanket *cobija*
sheets *sábanas*
air-conditioned *aire acondicionado*
fan *ventilador*
swimming pool *piscina*
gym *gimnasio*
bike *bicicleta*
key *llave*
suitcase *maleta*
backpack *mochila*
lock *candado*
safe *caja de seguridad*
manager *gerente*
maid *empleada*
clean *limpio*
dirty *sucio*
broken *roto*
(not) included *(no) incluido*

SHOPPING

cash *efectivo*
money *dinero*
credit card *tarjeta de crédito*
debit card *tarjeta de débito*
money exchange office *casa de cambio*
What is the exchange rate? *¿Cuál es la tasa de cambio?*
How much is the commission? *¿Cuánto es la comisión?*

Do you accept credit cards? *¿Aceptan tarjetas de crédito?*
credit card installments *cuotas*
money order *giro*
How much does it cost? *¿Cuánto cuesta?*
expensive *caro*
cheap *barato; económico*
more *más*
less *menos*
a little *un poco*
too much *demasiado*
value-added tax *IVA*
discount *descuento*

HEALTH

Help me please. *Ayúdeme por favor.*
I am ill. *Estoy enferma/o.*
Call a doctor. *Llame un doctor.*
Take me to ... *Lléveme a ...*
hospital *hospital, clínica*
drugstore *farmacia*
pain *dolor*
fever *fiebre*
headache *dolor de cabeza*
stomachache *dolor de estómago*
burn *quemadura*
cramp *calambre*
nausea *náusea*
vomiting *vomitar*
medicine *medicina*
antibiotic *antibiótico*
pill *pastilla, pepa*
aspirin *aspirina*
ointment; cream *ungüento; crema*
bandage (big) *venda*
bandage (small) *cura*
cotton *algodón*
sanitary napkin *toalla sanitaria*
birth control pills *pastillas anticonceptivas*
condoms *condones*
toothbrush *cepillo de dientes*
dental floss *hilo dental*
toothpaste *crema dental*
dentist *dentista*
toothache *dolor de muelas*
vaccination *vacuna*

COMMUNICATIONS

Wi-Fi *wifi*
cell phone *celular*
username *usuario*
password *contraseña*
laptop computer *portátil*
prepaid cellphone *celular prepago*
post office *4-72*
phone call *llamada*
letter *carta*
stamp *estampilla*
postcard *postal*
package; box *paquete; caja*

AT THE BORDER

border *frontera*
customs *aduana*
immigration *migración*
inspection *inspección*
ID card *cédula*
passport *pasaporte*
profession *profesión*
vacation *vacaciones*
I'm a tourist. *Soy turista.*
student *estudiante*
marital status *estado civil*
single *soltero*
married; divorced *casado; divorciado*
widowed *viudado*
insurance *seguro*
title *título*
driver's license *pase de conducir*

AT THE GAS STATION

gas station *estación de gasolina*
gasoline *gasolina*
full, please *lleno, por favor*
tire *llanta*
air *aire*
water *agua*
oil (change) *(cambio de) aceite*
My ... doesn't work. *Mi ... no funciona.*
battery *batería*
tow truck *grúa*
repair shop *taller*

VERBS

Verbs are the key to getting along in Spanish. They employ mostly predictable forms and come in three classes, which end in *ar, er,* and *ir,* respectively:

to buy *comprar*
I buy, you (he, she, it) buys *compro, compra*
we buy, you (they) buy *compramos, compran*

to eat *comer*
I eat, you (he, she, it) eats *como, come*
we eat, you (they) eat *comemos, comen*

to climb *subir*
I climb, you (he, she, it) climbs *subo, sube*
we climb, you (they) climb *subimos, suben*

Here are more (with irregularities indicated):
to do or make *hacer* (regular except for *hago,* I do or make)
to go *ir* (very irregular: *voy, va, vamos, van*)
to walk *caminar*
to wait *esperar*
to love *amar*
to work *trabajar*
to want *querer* (irregular: *quiero, quiere, queremos, quieren*)
to need *necesitar*
to read *leer*
to write *escribir*
to send *enviar*
to repair *reparar*
to wash *lavar*
to stop *parar*
to get off (the bus) *bajar*
to arrive *llegar*
to stay (remain) *quedar*
to stay (lodge) *hospedar*
to rent *alquilar*
to leave *salir* (regular except for *salgo,* I leave)
to look at *mirar*
to look for *buscar*
to give *dar* (regular except for *doy,* I give)

to give (as a present or to order something) *regalar*
to carry *llevar*
to have *tener* (irregular: *tengo, tiene, tenemos, tienen*)
to come *venir* (irregular: *vengo, viene, venimos, vienen*)

Spanish has two forms of "to be":
to be *estar* (regular except for *estoy,* I am)
to be *ser* (very irregular: *soy, es, somos, son*)

Use *estar* when speaking of location or a temporary state of being: "I am at home." *"Estoy en casa."* "I'm happy." *"Estoy contenta/o."* Use *ser* for a permanent state of being: "I am a lawyer." *"Soy abogada/o."*

NUMBERS

zero *cero*
one *uno*
two *dos*
three *tres*
four *cuatro*
five *cinco*
six *seis*
seven *siete*
eight *ocho*
nine *nueve*
10 *diez*
11 *once*
12 *doce*
13 *trece*
14 *catorce*
15 *quince*
16 *dieciseis*
17 *diecisiete*
18 *dieciocho*
19 *diecinueve*
20 *veinte*
21 *veinte y uno* or *veintiuno*
30 *treinta*
40 *cuarenta*
50 *cincuenta*
60 *sesenta*
70 *setenta*
80 *ochenta*
90 *noventa*

100	*cien*
101	*ciento y uno*
200	*doscientos*
500	*quinientos*
1,000	*mil*
10,000	*diez mil*
100,000	*cien mil*
1,000,000	*millón*
one-half	*medio*
one-third	*un tercio*
one-fourth	*un cuarto*

TIME

What time is it? *¿Qué hora es?*
It's one o'clock. *Es la una.*
It's three in the afternoon. *Son las tres de la tarde.*
It's 4am. *Son las cuatro de la mañana.*
six-thirty *seis y media*
quarter till eleven *un cuarto para las once*
quarter past five *las cinco y cuarto*
hour *una hora*
late *tarde*

DAYS AND MONTHS

Monday *lunes*
Tuesday *martes*
Wednesday *miércoles*
Thursday *jueves*
Friday *viernes*
Saturday *sábado*
Sunday *domingo*
today *hoy*
tomorrow *mañana*
yesterday *ayer*
day before yesterday *antier*
January *enero*
February *febrero*
March *marzo*
April *abril*
May *mayo*
June *junio*
July *julio*
August *agosto*
September *septiembre*
October *octubre*
November *noviembre*
December *diciembre*
week *una semana*
month *un mes*
after *después*
before *antes*
holiday *festivo*
long weekend *puente*

Suggested Reading

HISTORY

Bushnell, David. *The Making of Modern Colombia: A Nation in Spite of Itself.* Berkeley: University of California Press, 1993. Mandatory reading for students of Colombian history. Bushnell, an American, is considered the "Father of the Colombianists."

Hemming, John. *The Search for El Dorado.* London: Joseph, 1978. Written by a former director of the Royal Geographical Society, this book explores the Spanish gold obsession in the New World. It's a great companion to any visit to the Gold Museum in Bogotá.

Lynch, John. *Simón Bolívar: A Life.* New Haven, CT: Yale University Press, 2007. This biography of the Liberator is considered one of the best ever written in English, and is the result of a lifetime of research by renowned English historian John Lynch.

Palacios, Marco. *Between Legitimacy and Violence: A History of Colombia, 1875-2002.* Durham, NC: Duke University Press, 2006. Written by a Bogotano academic who was a former head of the Universidad Nacional, this book covers Colombia's economic, political, cultural, and social history from the late 19th century to the complexities of the late 20th century, and drug-related violence.

THE DRUG WAR AND ARMED CONFLICTS

Bowden, Mark. *Killing Pablo: The Hunt for the World's Greatest Outlaw.* New York: Grove Press, 2001. This account of U.S. and Colombian efforts to halt drug trafficking and terrorism committed by drug lord Pablo Escobar was originally reported in a 31-part series in the *Philadelphia Inquirer.*

Dudley, Steven. *Walking Ghosts: Murder and Guerrilla Politics in Colombia.* New York: Routledge Press, 2004. Essential reading for anyone interested in understanding the modern Colombian conflict, this book is written by an expert on organized crime in the Americas.

Gonsalves, Marc, Tom Howes, Keith Stansell, and Gary Brozek. *Out of Captivity: Surviving 1,967 Days in the Colombian Jungle.* New York: Harper Collins, 2009. Accounts of three U.S. military contractors who were held, along with former presidential candidate Ingrid Betancourt, by FARC guerrillas for over five years in the Colombian jungle.

Leech, Garry. *Beyond Bogotá: Diary of a Drug War Journalist in Colombia.* Boston: Beacon Press, 2009. The basis for this book is the author's 11 hours spent as a hostage of the FARC.

Otis, John. *Law of the Jungle: The Hunt for Colombian Guerrillas, American Hostages, and Buried Treasure.* New York: Harper, 2010. This is a thrilling account of the operation to rescue Ingrid Betancourt and U.S. government contractors held by the FARC. It covers the flip side of *Out of Captivity.*

NATURAL HISTORY

Hilty, Steven L., William L. Brown, and Guy Tudor. *A Guide to the Birds of Colombia.* Princeton, NJ: Princeton University Press, 1986. This massive 996-page field guide to bird-rich Colombia is a must for any serious bird-watcher.

McMullan, Miles, Thomas M. Donegan, and Alonso Quevedo. *Field Guide to the Birds of Colombia.* Bogotá: Fundación ProAves, 2010. This pocket-sized field guide published by ProAves, a respected bird conservation society, is a more manageable alternative to Hilty's guide.

ETHNOGRAPHY

Davis, Wade. *One River: Explorations and Discoveries in the Amazon Rain Forest.* New York: Simon & Schuster, 1997. From the author of *The Serpent and the Rainbow,* this is a rich description of the peoples of the Amazonian rainforest, and the result of Davis's time in the country alongside famed explorer Richard Evan Schultes.

Reichel-Dolmatoff, Gerardo. *Colombia: Ancient Peoples & Places.* London: Thames and Hudson, 1965. A thorough anthropological investigation of the indigenous cultures across Colombia by an Austrian-born anthropologist who immigrated to Colombia during World War II.

The Shaman and the Jaguar: A Study of Narcotic Drugs Among the Indians of Colombia. Philadelphia: Temple University Press, 1975. An examination of shamanic drug culture in Colombia, particularly among indigenous tribes from the Amazon jungle region.

TRAVEL

Mann, Mark. *The Gringo Trail.* West Sussex: Summersdale Publishers, 2010. A darkly comic tale of backpacking around South America.

Nicholl, Charles. *The Fruit Palace.* New York: St. Martin's Press, 1994. A wild romp that follows the cocaine trail from Bogotá bars to Medellín to the Sierra Nevada and a fruit stand called the Fruit Palace during the wild 1980s. The English author was jailed in Colombia for drug smuggling as he conducted research for the book.

PHOTOGRAPHY

Díaz, Hernán. *Cartagena Forever*. Bogotá: Villegas Editores, 2002. Beautiful photography of Cartagena's architecture and residents by a member of the American Society of Magazine Photographers in New York. The original Spanish text has been lovingly translated by author Jimmy Weiskopf, who lives in Bogotá and writes for *The City Paper Bogotá*.

Internet Resources

ACCOMMODATIONS

Hostel Trail
www.hosteltrail.com
Run by a Scottish couple living in Popayán, this is an excellent resource on hostels throughout South America.

BIRDING

ProAves
www.proaves.org
Excellent website for the largest birding organization in the country.

CARTAGENA

This Is Cartagena
www.ticartagena.com
Experience Cartagena like a local.

ECOTOURISM

Aviatur Ecoturismo
www.aviaturecoturismo.com
Package tours available from one of Colombia's most respected travel agencies.

Fundación Natura
www.natura.org.co
The Fundación Natura operates several interesting ecotourism reserves in the country.

Parques Nacionales Naturales de Colombia
www.parquesnacionales.gov.co
Colombia's national parks website has information on all of the natural parks and protected areas in the country.

EMBASSIES AND VISAS

Colombian Ministry of Foreign Affairs
www.cancilleria.gov.co
The website for the Ministry of Foreign Affairs offers information on visas and other travel information.

U.S. Embassy in Colombia
http://bogota.usembassy.gov
The Citizen Services page often has security information for visitors, and is where you can register your visit in case of an emergency.

ENTERTAINMENT, CULTURE, AND EVENTS

Banco de la República
www.banrepcultural.org
Information on upcoming cultural activities sponsored by the Banco de la República in 28 cities in the country.

Tu Boleta
www.tuboleta.com
The top event ticket distributor in the country, Tu Boleta is a good way to learn about concerts, theater, parties, and sporting events throughout Colombia.

HISTORY AND HUMAN RIGHTS ISSUES

Centro de Memoria Histórica
www.centrodememoriahistorica.gov.co
Excellent website on the human toll of the Colombian conflict.

CIA World Factbook Colombia
www.cia.gov
Background information on Colombia from those in the know.

Colombia Diversa
www.colombiadiversa.org
Covers LGBT rights in Colombia.

International Crisis Group
www.crisisgroup.org
In-depth analysis of the human rights situation in Colombia.

LANGUAGE COURSES
Spanish in Colombia
www.spanishincolombia.gov.co
Official government website on places to study Spanish in Colombia.

NEWS AND MEDIA
The City Paper Bogotá
www.thecitypaperbogota.com
Website of the capital city's English-language monthly.

Colombia Calling
www.richardmccoll.com/
colombia-calling
Weekly online radio program on all things Colombia from an expat perspective.

Colombia Reports
http://colombiareports.co
Colombian news in English.

El Espectador
www.elespectador.com.co
This is Colombia's second national newspaper.

El Tiempo
www.eltiempo.com
El Tiempo is the country's leading newspaper.

Revista Semana
www.semana.com
Semana is the top newsmagazine in Colombia.

TRANSPORTATION
Easy Taxi
http://cabify.com
To order a safe taxi in Colombia's large cities, upload this app, run by Cabify.

Moovit
http://moovitapp.com
This app will help you figure out public transportation in Bogotá.

TRAVEL INFORMATION
Colombia Travel
www.colombia.travel
This is the official travel information website of Proexport, Colombia's tourism and investment promotion agency.

Pueblos Patrimoniales
www.pueblospatrimoniodecolombia.
travel
Find a pueblo that suits your needs at this informative website.

VOLUNTEERING
Conexión Colombia
www.conexioncolombia.com
This website is one-stop shopping for the nonprofit sector in Colombia.

Index

222

LIST OF MAPS

List of Maps

Photo Credits

ROAD TRIPS AND DRIVE & HIKE GUIDES

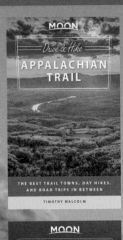

MOON

Drive & Hike
APPALACHIAN
TRAIL

THE BEST TRAIL TOWNS, DAY HIKES,
AND ROAD TRIPS IN BETWEEN

TIMOTHY MALCOLM

MOON

BLUE RIDGE
PARKWAY
Road Trip

INCLUDING SHENANDOAH & GREAT SMOKY
MOUNTAINS NATIONAL PARKS

JASON FRYE

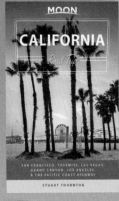

MOON

CALIFORNIA
Road Trip

SAN FRANCISCO, YOSEMITE, LAS VEGAS,
GRAND CANYON, LOS ANGELES,
& THE PACIFIC COAST HIGHWAY

STUART THORNTON

MOON

NASHVILLE TO
NEW ORLEANS
Road Trip

NATCHEZ TRACE PARKWAY • MEMPHIS •
TUPELO • MISSISSIPPI BLUES TRAIL

MARGARET LITTMAN

MOON

NEW ENGLAND
Road Trip

BOSTON, ACADIA NATIONAL PARK, WHITE
MOUNTAINS, BERKSHIRES, NEWPORT, AND CAPE COD

JEN ROSE SMITH

MOON

NORTHERN
CALIFORNIA
Road Trips

DRIVES ALONG THE COAST, REDWOODS, AND MOUNTAINS
WITH THE BEST STOPS ALONG THE WAY

STUART THORNTON & KAYLA ANDERSON

MOON

OREGON
TRAIL
Road Trip

HISTORIC SITES, SMALL TOWNS, AND
SCENIC LANDSCAPES ALONG THE LEGENDARY
WESTWARD ROUTE

KATRINA EMERY

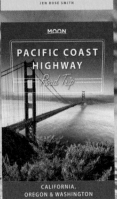

MOON

PACIFIC COAST
HIGHWAY
Road Trip

CALIFORNIA,
OREGON & WASHINGTON

IAN ANDERSON

MOON

Drive & Hike
PACIFIC CREST
TRAIL

THE BEST TRAIL TOWNS, DAY HIKES,
AND ROAD TRIPS IN BETWEEN

CAROLINE HINCHLIFF

MOON.COM | ROADTRIPUSA.COM

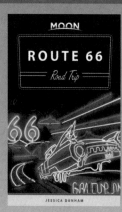

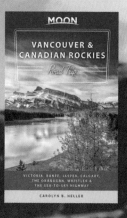

FIND YOUR ADVENTURE

MOON

USA NATIONAL PARKS

THE COMPLETE GUIDE TO ALL

62 PARKS

BECKY LOMAX

ACADIA
NATIONAL PARK
HILARY NANGLE

ARCHES &
CANYONLANDS
NATIONAL PARKS
W. C. McRAE & JUDY JEWELL

MOON
BANFF
NATIONAL
PARK
HIKE·CAMP
SEE WILDLIFE
ANDREW HEMPSTEAD

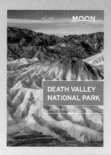

DEATH VALLEY
NATIONAL PARK
JENNA BLOUGH

MOON
GLACIER
NATIONAL PARK
HIKING · CAMPING
LAKES & PEAKS
BECKY LOMAX

MOON
GRAND
CANYON
HIKE·CAMP
RAFT THE
COLORADO RIVER
TIM HULL

MOON
GREAT SMOKY
MOUNTAINS
NATIONAL PARK
HIKING · CAMPING
SCENIC DRIVES
JASON FRYE

JOSHUA TREE
& PALM SPRINGS
JENNA BLOUGH

MOUNT RUSHMORE
& THE BLACK HILLS
Including the Badlands
LAURA A. BIDWELL

MOON
ROCKY
MOUNTAIN
NATIONAL PARK
HIKE·CAMP
SEE WILDLIFE
ERIN ENGLISH

MOON
SEQUOIA &
KINGS CANYON
HIKE·CAMP
SEE REDWOODS
LEIGH BERNACCHI

MOON
YELLOWSTONE
& GRAND TETON
HIKE, CAMP,
SEE WILDLIFE
BECKY LOMAX

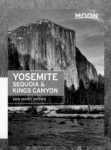

YOSEMITE
SEQUOIA &
KINGS CANYON
ANN MARIE BROWN

MOON
ZION &
BRYCE
Including Arches, Canyonlands,
Capitol Reef, Grand Staircase-
Escalante & More
W. C. McRAE & JUDY JEWELL

In these books:

- Full coverage of gateway cities and towns
- Itineraries from one day to multiple weeks
- Advice on where to stay (or camp) in and around the parks

For when your friends want your recommendations.
Keep track of your favorite...

Restaurants and Meals

Neighborhoods and Regions

Cultural Experiences

Outdoor Recreation

Day Trips or Scenic Drives

Travel Memories

Get inspired for your next adventure

Follow @**moonguides** on Instagram or
subscribe to our newsletter at **moon.com**

#TravelWithMoon

MAP SYMBOLS

▤▤▤	Expressway	○	City/Town	✗	Airport	⚓	Golf Course
▤▤▤	Primary Road	◉	State Capital	✗	Airfield	Ⓟ	Parking Area
▤▤▤	Secondary Road	⊛	National Capital	▲	Mountain	≞	Archaeological Site
∷∷∷	Unpaved Road	✪	Highlight	✦	Unique Natural Feature	⛪	Church
- - -	Trail	★	Point of Interest			🅶	Gas Station
⋯⋯	Ferry	•	Accommodation	🗻	Waterfall		
▰▰▰	Railroad	▼	Restaurant/Bar			⬮	Glacier
▨▨▨	Pedestrian Walkway	■	Other Location	♠	Park		Mangrove
▥▥▥	Stairs	Λ	Campground	🆃🅷	Trailhead		Reef
				⛷	Skiing Area		Swamp

CONVERSION TABLES

°C = (°F – 32) / 1.8
°F = (°C x 1.8) + 32
1 inch = 2.54 centimeters (cm)
1 foot = 0.304 meters (m)
1 yard = 0.914 meters
1 mile = 1.6093 kilometers (km)
1 km = 0.6214 miles
1 fathom = 1.8288 m
1 chain = 20.1168 m
1 furlong = 201.168 m
1 acre = 0.4047 hectares
1 sq km = 100 hectares
1 sq mile = 2.59 square km
1 ounce = 28.35 grams
1 pound = 0.4536 kilograms
1 short ton = 0.90718 metric ton
1 short ton = 2,000 pounds
1 long ton = 1.016 metric tons
1 long ton = 2,240 pounds
1 metric ton = 1,000 kilograms
1 quart = 0.94635 liters
1 US gallon = 3.7854 liters
1 Imperial gallon = 4.5459 liters
1 nautical mile = 1.852 km

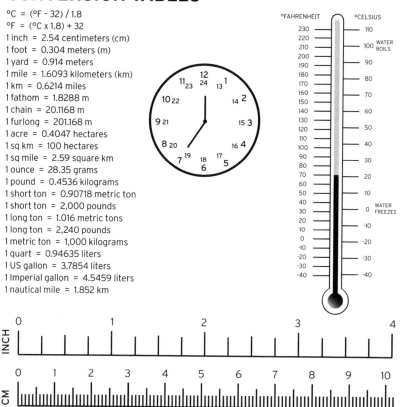

MOON CARTAGENA & COLOMBIA'S CARIBBEAN COAST

Avalon Travel
Hachette Book Group
1700 Fourth Street
Berkeley, CA 94710, USA
www.moon.com

Editor: Kristi Mitsuda
Acquiring Editor: Nikki Ioakimedes
Series Manager: Kathryn Ettinger
Copy Editor: Brett Keener
Graphics and Production Coordinator:
   Suzanne Albertson
Cover Design: Faceout Studios, Charles Brock
Interior Design: Domini Dragoone
Moon Logo: Tim McGrath
Map Editor: Kat Bennett
Cartographer: Brian Shotwell
Indexer: Greg Jewett

ISBN-13: 9781640499409

Printing History
1st Edition — 2016
2nd Edition — January 2021
5 4 3 2 1

Front cover photo: residents stroll a wide plaza in Cartagena, Colombia © KenWiedemann/Getty
Back cover photo: Cabo San Juan, Parque Nacional Natural Tayrona © Coughlandarragh | Dreamstime.com

Printed in China by RR Donnelley

Avalon Travel is a division of Hachette Book Group, Inc. Moon and the Moon logo are trademarks of Hachette Book Group, Inc. All other marks and logos depicted are the property of the original owners.